Mary Ann Shadd Cary

T0355156

OXFORD NEW HISTORIES OF PHILOSOPHY

*

Oxford New Histories of Philosophy provides essential resources for those aiming to
diversify the content of their philosophy courses, revisit traditional narratives about the
history of philosophy, or better understand the richness of philosophy's past. Examining
previously neglected or understudied philosophical figures, movements, and traditions,
the series includes both innovative new scholarship and new primary sources.

*

Mary Ann Shadd Cary

*Essential Writings of a Nineteenth-Century
Black Radical Feminist*

EDITED BY NNEKA D. DENNIE

OXFORD
UNIVERSITY PRESS

OXFORD
UNIVERSITY PRESS

Oxford University Press is a department of the University of Oxford. It furthers
the University's objective of excellence in research, scholarship, and education
by publishing worldwide. Oxford is a registered trade mark of Oxford University
Press in the UK and certain other countries.

Published in the United States of America by Oxford University Press
198 Madison Avenue, New York, NY 10016, United States of America.

© Oxford University Press 2024

Library of Congress Cataloging-in-Publication Data
Names: Cary, Mary Ann Shadd, 1823-1893. | Dennie, Nneka D., editor.
Title: Mary Ann Shadd Cary : essential writings of a nineteenth century
black radical feminist / [edited by] Nneka D. Dennie.
Other titles: Essential writings of a nineteenth century black radical feminist
Description: New York, NY : Oxford University Press, [2024] |
Series: Oxford new histories philosophy |
Includes bibliographical references and index.
Identifiers: LCCN 2023025349 (print) | LCCN 2023025350 (ebook) |
ISBN 9780197609477 (paperback) | ISBN 9780197609460 (hardback) |
ISBN 9780197609491 (epub)
Subjects: LCSH: Cary, Mary Ann Shadd, 1823-1893. | Feminism—
United States—History—19th century. | African American women civil rights
workers—History—19th century. | Civil rights workers—
United States—History—19th century. | Free African Americans. |
African Americans—Civil rights—History—19th century. | Blacks—Civil
rights—Canada—History—19th century.
Classification: LCC E185.97.C32 A25 2024 (print) | LCC E185.97.C32 (ebook) |
DDC 305.48/896073—dc23/eng/20230525
LC record available at https://lccn.loc.gov/2023025349
LC ebook record available at https://lccn.loc.gov/2023025350

DOI: 10.1093/oso/9780197609460.001.0001

Paperback printed by Marquis Book Printing, Canada
Hardback printed by Bridgeport National Bindery, Inc., United States of America

MIX
Paper from
responsible sources
FSC® C103567

For Isola Liverpool, my Granny,
In memory of the nights we spent watching the water and staring at the stars.

Contents

Series Editors' Foreword

Oxford New Histories of Philosophy (ONHP) speaks to a new climate in philosophy.

There is a growing awareness that philosophy's past is richer and more diverse than previously understood. It has become clear that canonical figures are best studied in a broad context. More exciting still is the recognition that our philosophical heritage contains long-forgotten innovative ideas, movements, and thinkers. Sometimes these thinkers warrant serious study in their own right; sometimes their importance resides in the conversations they helped reframe or problems they devised; often their philosophical proposals force us to rethink long-held assumptions about a period or genre; and frequently they cast well-known philosophical discussions in a fresh light.

There is also a mounting sense among philosophers that our discipline benefits from a diversity of perspectives and a commitment to inclusiveness. In a time when questions about justice, inequality, dignity, education, discrimination, and climate (to name a few) are especially vivid, it is appropriate to mine historical texts for insights that can shift conversations and reframe solutions. Given that philosophy's very long history contains astute discussions of a vast array of topics, the time is right to cast a broad historical net.

Lastly, there is increasing interest among philosophy instructors in speaking to the diversity and concerns of their students. Although historical discussions and texts can serve as a powerful means of doing so, finding the necessary time and tools to excavate long-buried historical materials is challenging.

Oxford New Histories of Philosophy is designed to address all these needs. It contains new editions and translations of significant historical texts. These primary materials make available, often for the first time, ideas and works by women, people of color, and movements in philosophy's past that were groundbreaking in their day, but left out of traditional accounts. Informative introductions help instructors and students navigate the new material. Alongside its primary texts, ONHP also publishes monographs and collections of essays that offer philosophically subtle analyses of understudied topics, movements, and figures. In combining primary materials and astute philosophical analyses, ONHP makes it easier for philosophers, historians, and instructors to include in their courses and research exciting new materials drawn from philosophy's past.

ONHP's range is wide, both historically and culturally. The series includes, for example, the writings of African American philosophers, twentieth-century Mexican philosophers, early modern and late medieval women, Islamic and Jewish authors, and non-western thinkers. It excavates and analyses problems and ideas that were prominent in their day, but forgotten by later historians. And it serves as a significant aid to philosophers in teaching and researching this material.

As we expand the range of philosophical voices, it is important to acknowledge one voice responsible for this series. Eileen O'Neill was a series editor until her death, December 1, 2017. She was instrumental in motivating and conceptualizing ONHP. Her brilliant scholarship, advocacy, and generosity made all the difference to the efforts that this series is meant to represent. She will be deeply missed, as a scholar and a friend.

We are proud to contribute to philosophy's present and to a richer understanding of its past.

Christia Mercer and Melvin Rogers
Series Editors

Acknowledgments

I wasn't supposed to write this book yet. But when my undergraduate adviser, Neil Roberts—who probably didn't think he would still be stuck with me years after I walked into his office as a first-year student—told me about the Oxford New Histories of Philosophy series, I saw an opportunity that I couldn't pass up. I first encountered Mary Ann Shadd Cary in graduate school. I kept seeing her name alongside other abolitionists—a passing reference here, a book chapter there, and a handful of journal articles—but only saw one book, Jane Rhodes's 1998 biography, that was specifically about her. I am thankful for earlier generations of scholars who have facilitated Shadd Cary's historical recovery. I began my research into Shadd Cary while writing a dissertation on nineteenth-century Black women under the direction of Manisha Sinha. She encouraged me to stand firm in my belief that I can, in fact, call certain nineteenth-century Black women "feminists" *and* "radicals." As I wrote my dissertation, I noticed that there were documentary readers for many of the other figures who I wrote about, but not Shadd Cary. At the time, I thought I might edit one eventually if it hadn't been done yet once I was ready to do so. I turned my attention to other research projects. But when Melvin Rogers and I noticed that the two-hundred-year anniversary of Shadd Cary's birth would be in 2023, a fleeting idea suddenly became both concrete and urgent. With the help of Oxford University Press editor Peter Ohlin and series editor Christia Mercer, my "second" book accidentally became my first book.

This research was supported by a Consortium for Faculty Diversity Postdoctoral Fellowship at Davidson College; the Summer Institute on Tenure and Professional Advancement at Duke University; a Lenfest Grant at Washington and Lee University (W&L); and a Mellon Just Transformations Fellowship in the Center for Black Digital Research at Pennsylvania State University. The W&L Department of History and Dean's Office also supported my sabbatical to complete this manuscript.

Archivists and staff at the Amistad Research Center at Tulane University, the Archives of Ontario, and the Moorland-Spingarn Research Center provided essential guidance on identifying documents by and about Shadd Cary, and processed permission requests to include some of the material included in this text. I appreciate the contributions that Jamie Lee, Jackie Martin, Lisa Moore, Lela Sewell-Williams, and Sean Smith have made to this book.

Former undergraduate research assistants were invaluable during the early stages of this project. Niani Benjamin, P. T. Meadors, and Bry Reed transcribed many documents for this manuscript, and helped to search for relevant newspaper articles. They also reminded me of the joys of seeing new historical material for the first time.

I am indebted to those who offered feedback on portions of this work, including Gabrielle Foreman, Sarah Horowitz, Chike Jeffers, Shirley Moody Turner, Michael Sawyer, peer reviewers, participants in the Rutgers Seminar in Literature and Political Theory, and participants in the Penn State Just Transformation Fellows Workshop. I am also thankful to members of the Douglass Day Team, particularly Jim Casey, Denise Burgher, Kristin Moriah, and Summer Hamilton. Our collective conversations about Shadd Cary and her digital archives allowed me to think about this research in new ways.

My mentors empowered me to pursue this particular project at this particular time. I am deeply grateful to Tanisha Ford, Bayyinah Jeffries, and Molly Michelmore for affirming that my decisions about what and when to publish do not need to be bound by conventional academic expectations.

Many colleagues at W&L, particularly Kameliya Atanasova, Diego Millan, Franklin Sammons, Melissa Vise, Taylor Walle, and Brenna Womer, helped me make time to write throughout the school year, even on teaching days when I usually didn't feel like it. Our weekly Junior Humanists Write sessions always gave me something to look forward to. I value the ways that Henryatta Ballah, Mikki Brock, Carliss Chatman, and Carla LaRoche have modeled how best to distribute my time and energy. I'm also glad that the National Center for Faculty Diversity and Development introduced me to Keona Ervin, Niwaeli Kimambo, and Bryn Meché. Our small group encouraged me to develop a daily writing practice and determine which work habits would be most sustainable for me. I wouldn't have been able to find a way to balance teaching and research without all of you!

This is a project that was started and finished in community. Writing alongside Crystal Donkor, Kenton Rambsy, Jacinta Saffold, and Crystal Webster on a consistent basis over the past few years has been one of the greatest privileges of completing this manuscript. They all inspire me, push me to think more creatively, and share in my joys and challenges. They also forgive me when I accidentally oversleep our morning writing sessions. For that, I rejoice.

Finally, my partner and family have nurtured me throughout this journey in ways that only loved ones can. Whether they cooked for me, tolerated my complaints, asked questions, or simply spent time with me when I needed a break, Joseph Williams, Debbie Dennie, Michael Dennie, Madiba Dennie, Nai-Andra Fleuranvil, Cathy Liverpool, Paul Phillips, and Keba Walker have all helped bring this book to fruition. I couldn't have done this without you.

A Note on the Cover Illustration

The portrait of Mary Ann Shadd Cary on this cover is titled "Luminary: Mary Ann Shadd." It is by a Canadian Afrofuturist artist, Adeyemi Adegbesan, also known as Yung Yemi. Adegbesan created this portrait as a mural for the Toronto History Museums' *Awakenings* series, and it was installed in the fall of 2021.[1] There is only one extant photograph of Mary Ann Shadd Cary from the mid-nineteenth century. In the image, she appears unsmiling with a look of steely determination on her face. "Luminary: Mary Ann Shadd" adopts this photograph as its foundation and incorporates several aspects of Shadd Cary's life and work into its symbolic representation of her. Adegbesan has noted, for instance, that the asterisks dangling along the bottom of the portrait are derived from the asterisks that Shadd Cary used to sign articles anonymously in her newspaper, the *Provincial Freeman*. Similarly, the flowers above Shadd Cary's ear, on her neck, and across her chest are the state flowers of Delaware, Pennsylvania, and Ontario, three locations that were formative to her development as a thinker and activist.[2]

One of Adegbesan's artistic goals is to allow the audience to see themselves reflected in his work. In relation to Shadd Cary, he explains, "All of the adversity that she faced is probably more . . . adversity than I or most people are facing in 2021. If she could find that sense of strength and inner purpose I think we can do it in 2021 as well."[3] This rendering of Shadd Cary not only aims to inspire, but also encourages viewers to have twenty-first-century interpretations of her—interpretations that, as this book illustrates—can deepen contemporary understandings of Shadd Cary's Black, radical, feminist politics.

[1] Toronto History Museums, "Luminary: Mary Ann Shadd," accessed October 22, 2021, https://www.toronto.ca/explore-enjoy/history-art-culture/museums/luminary-mary-ann-shadd/.

[2] Toronto History Museums, "Awakenings Reflections with Adeyemi Adegbesan," August 10, 2021, 6:07, https://www.youtube.com/watch?v=5tqvYAGlTIQ.

[3] Toronto History Museums, "Awakenings Reflections with Adeyemi Adegbesan."

Introduction

"We Should Do More, and Talk Less"

In 1849, Mary Ann Shadd Cary had not yet become one of the first Black woman newspaper editors in North America. She was decades away from being admitted to Howard University's Law School and becoming the first Black woman to enroll in law school in the United States. She had not yet begun to lobby for women's right to vote, and she had not yet emigrated to Canada, where she would soon rise to prominence as a formidable abolitionist and emigrationist. Though many years would pass before Shadd Cary made a name for herself as a gifted writer, editor, lecturer, educator, lawyer, and suffragist, in 1849, she was already certain of one thing: "We should do more, and talk less."[1] On March 23, 1849, Shadd Cary wrote a letter to Frederick Douglass published in the *North Star* in agreement with Henry Highland Garnet's January 19, 1849, letter to the editor, which argued that self-reliance is a vital component of Black people's struggle for liberation. She expressed frustration that, despite holding colored conventions for the past two decades, where they "have been assembling together and whining over our difficulties and afflictions, passing resolutions on resolutions to any extent . . . it does really seem that we have made but little progress, considering our resolves."[2] She therefore implored African Americans to take stronger action, which she would continue to do for the next forty years.

Shadd Cary's 1849 letter was prescient in many ways. In addition to foreshadowing her lifelong commitment to civil rights advocacy, it foretold the methods that her activism would often take. She established that

---

[1] Mary Ann Shadd, letter to Frederick Douglass, *North Star*, March 23, 1849, included in Part 1.

[2] Shadd, letter to Frederick Douglass. Beginning in 1830, African Americans held state and national colored conventions to mobilize for abolition. Attendees frequently delivered speeches, debated activist strategies, and voted on resolutions. The Colored Conventions Movement continued into the 1890s as African Americans continued to grapple with their new status as citizens and persistent social, political, and economic racism. For more, see the Colored Conventions Project (CCP), https://coloredconventions.org/, accessed June 13, 2020. The CCP is a digital humanities collective that has transcribed and archived documents from over one hundred colored conventions. It was created by P. Gabrielle Foreman and graduate students at the University of Delaware in 2012.

Mary Ann Shadd Cary. Nneka D. Dennie, Oxford University Press. © Oxford University Press 2024.
DOI: 10.1093/oso/9780197609460.003.0001

"in anything relating to our people, I am insensible of boundaries." Indeed, this statement would hold true as Shadd Cary transgressed racial and gender boundaries concerning appropriate forms of activism for Black women, and traversed geographic boundaries through her emigrationism and transnational publishing. Shadd Cary was steadfastly committed to creating better lives for Black people and Black communities, regardless of how she did so or where those efforts may have led her.

Three years later, Shadd Cary published her landmark pamphlet, *A Plea for Emigration, or, Notes of Canada West* (1852), in which she proposed that African Americans pursue a simple solution to the problem of racism in the United States: leave. Shadd Cary's disavowal of the American nation-state situated her among a cadre of well-known Black thinkers and activists such as Douglass, Garnet, and Martin Delany, who vigorously debated whether African Americans should remain in the United States. Shadd Cary continued to advocate for emigration in the *Provincial Freeman*, the newspaper that she founded and edited beginning in 1853. Today, Shadd Cary's emigrationism continues to dominate her historical and philosophical framing. However, throughout her decades-long career, Shadd Cary also examined a range of topics including labor, women's rights, and racial uplift. Although scholars tend to emphasize the earlier period of Shadd Cary's work, her writing and activism continued into the 1880s.

Shadd Cary had a prolific career as a writer, lecturer, and public intellectual, but her legacy is continually overshadowed by that of other African American thinkers during the mid- to late nineteenth century, such as Delany and Frances Harper. Over the course of forty years Shadd Cary both produced and disseminated knowledge about emigration, racial uplift, labor, education, and women's rights. Accordingly, it is worth returning to Shadd Cary and her written work in order to develop a more comprehensive understanding of the ways that African American women's intellectual thought advanced early Africana philosophies.

Life and Context

Mary Ann Shadd Cary, pictured in Figure 0.1, was born in 1823 to free African Americans in Delaware. She was the eldest of thirteen children.[3]

---

[3] Jane Rhodes, *Mary Ann Shadd Cary: The Black Press and Protest in the Nineteenth Century* (Bloomington: Indiana University Press, 1998), 13.

Figure 0.1 Portrait of Mary Ann Shadd Cary, Library and Archives Canada/ Mary Ann Shadd Cary collection/e011536885

Unlike many African Americans in the antebellum era, Shadd Cary was born to a relatively wealthy and politically active family. For example, her father, Abraham Shadd, launched early opposition to the Union Colonization Society of Wilmington, an organization primarily comprised of white community members who aimed to remove Black people from the United States.[4] He and several other relatives, including Shadd Cary's brother Isaac D. Shadd, sister-in-law Amelia Freeman Shadd, and cousin Furman J. Shadd, attended colored conventions throughout the nineteenth century.[5] The Shadd family were free African Americans in a slave state. Despite their status as free, they were nevertheless subject to Black codes—racially restrictive laws that limited African American freedoms. For example, the state of Delaware barred Black students from attending public schools, which perhaps influenced the Shadd family's decision to move to Pennsylvania in 1833.[6] Shadd Cary attended a Quaker school in Pennsylvania and later became a teacher. In the 1850s, she became a vocal proponent of emigration. Shadd Cary argued

---

[4] Brandi Locke et al., "Mary Ann Shadd Cary's Herstory in the Colored Conventions: Abraham Shadd," in Colored Conventions Project, Center for Black Digital Research, https://coloredconventions.org/mary-ann-shadd-cary/making-a-delegate/abraham-shadd/.

[5] Locke et al., "Shadd Cary's Herstory."

[6] Rhodes, *Mary Ann Shadd Cary*, 8.

that African Americans should relocate to Canada rather than tolerate white supremacy and racial discrimination in the United States. To Shadd Cary, the solution to American racism was inherently a transnational one, as the documents in this reader illustrate.

Shadd Cary emigrated to Canada in 1851 amid an increasingly dangerous racial environment in the United States. In 1850, approximately 3.2 million Black people were being held captive in slavery, and fewer than 435,000 were free.[7] That year saw the passage of a new Fugitive Slave Law. This measure was preceded by the Fugitive Slave Act of 1793. The first act protected enslavers' rights to recapture enslaved persons who ran away, and penalized those who assisted fugitives from slavery in their escape. This law was enforced within state courts. The Fugitive Slave Law of 1850, however, allowed for stronger enforcement of the law and for cases to be tried in federal court. It also incentivized the return of formerly enslaved persons to slavery, as special commissioners who ruled on these cases were paid twice as much for ruling that an alleged fugitive was enslaved rather than free.[8] Under the Fugitive Slave Laws, any free Black person was at risk of being captured and sold into slavery, regardless of whether they had fled slavery, had never been enslaved, or were manumitted legally.[9] The threats posed by the Fugitive Slave Act of 1850 motivated many African Americans, including Shadd Cary, to flee to Canada.[10]

In 1853 she founded a newspaper, the *Provincial Freeman*, that ran regularly until 1857. Although the newspaper was thought to have published issues sporadically before folding in 1860 due to financial strain, the latest known issue of the paper was published in the spring of 1866.[11] Shadd Cary used the *Provincial Freeman* as a tool to build community among Black

---

[7] J. D. B. DeBow, *Statistical View of the United States, Embracing its Territory, Population—White, Free Colored, and Slave—Moral and Social Condition, Industry, Property, and Revenue; The Detailed Statistics of Cities, Towns, and Counties; Being a Compendium of the Seventh Census; To Which Are Added The Results of Every Previous Census, Beginning with 1790, in Comparative Tables, with Explanatory and Illustrative Notes, Based upon the Schedules and Other Official Sources of Information* (Washington, DC: Beverley Tucker, Senate Printer, 1854), 82–83.

[8] Sharon A. Roger Hepburn, "Following the North Star: Canada as a Haven for Nineteenth-Century American Blacks," *Michigan Historical Review* 25, no. 2 (1999): 101.

[9] One notable example is that of Solomon Northrup (b. 1807) a free Black man who recounted his experience of being kidnapped and sold into slavery in his memoir, *Twelve Years a Slave* (Auburn: Derby and Miller, 1853).

[10] Approximately thirty-thousand African Americans migrated to Canada during the 1850s. See Fred Landon, "The Negro Migration to Canada after the Passing of the Fugitive Slave Act," *Journal of Negro History* 5, no. 1 (1920): 22.

[11] Rhodes, *Mary Ann Shadd Cary*, 135; ARC Vertical File, Box 31, Folder 8, Shadd Family Papers, Amistad Research Center, Tulane University, New Orleans, LA. Thanks are due to Jim Casey for calling my attention to the existence of the 1866 issue of the *Provincial Freeman*.

Canadians. It was also a vehicle for her to levy critiques against American racism and certain Black male leaders, like Henry Bibb, who she believed were self-interested or otherwise incompetent. Shadd Cary was cognizant that as a Black woman, her political activity was not socially acceptable. She initially attempted to obscure the fact that the *Provincial Freeman* was published by a woman by refusing to print her name on the paper. Instead, she listed four African American men as the paper's managing editors and often enlisted men's assistance to solicit donations to fund the *Provincial Freeman*. Despite her attempts to avoid gendered scrutiny, Shadd Cary's statements often sparked controversy, both for their radicalism and for Shadd Cary's refusal to limit her activism to roles that were deemed appropriate for women, such as clerical work in political organizations or participating in women's auxiliaries to abolitionist associations.

Shadd Cary became a naturalized Canadian citizen in 1862. She returned to the United States in 1863 at the height of the Civil War, at which point she began recruiting Black soldiers for the Union army at Delany's request.[12] Following Emancipation, she turned her attention more directly toward women's suffrage, although her abolitionist work had always advocated for women's rights alongside Black people's freedom. Throughout the 1870s and 1880s, she published in newspapers such as the *New National Era*, delivered lectures around the country, taught in public schools in Detroit and Washington, DC, and earned a law degree from Howard University. During this time period, Shadd Cary also expanded her organizational work by working with the Colored National Labor Union, serving on the executive board of the National Woman Suffrage Association, and founding the short-lived Colored Women's Progressive Franchise Association. Shadd Cary remained politically active in DC until her death in 1893.

Jane Rhodes published a groundbreaking biography of Shadd Cary in 1998; however, in the past twenty-five years, there have been no book-length projects about Shadd Cary's political thought.[13] In excavating Shadd Cary's work, Rhodes charted her path from the United States, to Canada, and back again with great detail. *Mary Ann Shadd Cary: The Black Press and Protest in the Nineteenth Century* shed new light on Shadd Cary's writings, some of

[12] "Naturalization Certificate of Mary Ann Shadd Cary," September 9, 1862, R4182-1-1-E, Mary Ann Shadd Cary Collection, Library and Archives of Canada, https://recherche-collection-search.bac-lac.gc.ca/eng/home/record?app=fonandcol&IdNumber=5793102. In addition to being a physician, an abolitionist, and a writer, Martin R. Delany (1812–1885) was a recruiting agent and the first Black field officer of the US Army.
[13] Rhodes, *Mary Ann Shadd Cary*.

which are included in this book. It documents her early life, support for em-igration, successes and challenges with publishing the *Provincial Freeman*, and her activism after returning to the United States. Given the scarcity of scholarship on Shadd Cary since the publication of Rhodes's biography, this documentary reader aims to reveal new dimensions of Shadd Cary's lifework and promote further research into her philosophical contributions.

Several scholars of African American women's literature and history, including Carla Peterson, Gabrielle Foreman, and Martha Jones, have endeavored to treat nineteenth-century Black women's intellectual thought with rigor.[14] Additional work by Kathy Glass and Teresa Zackodnik reveals how nineteenth-century African American women pursued various modes of Black nationalism.[15] Their scholarship gestures toward Shadd Cary's rad-ical roots in ways that are instructive for developing a more precise inter-pretation of the questions, methods, and actors that shaped Black radicalism in the nineteenth century. In particular, such work demonstrates that Black

[14] Carla Peterson, *"Doers of the Word": African American Women Speakers and Writers in the North (1830–1880)* (New York: Oxford University Press, 1995); P. Gabrielle Foreman, *Activist Sentiments: Reading Black Women in the Nineteenth Century* (Urbana: University of Illinois Press, 2009); Martha Jones, *All Bound Up Together: The Woman Question in African American Public Culture, 1830–1900* (Chapel Hill: University of North Carolina Press, 2007). Peterson reveals how Black women theorized a Black cultural nationalism through writing from and about liminal spaces produced by their racial and gendered marginalization. She locates Shadd Cary within a Black women's literary tradition in order to examine nineteenth-century Black women's constructions of Blackness and womanhood in their speeches and writings. Foreman's work considers how Black women drew on the sentimental tradition to articulate their politics in their writing. Black women's sentimental texts, like slave narratives and novels, allowed them to discuss social injustice in a manner that was compatible with women's domesticity, particularly among white, female audiences that were invested in affective expressions of human experience. Both Peterson and Foreman illu-minate the literary strategies that informed Black women's writing throughout the nineteenth cen-tury. Peterson's and Foreman's work helps to contextualize the rhetorical strategies that Shadd Cary used throughout the course of her career, which varied based on her audience, arguments, mode of engaging the public, and more. Jones extends scholarship on nineteenth-century Black women's writing by tracing how Black women inserted themselves into Black public culture from the 1830s to 1890s. In addition to examining Black print culture, she considers how Black women insisted on their right to be politically active in the public sphere. Jones is attentive to how Black women fash-ioned themselves as activists through raising "the woman question" within antislavery societies, col-ored conventions, churches, literary societies, and other institutions. From 1849 onward, Shadd Cary employed many of the strategies that Jones identifies as ways that Black women engaged in African American public culture.

[15] Kathy Glass, *Courting Communities: Black Female Nationalism and "Syncre-Nationalism" in the Nineteenth-Century North* (New York: Routledge, 2006); Teresa Zackodnik, *Press, Platform, Pulpit: Black Feminist Publics in the Era of Reform* (Knoxville: University of Tennessee Press, 2011). Glass coins the term "syncre-nationalism" to describe how nineteenth-century Black women crafted Black nationalist imagined communities in ways that emphasized ideological ties and transcended geographic boundaries. Zackodnik suggests that Black women used the Black press to practice and popularize Black feminist nationalism. Their attention to the forms of Black nationalism that women embraced during the nineteenth century invites further inquiry into the ways that Shadd Cary and her contemporaries crafted radical thought.

radicalism is not static, and that Black women have always had the capacity to become radicals. This book hopes to continue their work by solidifying Shadd Cary's status as an early Black radical thinker.

Many works examine Shadd Cary alongside other nineteenth-century Black thinkers and activists; however, there are few stand-alone texts dedicated to her intellectual thought.[16] Shadd Cary frequently appears alongside other figures, but rarely as a thinker whose work is assessed in its own right. Some edited collections include chapters dedicated to Shadd Cary, which successfully positions her among her African American contemporaries. Other documentary readers, like the five-volume *The Black Abolitionist Papers* and Teresa Zackodnik's impressive six-volume collection, *African American Feminisms, 1828–1923*, contain some of Shadd Cary's work.[17] Both readers are quite comprehensive, however, and within their pages, other texts can easily overshadow Shadd Cary's work.

To date, there have been two reprints of *A Plea for Emigration*, edited by Richard Almonte and Phanuel Antwi, respectively.[18] Almonte's 1998 revival of the pamphlet was the first time it was reproduced since its original publication nearly 150 years prior. The edition pairs *A Plea for Emigration* with an excerpt from one of Shadd Cary's lectures, "Obstacles to the Progress of Coloured Canadians." Almonte locates Shadd Cary's pamphlet within early Canadian literature and discusses its significance as a settlement journal.[19] He is particularly attentive to questions of genre as he describes Shadd Cary's significance to Black Canadian literature. Of note are the ways that Shadd Cary portrayed Canada as a safe haven for African Americans and actively encouraged emigration in ways that departed from other nineteenth-century Canadian settler guides. Almonte explains,

---

[16] Kathryn Kish Sklar and James Brewer Stewart, eds., *Women's Rights and Transatlantic Antislavery in the Era of Emancipation* (New Haven: Yale University Press, 2007); Kristin Waters and Carol B. Conaway, eds., *Black Women's Intellectual Traditions: Speaking Their Minds* (Burlington: University of Vermont Press, 2007); Mia Bay et al., eds., *Toward an Intellectual History of Black Women* (Chapel Hill: University of North Carolina Press, 2015); Brigitte Fielder and Jonathan Senchyne, eds., *Against a Sharp White Background: Infrastructures of African American Print* (Madison: University of Wisconsin Press, 2019).

[17] C. Peter Ripley et al., eds., *The Black Abolitionist Papers* (Chapel Hill: University of North Carolina Press, 1985); Teresa Zackodnik, ed., *African American Feminisms, 1828–1923* (New York: Routledge, 2007).

[18] Mary A. Shadd, *A Plea for Emigration; Or Notes of Canada West*, ed. Richard Almonte (Toronto: Mercury Press, 1998). Mary Ann Shadd, *A Plea for Emigration; Or Notes of Canada West*, ed. Phanuel Antwi (Peterborough: Broadview Press, 2016). Hereinafter referred to as Almonte, ed., *A Plea for Emigration* and Antwi, ed., *A Plea for Emigration* for clarity.

[19] Almonte, ed., *A Plea for Emigration*, 26–33.

Whereas for white Canadian writers the garrison mentality (re-creation of the past for fear of the present) holds, in the case of Shadd, there is a distinction: Shadd hopes Blacks will assimilate so that they can *benefit* from Canadian-British institutions. This is about repudiating a troubling past to make a better present. In other words, a strictly utilitarian decision.[20]

To Almonte, *A Plea for Emigration* is simultaneously a vital part of early Canadian literature and a notable departure from other settlement journals. Likewise, Antwi establishes that *A Plea for Emigration* is unique among Canadian settler guides. Settler guides often fell into one of two camps: "glowing in their depiction of life in the New World—and economical with the truth, downplaying such things as the realities of winter in northern North America," or "painting a far less rosy picture of life in the colonies, and aiming to dampen the 'vain expectations'" of potential emigrants.[21] Both types of guides, however, were typically directed toward white Europeans, where Shadd Cary instead wrote for a Black audience. In addition to situating *A Plea for Emigration* within Canadian literature, Antwi's edition places Shadd Cary in conversation with other authors, including Harriet Martineau and Frederick Douglass. His approach offers useful context about American racism and Canadian life in the nineteenth century.

This documentary reader centers Shadd Cary in an effort to promote concentrated engagement with her intellectual thought both within and beyond *A Plea for Emigration*. It aims to illuminate the original elements of Shadd Cary's perspectives on dominant philosophical problems that African Americans engaged during the mid- to late nineteenth century, most notably, racial uplift, women's rights, and emigration. Of particular import are two points: that Shadd Cary's activism extended beyond editorship, and that she participated in public discourse on a range of topics beyond emigration. This book seeks to expand our interpretations of the modes in which Africana theorists articulated their intellectual thought, and to foreground how nineteenth-century Black women, who are frequently characterized as *doers* rather than *thinkers*, laid the foundation for Africana philosophy. Through examining the breadth and depth of Shadd Cary's intellectual work, it is possible to arrive at a fuller understanding of how African American women shaped early Africana philosophy.

---

[20] Almonte, ed., *A Plea for Emigration*, 29.
[21] Antwi, ed., *A Plea for Emigration*, 11–12.

Reading Shadd Cary's Radicalism

When I taught an undergraduate course, Black Radical Women, on the first day of class, I asked students to write their own definitions of Black radicalism. One definition in particular stuck with me. A first-year student, Johny McGrath, astutely suggested that Black radicalism is an ideology comprised of things that should not actually be considered radical. In some ways, I tend to agree. It should not be considered radical for Black people to want to live lives free of state violence. It should not be considered radical for Black people to want economic self-determination, or to be free from class exploitation. It should not be considered radical for Black people to want to be able to exercise some measure of control or self-governance in their own communities. Yet to achieve those goals would necessitate a radical reorganization of society as we know it, and as we have known it for the past four hundred years. It would require a dramatic reordering of legal, political, and social systems. It would call for a large-scale unlearning of racial logics, as well as education about antiblackness and white supremacy. I suggest, then, that it is inherently radical to fight for Black people's liberation from systemic oppression and the freedom to define ourselves in a world designed to deny these rights to us.

I prefer to think not of Black radicalism as a cohesive ideology, but of Black radicalisms, in the plural, as a set of overlapping ideologies and methods oriented toward securing Black people's political, economic, and civil rights. Black radicals do not always agree with each other. They at times have competing goals and pursue divergent strategies. They engage in fervent debates with one another, and the dynamics between various thinkers and activists over time illustrate that Black radicalism is not fixed; it holds a variety of meanings in the nineteenth, twentieth, and twenty-first centuries. Some scholars might locate nineteenth-century Black radicalism in thinkers like Martin Delany, who has often been hailed as the "father of Black nationalism."[22] Others might conceptualize the Black radical tradition during the twentieth century as one that is necessarily linked to socialist and communist thought.[23] However, both of these formations elide the ways that nineteenth-century Black women, too, conceptualized and enacted their own forms of

[22] Victor Ullman, *Martin R. Delany: The Beginnings of Black Nationalism* (Boston: Beacon Press, 1971).
[23] Cedric Robinson, *Black Marxism: The Making of the Black Radical Tradition* (Chapel Hill: University of North Carolina Press, 2005).

Black radicalism, often in ways that explicitly critiqued masculinist notions about citizenship *and* in ways that predated Marxist interpretations of race and labor.

The trouble with conceptualizing Black radicalism as a single intellectual formation is that Black people have never embraced a singular understanding of our condition, needs, and hopes for the future. Conversely, identifying multiple Black radicalisms runs the risk of creating an umbrella so wide that "radicalism" becomes devoid of meaning. As David Scott suggests, identifying who and what belongs to an intellectual tradition "does not pre-suppose agreement, a uniformity of perspective, [or] an ultimate consensus" on a set of ideas.[24] Instead, to include work in a tradition—or in this case, to write Shadd Cary into the Black radical tradition—is "to take a stand on what is to be valued, preserved, transmitted, inculcated, and remembered."[25] Without a doubt, Shadd Cary should be remembered. Scott asks: "Is there a genealogy waiting to be written about the idea of a black radical tradition that would traverse—and therefore connect—the discontinuous uses to which it has been put in the historical times and geopolitical spaces of black intellectual life?"[26] Here I offer an answer.

I suggest that what unites various forms of Black radicalism is a concept I term *a Black radical ethic of care*. A Black radical ethic of care, at its core, represents the convergence between recognizing the multilayered forms of oppression that target Black communities; critiquing the micro- and macro-level manifestations of antiblackness and white supremacy; and articulating or acting on a desire to realize change on behalf of Black communities. Work on Black feminist ethics of caring and Black radical love tends to privilege emotions and interpersonal relationships. In *Black Feminist Thought: Knowledge, Consciousness, and the Politics of Empowerment*, Patricia Hill Collins explores how Black women have embraced an ethic of caring in their families and communities. She identifies three central features that inform what she describes as "an alternative epistemology used by Black women."[27] According to Collins, Black women's ethic of caring entails "the value placed on individual expressiveness, the appropriateness of emotions, and the capacity for empathy," which all "reappear in varying combinations

---

[24] David Scott, "On the Very Idea of a Black Radical Tradition," *Small Axe* 17, no. 1 (2013): 3.
[25] Scott, "On the Very Idea," 3.
[26] Scott, "On the Very Idea," 1.
[27] Patricia Hill Collins, *Black Feminist Thought: Knowledge, Consciousness, and the Politics of Empowerment* (New York: Routledge, 2000), 262–263.

throughout Black civil society."[28] She argues that this reflects both African and feminist epistemologies. Collins's formulation of Black women's ethics of caring is valuable for identifying how Black feminist ways of knowing become linked to larger political projects.

Likewise, Darnell Moore explores how love precipitates action. In "Black Radical Love: A Practice," he suggests that "nothing but an unwavering love for Black people can catalyze and sustain the protracted struggle for Black liberation and its various iterations across time."[29] Moore posits that Black radical love is the driving force behind Black people's mobilization in support of Black communities. He identifies Black radical love as the central motivation for twenty-first-century protests, like those around the killings of Trayvon Martin and Michael Brown. Above all, Moore frames Black radical love as a daily practice that requires standing in solidarity with and in defense of multiply marginalized Black populations, like LGBTQ Black people, Black women, and disabled Black people.[30]

I put forth a Black radical ethic of care as a bridge between Black feminist ethics of caring, Black radical love, and Black radical theory and praxis over time. I understand the three aforementioned characteristics—grappling with intersectional oppressions, confronting various forms of antiblackness, and theorizing or enacting Black liberation—not as motivations for pursuing Black radicalism, but as its defining features. Where Collins and Moore explore how ethics of caring and Black radical love are the roots of Black activism and community-building, I suggest that a Black radical ethic of care, in and of itself, is Black radicalism.

Studying the work of Black thinkers and activists through the lens of a Black radical ethic of care creates epistemological space to identify continuities within Black radicalism across space and time, without minimizing specific points of departure that emerge based on historically located conditions. A Black radical ethic of care ties together existing strains of thought while highlighting how Black radicalism can take many different forms. Rather than orienting a Black radical ethic of care around emotion, feeling, or affective labor and bonds in the ways that some theorists have framed feminist ethics at large, a Black radical ethic of care considers how Black radical practices of community care can take a variety of forms. The ways that Black

[28] Collins, *Black Feminist Thought*, 264.
[29] Darnell L. Moore, "Black Radical Love: A Practice," *Public Integrity* 20, no. 4 (2018): 325–328.
[30] Moore, "Black Radical Love," 326.

women embraced a Black radical ethic of care during the nineteenth century might not necessarily reflect the forms of Black radicalism that were popularized during the twentieth century, like militancy among the Black Panther Party for Self-Defense or communism among Black radical women like Claudia Jones. Nevertheless, nineteenth-century Black women adopted their own strategies and stances that, within the context of racialized gender throughout the 1800s, *must* be considered radical.

The long nineteenth century produced a Black radical feminist tradition that becomes legible through its interlocutors' Black radical ethic of care. Shadd Cary's work exists alongside that of other women who shared many of the same priorities and employed many of the same strategies that came to define her life's work—figures like Maria W. Stewart, who was the first Black woman public speaker in the United States; Sojourner Truth, who was an abolitionist and suffragist lecturer; Sarah Parker Remond, an abolitionist who traveled and lectured abroad; Anna Julia Cooper, a writer and an educator; and Ida B. Wells, a journalist and antilynching activist. Their interrogations of how slavery specifically impacted women; how Black people could obtain civil rights; how African Americans could benefit from education; how to protect themselves from violence; how transnationalism could facilitate Black freedom; and the conditions that shaped Black people's labor situated them within debates that animated nineteenth-century Black radical thought. They examined such questions with Black men who also displayed a Black radical ethic of care, like Delany, Douglass, and Garnet. Black women were not peripheral, but central, to early Black radical theorizing.

Black women's radicalism took several forms throughout the nineteenth century. In some ways, their radicalism appears muted due to the racial and gendered constraints that required them to couch their intellectual interventions in the language of religion, domesticity, and middle-class standards of womanhood. Take, for instance, Frances Ellen Watkins Harper's 1855 article, "The Free Labor Movement." It begins by drawing on the sentimental tradition, explaining, "One of the saddest features of American Slavery, is its mournful reaction upon the whole country, both north and south."[31] However, Harper then calls on readers to abstain from consuming goods that were produced with slave labor. Her reflections on morality were

---

[31] Frances Ellen Watkins, "The Free Labor Movement," *Frederick Douglass' Paper*, June 29, 1855.

deeply entangled with her analyses of American economics. In other ways,
nineteenth-century Black radical women adopted strategies and stances that
were a prelude to twentieth-century Black radicalism. Some nineteenth-
century Black women embraced armed resistance. As Rebecca Hall and Kellie
Carter Jackson have shown, Black women were willing to take up arms in defense of themselves and Black communities, particularly in slave revolts.[32] It
is precisely because of the multifaceted nature of nineteenth-century Black
women's radicalism, like that of Shadd Cary, that I hope to reevaluate the
bounds of Black radicalism.

A Black radical ethic of care allows us to craft a definition of Black radicalism that is inclusive of Black feminisms. It also enables scholars to trace
the lineage of Black radicalism to the nineteenth century, and to account
for the different modes of theorizing and practicing Black radicalism at
varying points in time. Furthermore, this approach decenters masculinity in
histories of nineteenth-century Black radicalism by shifting attention away
from how Black men attempted to assert their manhood and humanity, to
how they adopted a Black radical ethic of care even though ethics of care
are traditionally conceived of as feminine. As Barbara Christian explains in
"The Race for Theory," there is a "tendency toward the monolithic, monothe-
istic, and so on" that obscures non-Western theorizing.[33] It is in the spirit of
exploring how the race for Black radical theory, too, has marginalized Black
radical women, particularly those of the nineteenth century, that I turn to a
Black radical ethic of care. Where Christian establishes that "people of color
have always theorized—but in forms quite different from the Western form
of abstract logic," I maintain that Black women have always theorized—even
in the nineteenth century, and even in ways that may not initially read as
radical.[34]

[32] Rebecca Hall, "Not Killing Me Softly: African American Women, Slave Revolts, and Historical
Constructions of Racialized Gender," *Freedom Center Journal* 1, no. 2 (2009): 1–44; Kellie Carter
Jackson, "'Dare You Meet a Woman': Black Women, Abolitionism, and Protective Violence, 1850–
1859," *Slavery and Abolition* 42, no. 2 (2021): 269–292.

[33] Barbara Christian, "The Race for Theory," *Feminist Studies* 14, no. 1 (1987): 75.

[34] For additional work on nineteenth-century Black women's radicalism, see Elizabeth A. Petrino,
"'We Are Rising as a People': Frances Harper's Radical Views on Class and Racial Equality in *Sketches
of Southern Life*," *ATQ: 19th Century American Literature and Culture* 19, no. 2 (2005): 133–154, and
Elizabeth Cali, "'Why Does Not SOMEBODY Speak Out?': Mary Ann Shadd Cary's Heteroglossic
Black Protofeminist Nationalism, *Vitae Scholastic* 32, no. 2 (2015): 32–48.

Two-Faced Archive

In an effort to reveal the contours of Shadd Cary's Black radical ethic of care, this text evaluates what K. T. Ewing terms a "two-faced archive," or alternatively, Black women's deliberate curation of how their public and private selves enter the historical record.[35] Ewing rightly notes that "a range of Black women have used practices of hiding, tricking, and obscuring towards the end of resistance" as they documented their own lives.[36] Shadd Cary herself was no stranger to these practices. As a writer and editor, she was incredibly attentive to questions of authorship and attribution, alternately writing anonymously in order to conceal her identity (however futilely); signing her initials; or publishing under her own name, which deliberately made her contributions known to the public.[37] Shadd Cary also did not publish under her married name until six months after her wedding.[38] These efforts to strike a balance between crediting herself for her intellectual work and maintaining some measure of privacy are best understood as acts of personal and archival self-preservation. Shadd Cary's two-faced archive suggests that her public portrayal—one of unshakable, fiery determination—was occasionally at odds with the anxieties, nervousness, or even desperation that she expressed privately over her ability to sustain herself and her work.

For instance, as early as January 1851, Shadd Cary wrote to George Whipple, who was corresponding secretary of the American Missionary Association (AMA), to express her commitment to educating Black children in interracial schools. However, by this point in time, she was already worried that students' school fees would not allow her to provide for herself unless she also received foreign aid, and she repeatedly wrote to Whipple about her need for financial support.[39] Over the next two years, Shadd Cary had grown uneasy about the stability of her relationship with the AMA, which she feared had soured due to her ongoing conflicts with Henry Bibb and Reverend C. C.

---

[35] K. T. Ewing, "Tricksters, Biographies, and Two-Faced Archives," *Black Perspectives*, African American Intellectual History Society, June 2, 2022, https://www.aaihs.org/tricksters-biographies-and-two-faced-archives/.

[36] Ewing, "Tricksters, Biographies."

[37] Jim Casey, "Parsing the Special Characters of African American Print Culture: Mary Ann Shadd and the * Limits of Search," in Fielder and Senchyne, *Sharp White Background*, 109–126.

[38] Rhodes, *Mary Ann Shadd Cary*, 113.

[39] Mary A. Shadd to George Whipple, November 27, 1851, American Missionary Association Archive, Amistad Research Center, New Orleans, LA (included in Part 1); Mary A. Shadd to George Whipple, February 14, 1852, American Missionary Association Archive, Amistad Research Center, New Orleans, LA.

Foote.[40] By March 1853, Shadd Cary was disenchanted by the unpredicta-
bility of receiving foreign aid to run her school, and was deeply frustrated
that she needed to rely on white benefactors to educate a community of Black
students in Canada. She reluctantly explains, "Not knowing the determination of your Ex. Committee concerning the school here I closed on the 22. So
long as there is uncertainty in regard to support for the school not much will
be done for the people." Shadd Cary notes that although "the school has been
very full this winter," the funds from the AMA "have not sufficed to support a
teacher one month. . . . I do not feel justifiable in contracting debts on my own
accord further than I have done when I know that the rates charged parents
will not meet the same by half."[41] She was willing to make personal sacrifices
in order to pursue work that was incredibly meaningful to her, but in the face
of mounting disappointment, remained firm that the burden should not be
hers to shoulder alone.

Where Shadd Cary's public writings often spoke to the necessity of Black
self-reliance and critiqued the political economy of Black activism, Shadd
Cary did not publicly address her personal financial difficulties with great
specificity. Any public discussion of finances in the *Provincial Freeman*
pertained to the paper's viability and occasionally scolded subscribers for
their unpaid bills.[42] In this instance, interpreting Shadd Cary's two-faced
archive of public writings alongside letters to benefactors grants further
insight into her self-fashioning as an educator, editor, activist, and intellectual. Shadd Cary's personal correspondence and her handwritten drafts of
published pieces, including the subsequent strikeouts, rewordings, or notes
in the margins, also grant insight into the meticulous revisions she made as
she considered how to plead her cause most effectively. The surviving documentation of Shadd Cary's public and personal life demonstrates how she
intentionally crafted a persona that would enter the historical record for
centuries to come.

[40] Mary A. Shadd to George Whipple, December 5, 1852, American Missionary Association
Archive, Amistad Research Center, New Orleans, LA.; Mary A. Shadd to George Whipple, April 2,
1853, American Missionary Association Archive, Amistad Research Center, New Orleans, LA.

[41] Mary A. Shadd to George Whipple, March 28, 1853, American Missionary Association Archive,
Amistad Research Center, New Orleans, LA.

[42] "To Travelling Agents and Subscribers," *Provincial Freeman*, May 13, 1854; "The Extension of the
Provincial Freeman," *Provincial Freeman*, March 1, 1856; "Pay us what you Owe," *Provincial Freeman*,
February 28, 1857.

Parts and Sources

This book contains four parts; a conclusion; and a recommended reading list with texts about Shadd Cary in particular and nineteenth-century Black women thinkers in general. The first three parts include writings by Shadd Cary on three key themes that become legible from her two-faced archive: racial uplift, women's rights, and emigration. Because Shadd Cary's conception of racial uplift was necessarily inclusive of women's rights and emigration, there is some thematic overlap between the parts. The final part includes observations that Shadd Cary's contemporaries made about her, including both praise and criticism. Sources are organized chronologically within each part. Rather than correcting typographical errors in the texts, I have reproduced the original documents as faithfully as possible. In some instances, I have added missing letters, words, or punctuation in brackets for clarity.

Shadd Cary was a versatile activist and intellectual who used a variety of methods to advocate for Black citizenship and liberation. Although she was immersed in Black print culture throughout her lifetime, the 1850s is the decade when she published her written work most frequently. Accordingly, many of the enclosed documents span 1850–1859. This was also a formative period for Shadd Cary's intellectual thought. Racial uplift, women's rights, and emigration first emerged as central frameworks in Shadd Cary's work as she considered how African Americans could be shielded from slavery. Her preoccupation with racial uplift and women's rights outlived the institution of slavery, and she continued to address issues including education, labor, and women's suffrage in the decades following abolition. Shadd Cary's support for emigration waned in the early years of the Civil War, as she was sufficiently optimistic about the possibility of abolition to return to the United States in 1863.

The 1860s proved to be a tumultuous decade for the nation at large and for Shadd Cary in particular. She published less frequently during the 1860s than the 1850s, which is likely a result of the numerous transitions she experienced. The *Provincial Freeman* had virtually dissolved by early 1860. Shadd Cary's husband, Thomas Cary, died in November 1860, and she gave birth to their second child in the months following his death.[43] Shadd Cary occasionally published her objections to Haitian emigration in newspapers during

---

[43] Rhodes, *Mary Ann Shadd Cary*, 135–136.

1861 and 1862, but her labor and role in public discourse largely shifted during the Civil War. She "juggled several jobs as she remained in the States to help the war effort."[44] Shadd Cary was also very mobile, having lived or worked in regions including Chatham, Indiana, Detroit, and Washington, DC, over the course of a decade. For these reasons, there are few surviving documents authored by Shadd Cary from this time period.

Reconstruction prompted additional shifts in the nature of Shadd Cary's advocacy on behalf of Black communities. During the late 1860s and 1870s, she taught in public schools in Detroit and Washington, DC; enrolled in Howard University Law School; sat on the executive board of the National Women's Suffrage Association; traveled around the country delivering lectures; and continued to write for newspapers in the nation's capital. The organizational records, unpublished work, and newspaper articles from the 1870s that are contained within reflect how Shadd Cary sought to fully integrate Black people, women, and indeed, *Black women*, into the US citizenry during this time period. Assorted unpublished writings, in particular, lend insight into Shadd Cary's willingness to reflect, revise, and evolve in her thinking. The latest documents in this reader, which were written after Reconstruction, highlight how Shadd Cary sharpened her specific focus on Black women's rights into the 1880s and how her work impacted DC's Black community.

This volume primarily includes texts that Shadd Cary signed or initialed. While most of the materials contained within are verified to have been written by Shadd Cary, it is well documented that she at times wrote unsigned editorials and authored anonymous pieces for other newspapers. There are editorials appearing in the *Provincial Freeman* where the authentication of the author is unsettled, although they were very likely written by Shadd Cary. "Woman's Rights" (1854), "To Our Readers West" (1855), and "Adieu" (1855) may be reasonably attributed to Shadd Cary because of the subject matter and writing style, like a biting discussion of the experience of women editors in the latter two pieces. Scholars generally agree that Shadd Cary authored these three texts. Zackodnik credits Shadd Cary for "Woman's Rights"; Rhodes and Rodger Streitmatter determine that Shadd Cary wrote "To Our Readers West"; and Streitmatter and Rinaldo Walcott acknowledge that Shadd Cary penned "Adieu."[45] Nevertheless, in order to avoid possible

[44] Rhodes, *Mary Ann Shadd Cary*, 158.
[45] Zackodnik, *African American Feminisms*; Rhodes, *Mary Ann Shadd Cary*, 98; Rodger Streitmatter, *Raising Her Voice: African-American Women Journalists Who Changed History*

misrepresentations of Shadd Cary's authorship, these three documents include footnotes that identify them as being unsigned.

Through her writings and activism, Shadd Cary put forth a comprehensive vision of racial uplift. Hers was one that centered Black independence, which she thought could be achieved through a combination of education, labor, honest leadership, and temperance. Part 1, "'Our Women Must Speak Out; The Boys Must Have Trades': Visions of Racial Uplift," includes newspaper articles, letters, and unpublished essay drafts that offer a cohesive snapshot of Shadd Cary's approaches to racial uplift. The documents illuminate her perspectives on labor and the importance of self-reliance. They also reveal her disillusionment with Reconstruction and demonstrate how her philosophies for racial uplift prioritized Black women. Shadd Cary's correspondence with and criticisms of her contemporaries also show how she participated in networks and conflicts with Black activists and white beneficiaries.

Shadd Cary theorized racial uplift as a process that must be rooted in community-centered advocacy. She regularly encouraged African Americans to prioritize action, like emigration or mutual aid, instead of passing toothless resolutions at meetings. However, Shadd Cary never divorced theory from activism. While she was critical of those who offered "strong words only" and encouraged African Americans to "look at facts instead of everlastingly theorizing," she never discounted the importance of creating and participating in Black discursive spaces, as can be seen through her editorship of the *Provincial Freeman* and her reliance on Black print culture to debate issues relevant to African American communities.[46]

The documents in Part 1 illustrate how Shadd Cary promoted Black self-determination in theory and in practice. She sought to create the conditions that would allow Black people to live free from oppression and empower African Americans to make decisions on their own behalf. In her view, self-determination could be achieved through racial uplift, which included priorities like education, temperance, and self-reliance. Interwoven with this vision was her support for emigration, which would not simply shield

(Lexington: University Press of Kentucky, 1994), 32; Rinaldo Walcott, "'Who Is She and What Is She to You?'": Mary Ann Shadd Cary and the (Im)possibility of Black/Canadian Studies, *Atlantis: Critical Studies in Gender, Culture, and Social Justice* 24, no. 2 (2000): 145.

[46] Mary Ann Shadd Cary, "Meetings at Philadelphia," *Provincial Freeman*, April 18, 1857 (included in Part 1).

Black people from American racism, but provide the foundation for other components of her racial uplift ideology, including integration and equal labor opportunities.

According to Shadd Cary, racism was virtually absent from Canada, a conclusion that she likely embraced because Britain's Slavery Abolition Act brought an end to slavery throughout all of its territories in 1834. Her argument that racial discrimination was nonexistent in Canada is one that would justifiably be met with skepticism by contemporary readers, especially considering that slavery existed in Canada from the seventeenth to nineteenth centuries.[47] Nevertheless, the fact that slavery had been abolished prior to Shadd Cary's 1851 arrival allowed her to picture Canada (perhaps, naively so) as a promised land where integrated communities would flourish. As Rhodes and Carol B. Conaway have written, Shadd Cary was an avid integrationist.[48] She was confident that Black people "must participate in and benefit from the dominant culture if they were to become respected parts of society."[49] In Shadd Cary's view, integration in Canada would ensure that Black people were not relegated to second-class citizenship. Furthermore, because Canada was allegedly free of racial prejudice, Shadd Cary anticipated that Black refugees would thrive in any form of labor they pursued in interracial communities. For Black people to choose when to work, how to work, and how they would be fairly compensated for their work was an ambitious and incredibly meaningful goal, especially against the backdrop of slavery in the United States, which simultaneously dictated the labor of the enslaved and restricted labor opportunities for the free. Shadd Cary was not a racial separatist, but she believed that Africans Americans must "separate" from the United States in order to escape white supremacy and have autonomy over their labor.

Shadd Cary's analyses of Black people's labor intensified during Reconstruction, the period from 1865 to 1877 when the American

---

[47] For additional information on slavery and racism in Canada during the nineteenth century, see Ken Donovan, "Slavery and Freedom in Atlantic Canada's African Diaspora: Introduction," *Acadiensis* 43, no. 1 (2014): 109–15; Robyn Maynard, *Policing Black Lives: State Violence in Canada from Slavery to the Present* (Black Point: Fernwood Publishing, 2017); and Barrington Walker, *Race on Trial: Black Defendants in Ontario's Criminal Courts, 1858–1961* (Toronto: University of Toronto Press, 2010).

[48] Jane Rhodes, "At the Boundaries of Abolitionism, Feminism, and Black Nationalism: The Activism of Mary Ann Shadd Cary," in Sklar and Brewer Stewart, *Women's Rights*, 346–366; Carol B. Conaway, "Mary Ann Shadd Cary: Visionary of the Black Press," in *Black Women's Intellectual Traditions: Speaking Their Minds*, ed. Kristin Waters and Carol B. Conaway (Lebanon: University Press of New England, 2007), 216–248.

[49] Rhodes, "At the Boundaries," 355.

government sought to integrate African Americans into the body politic as the country's newest citizens. As a pair of 1872 "Letters to the People" demonstrate, Shadd Cary saw Black people's labor as an integral part of racial uplift. In her view, by having control over their labor, Black people could depend on themselves rather than on potentially racist whites. To Shadd Cary, economic self-determination could shield Black people from the effects of white supremacy. She was skeptical of African Americans' political gains under Reconstruction and sought the end of their labor exploitation in order to create lasting change. During Reconstruction and, indeed, throughout the entirety of her career, Shadd Cary also viewed women's rights as a barometer for racial progress, as shown by her 1871 "Letter from Wilmington, DE" and her continual demands for Black women to be involved in public affairs.

The letters and articles in Part 1 also reveal how Shadd Cary's collaborative networks and contentious relationships with prominent African American men impacted her writing and activism. Some men, including Garnet and Douglass, influenced Shadd Cary's philosophy of racial uplift and published her work. Meanwhile, Henry Bibb and his white colleague, Reverend C. C. Foote, were frequent targets of Shadd Cary's criticisms. Shadd Cary was engaged in a protracted feud with Bibb and Foote. She disapproved of how their charity, the Refugee Home Society, managed its funds and portrayed African American refugees to white donors. Bibb repeatedly used his newspaper, *Voice of the Fugitive*, to criticize the school that Shadd Cary founded and to describe Shadd Cary herself as an ill-informed, unruly, unladylike woman.[50] An 1852 editorial, for instance, proclaimed that "Miss Shadd has said and written many things which we think will add nothing to her credit as a lady."[51] Their conflict represented not simply a dispute over what form Black community leadership in Canada should take, but also the appropriate bounds of Black women's activism during the nineteenth century.

Part 2, "'Our Leaders Do Not Take the Women into Consideration': Empowering Black Women," demonstrates how Shadd Cary argued for women's rights, particularly women's right to be activists and women's right to vote, over a thirty-year period. The articles, reports, organizational records, and essays in this part illuminate how she conceptualized citizenship and its gendered limitations. This part also includes several

[50] For more on the conflict between Bibb and Shadd Cary, see Rhodes, *Mary Ann Shadd Cary* and Cali, "Why does not SOMEBODY speak out?"
[51] "Schools in Canada," *Voice of the Fugitive*, July 15, 1852.

never-before-published documents wherein Shadd Cary advocated for women's suffrage. Collectively, the documents in this part show how Shadd Cary explored what roles women should play in racial uplift and in public affairs at large.

During her decades-long career, Shadd Cary embraced a broad conception of women's rights that included women's right to vote, to receive an education, and to participate in abolition, as well as other forms of activism. Over the course of thirty years, she transitioned from writing anonymously about gender, to incorporating feminism into her discussions of racial uplift, to explicitly advocating for women's suffrage and critiquing Black women's subordination to male activists. Shadd Cary used three primary strategies as she addressed gendered oppression in the *Provincial Freeman* and in other writings.

First, early in her career, Shadd Cary penned unsigned editorials about women's roles in Black activism. Pieces like "Adieu" and "To Our Readers West" discuss the difficulties that Shadd Cary faced as a female editor in order to address women's status more generally. Both editorials attribute the *Provincial Freeman*'s financial challenges to public resistance to patronizing a newspaper edited by a woman. In so doing, she suggested that sexism toward Black women ultimately hinders movements for Black rights and freedom. Although Shadd Cary did not sign either piece, both are written in her voice and from the perspective of a woman who faced sexist opposition in her chosen career.

Second, Shadd Cary frequently made passing reference to women's rights in articles that were primarily focused on race. For example, her 1856 "Editorial Cor. for the *Provincial Freeman*" documented Shadd Cary's observations about abolitionism during her travels through Ohio, but it also addresses Black men's hostility to women's rights. Similarly, in her 1871 "Letter from Baltimore," which is included in Part 1 of this volume, Shadd Cary described her disillusionment with Reconstruction-era reforms in politics, education, and labor. In her analysis of the failures of the political system, she also identified women's suffrage and women's employment as two areas of concern. For Shadd Cary, women's rights were intertwined with overlapping political issues. She prioritized gender alongside race, ultimately determining that they must be addressed simultaneously.

Finally, by the 1880s, Shadd Cary deliberately centered Black women in her public and private writing. Two unpublished, handwritten documents, "Would Woman Suffrage Have a Tendency to Elevate the Moral Tone of

· Politics" (n.d.) and "The Last Day of the 43 Congress" (c. 1875), make the case for women's citizenship. Others, including records from the only known meeting of the Colored Women's Progressive Franchise Association in 1880 and an 1887 article, "Advancement of Women," illustrate Shadd Cary's willingness to openly write about gender later in her career. This evolution is simultaneously indicative of Shadd Cary's growth as a thinker and of the gradual expansion of opportunities for Black women's public engagement throughout the nineteenth century.[52]

Part 3, "'The Men Who Love Liberty Too Well to Remain in the States': Enabling Emigration," includes a letter that Shadd Cary wrote to her brother, Isaac, upon her 1851 arrival in Canada. It contains Shadd Cary's landmark pamphlet, A Plea for Emigration, as well as shorter articles that provide a comprehensive view of Shadd Cary's interpretation of the impacts that emigration would have on African Americans. These pieces show how emigration was an integral component of Shadd Cary's philosophies of racial uplift, as emigration was interwoven with her calls for self-reliance and economic self-determination. The part also highlights Shadd Cary's opposition to Haitian colonization.

Additionally, the third part demonstrates that despite her fervent support for emigration, Shadd Cary was an avid integrationist. As Shadd Cary upheld the benefits of integration, she emphasized that British political institutions would guarantee African Americans civil rights and allow for social integration if they so choose. For Shadd Cary, racial discrimination is a uniquely American invention; she associates racism and white supremacy nearly exclusively with the American nation-state, despite evidence that Black people in nineteenth-century Canada also suffered from racial oppression. Indeed, Shirley J. Yee is correct in her assertion that "Canada emerges as a problematic site for the formation of identity and community" for African Americans during the nineteenth century, particularly for Shadd Cary.[53] As Rhodes

---

[52] For more on the forms of activism that Black women participated in during the nineteenth century and the social conditions that mediated their political engagement, see Gayle Tate, Unknown Tongues: Black Women's Political Activism in the Antebellum Era, 1830–1860 (East Lansing: Michigan State University Press, 2003); Jane E. Dabel, A Respectable Woman: The Public Roles of African American Women in Nineteenth-Century New York (New York: Basic Books, 2010); Shirley Yee, Black Women Abolitionists: A Study in Activism, 1828–1860 (Knoxville: University of Tennessee Press, 1992); Stephanie M. H. Camp, Closer to Freedom: Enslaved Women and Everyday Resistance in the Plantation South (Chapel Hill: University of North Carolina Press, 2004); and Deborah Gray White, Too Heavy a Load: Black Women in Defense of Themselves, 1894–1994 (New York: Norton, 1999).

[53] Shirley J. Yee, "Finding a Place: Mary Ann Shadd Cary and the Dilemmas of Black Emigration to Canada, 1850–1870," Frontiers: A Journal of Women Studies 18, no. 3 (1997): 2.

has explained, Shadd Cary was critical of Black activists in Canada who she believed supported racial separatism over African Americans' full integration into Canadian civic life, such as rival editor Henry Bibb.[54] Racial separatism "ran counter to Shadd's beliefs that Blacks must participate in and benefit from the dominant culture if they were to become respected parts of society."[55] Like Rhodes, Carol B. Conaway positions Shadd Cary as an "emigrationist-integrationist." Conaway explains that Shadd Cary understood the racialized limitations of attempting to secure equality in the United States, but simultaneously "envisioned the benefits of a continuity of North American Black culture, and the practicality and basic fairness of racial integration."[56] Shadd Cary believed that Black Americans must divorce themselves from the American nation-state in order to escape structural racism, but she did not endorse the view that racial separatism would advance racial equality and eradicate racial discrimination. As such, Shadd Cary's brand of emigrationism was critical of racism in the United States while still allowing for the creation of interracial communities in Canada.

Shadd Cary ultimately determined that pursuing racial separatism in Canada would be counter to Black people's goal of securing racial equality. As an alternative, she suggested that racial integration would simultaneously incorporate African Americans into civic and political life in Canada, and increase Black people's engagement with white business owners and patrons. Shadd Cary insisted that in Canada, people of different races worked alongside each other seamlessly and Black people had opportunities to become successful business owners.[57] In Shadd Cary's estimation, emigration and integration would widen Black people's access to labor opportunities and offer Black business owners a larger customer base. This, in turn, would guarantee them economic self-determination. For Shadd Cary, emigration was a multifaceted tactic to promote abolition, integration, and Black labor.

Part 4, "Contextualizing Shadd Cary" comprises contemporaneous accounts of Shadd Cary's writings and activism. Some documents offer excerpts or summaries of Shadd Cary's work. Others include praise for her as a pioneering female activist. Still others offer criticism of Shadd Cary from the perspective of those with whom she shared a contentious relationship.

---

[54] Rhodes, "At the Boundaries."
[55] Rhodes, "At the Boundaries," 355.
[56] Conaway, "Mary Ann Shadd Cary," 217.
[57] Shadd Cary, *A Plea for Emigration; or, Notes of Canada West, in its Moral, Social, and Political Aspect: With Suggestions Respecting Mexico, West Indies, and Vancouver's Island, for the Information of Colored Emigrants* (Detroit: George W. Pattison, 1852), 16–17.

This part reflects how Shadd Cary was received in her time by activists and general audiences alike. It also highlights African American collective memory of Shadd Cary's abolitionism during the late nineteenth century.

The conclusion discusses the relationship between Shadd Cary's interior life and her public-facing work, as well as the implications of Shadd Cary's work for how contemporary scholars may understand the history of Africana philosophy. It explains how the nature of Shadd Cary's archive impacts scholarship about her life and work, then identifies potential areas for further research. The recommended reading list identifies texts that offer further insight into nineteenth-century Black women's intellectual thought and the debates that Shadd Cary engaged in her work. Ultimately, Shadd Cary's writings and activism illuminate where Black feminists have been and where we may continue to go.

Part I

"Our Women Must Speak Out; The Boys Must Have Trades"

Visions of Racial Uplift

1. Letter to Frederick Douglass, *North Star*, March 23, 1849

WILMINGTON, Jan. 25, 1849.

FREDERICK DOUGLASS:—Though native of a different State, still in anything relating to our people, I am insensible of boundaries. The statement of Rev. H. H. Garnet which appeared in the North Star of the 19th inst., relative to the very wretched condition of thirty thousand of our people in your State, and your willingness to listen to suggestions from any one interested, has induced me to send you these lines, which I beg you to insert if you think worthy.[1]

The picture he drew, sir, of thirty thousand, is a fair representation of many more thousands in this country. The moral and intellectual debasement portrayed, is true to the life. How, in view of everything, can it be otherwise? We bring a heavy charge against the church and people of this country, which they themselves can hardly deny; but have we not been, and are we not still, "adding fuel to the flame;" or do our efforts, to the contrary, succeed as we have reason to expect? We are not satisfied with the result in every way—may be we have reason for not being. With others, I have for some time doubted the efficiency of the means for the end. Do you not think, sir, that we should direct our attention more to the farming interest than hitherto? I suggest this, as concerning the entire people. The estimation in which we would be held by those in power, would be quite different, were we producers, and

---

[1] Shadd Cary was referring to an article by Henry Highland Garnet, "Self-help.—The Wants of Western New York," that was published in the *North Star* on January 19, 1849. Garnet's article upholds self-help as an essential tactic for liberating oppressed peoples.

Mary Ann Shadd Cary. Nneka D. Dennie, Oxford University Press. © Oxford University Press 2024. DOI: 10.1093/oso/9780197609460.003.0002

not merely, as now, consumers. He, sir, proposed a Convention without distinction of caste—a proposition which no doubt will be acceptable, because
by exchanging views with those who have every advantage, we are materially benefitted. Persons likely to associate with our people in such manner,
are generally educated people, and possessed of depth of sentiment. Their
influence on us should not be lightly considered. We have been holding
conventions for years—have been assembling together and whining over
our difficulties and afflictions, passing resolutions on resolutions to any extent; but it does really seem that we have made but little progress, considering
our resolves. We have put forth few practical efforts to an end. I, as one of
the people, see no need for our distinctive meetings, if we do not do something. We should do more, and talk less. What intellectually we most need,
and the absence of which we most feel, is the knowledge of the white man,
a great amount of which, by intercourse in public meetings, &c., we could
glean, and no possible opportunity to seize upon which should be allowed to
escape. Should not the importance of his literature upon us, and everything
tending to add to his influence, be forcibly impressed, and we be directed to
that course? The great fault of our people, is in imitating his follies; individual
enterprise and self-reliance are not sufficiently insisted upon. The influence
of a corrupt clergy among us, sapping our every means, and, as a compensation, inculcating ignorance as a duty, superstition as true religion—in short,
hanging like millstones about our necks, should be faithfully proclaimed.
I am willing to be convinced to the contrary, if possible; but it does really
seem to me that our distinctive churches and the frightfully wretched instruction of our ministers—their gross ignorance and insolent bearing, together with the sanctimonious garb, and by virtue of their calling, a character
for mystery they assume, is attributable more of the downright degradation
of the free colored people of the North, than from the effect of corrupt public
opinion; for, sir, not withstanding the cry of prejudice against color, some
think it will vanish by a change of condition, and that we can, despite this
prejudice, change that condition. The ministers assume to be instructors
in every matter, a thing we would not object to, provided they taught, even
in accordance with the age; but in our literature, they hang tenaciously to
exploded customs, (as if we were not creatures of progress as well as others,)
as they do in everything else. The course of some of our high priests, makes
your humble servant, and many others, think money, and not the good of the
people, is at the bottom.—The great aim of these gentlemen now, is secrecy
in all affairs where our spiritual welfare is being considered. Our conferences,

they say, are too public. The open-stated people and laymen learn, as they should not, the transactions in conference and sessions, of these men of God. Depend upon it, sir, "men love darkness rather than light, because their deeds are evil." One thing is clear: this hiding the light under a bushel, is not, to those who dare think, very satisfactory; their teaching tends to in-culcate submission to them in all things. "Pay no attention to your perishing bodies, children, but get your souls converted; prepare for heaven. The elec-tive franchise would not profit you; a desire for such things indicates worldly mindedness."—Thus any effort to a change of condition by our people is replied to, and a shrinking, priest-rid people, are prevented from seeing clearly. The possibility of final success, when using proper means, the means to be used, the possibility of bringing about the desired end ourselves, and not waiting for the whites of the country to do so, should be impressed on the people by those teachers, as they assume to be the only, true ones; or at least there should be no hindrance to their seeing for themselves.

Yours for a better condition,

M. A. SHADD.

2. Letter to George Whipple, November 27, 1851[*]

Windsor, CW
/ Nov 27, 1851

Professor G. Whipple
/ Sir:

  In reply to yours of Nov., 4th, which has been recd., I beg you will not con-sider my effort here, an attempt to encourage the spirit of caste. I am utterly opposed to such a thing, under any circumstances, and would consider an attempt to enlist the sympathy of your society in favor of a project of the kind, decidedly reprehensible.[2]

---

[*] Mary A. Shadd to George Whipple, November 27, 1851, American Missionary Association Archive, Amistad Research Center, New Orleans, LA.
  [2] Shadd Cary was requesting aid from the American Missionary Association to fund the school that she opened in 1851. Although she encouraged Black self-reliance and was critical of Black leaders/institutions that relied heavily on foreign aid, like Henry Bibb and the Refugee Home Society, she did, at times, concede that aid was necessary. Her reluctance to obtain financial support from white benefactors did not grow out of a desire for racial separatism; Shadd Cary repeatedly voiced her support for integration (see A Plea for Emigration, 1852, and "The Things Most Needed," both in Part 3). Rather, as she explained in her 1854 "Our Free Colored Emigrants," she was critical of any attempts to fundraise that portrayed emigrants as destitute or beggarly. Shadd Cary sought to

Whatever excuse may be offered in the states for exclusive institutions, I am convinced that in this country, and in this particular region, (the most opposed to emigration of colored people I have seen), none could be offered with a shadow of reason, and with this conviction, I opened school here with the condition of admission to children of all complexions.

In answer to your first question, there is no doubt, that colored children would be admitted into the Governmt. schools of this village, if a process of law were resorted to; the Trustees of those schools, base their refusal, at present, on a provision (not at all mandatory) for colored people, in the "School Act.["][3] The parents are indifferent to the necessary measures, hence their exclusion. 2. There are, at least, forty children of suitable age, and many grown persons, who would frequent the day school, and who plead inability to pay, as an excuse for not sending or attending now; the frequent arrivals, make an exact estimate a difficult matter, but in a sch. among fugitives, grown persons contribute largely to the numbers.

If I should receive foreign aid, my dependence on parents would be at an end, I am convinced, as the sum realized from a day school, at one shilling per week, and an evening school, for adults, at sixpence, is insufficient to support any one comfortably, and is accompanied with protestations of poverty. One might get on, for a time, with the very poor accommodations the Barracks afford for a school on a small sum, but if an estimate of expenses (as room fuel ect.,) is included, as would have to be, 250. per annum would be the smallest sum reasonable.[4] At present, parents furnish fuel, and take room rent out of it, the consequence is, a very cold, open apartment, unfurnished & objectionable in every way, and a scanty supply of fire-wood.

In the states, I was connected by membership, with the African Methodists but have not renewed my membership with that body of Christians in this country, because of its distinctive character and do not purpose to do so.

---

preserve Black people's dignity and, accordingly, rejected any fundraising efforts that exaggerated the difficulties Black refugees faced in Canada.

[3] The Common School Act of 1850 determined how public schools would be organized and funded in Canada West. It stipulated that separate schools would be established for Black Canadians if twelve heads of households in a given district submitted a request in writing. As a result, public schools were strictly segregated, while private schools, such as the one that Shadd Cary opened, were integrated. For more, see Kristin McLaren, "'We Had No Desire to Be Set Apart': Forced Segregation of Black Students in Canada West Public Schools and Myths of British Egalitarianism," in *The History of Immigration and Racism in Canada*, ed. Barrington Walker (Toronto: Canadian Scholars' Press, 2008), 73.

[4] Shadd Cary's school was held in military barracks remaining from the War of 1812. See Rhodes, *Mary Ann Shadd Cary*, 35–36.

By way of testimonial as to personal reputation, or qualifications for this employment, I take liberty to refer you to Rev. C. B. Ray or Professor Charles Reason of your City, to whom I am personally known, or to Dr. J. McCune Smith—Rev S. E. Cornish or Mr. Wm. P. Powell, members of the "Society for the Promotion of Education Among Cold. Children," in whose employ I was, as a teacher in the Centre St., School in July last.[5] I am unmarried.

Respectfully Sir,
Mary A. Shadd

3. "The Colored People in Canada—Do They Need Help?," *Liberator*, March 4, 1853[*]

MR. GARRISON: The incomparable letter of Rev. C. C. Foote has been given to your readers; but, as truth is mighty and will prevail, there is no reason to fear that the real friends of the colored race will be slow to award their due to those 'tall beggars,' who live by misrepresenting the condition of fugitives, after this matter shall have been thoroughly sifted, and the glaring falsehoods and sophistry resorted to, to sustain a rotten institution, fairly set forth.

I can claim no consideration from you on the score of personal acquaintance, whatever; but as the authorized representative of a large body of fugitives, some of whose names I herewith send, I trust that you will open your columns, that something may be said in answer to the letter referred to.

[5] Here, Shadd Cary referred to Charles Bennett Ray (1807–1886), James McCune Smith (1813–1865), Samuel E. Cornish (1795–1858), and William P. Powell (1834–1915). In addition to illustrating how she was active in networks comprised of prominent African American abolitionists and editors, this statement to Whipple (1805–1876) shows how Shadd Cary at times cited her relationships with Black male leaders in order to legitimate herself as an authority on the issues facing African American refugees in Canada. This is a strategy that Shadd Cary perhaps used in order to preempt gendered criticisms of her work, which frequently transgressed nineteenth-century expectations for women's activism to occur in the domestic sphere.

[*] Shadd Cary's article title appeared in quotation marks in the *Liberator* because it is a direct response to Reverend C. C. Foote's article of the same name, "The Colored People of Canada—Do They Need Help?" that appeared in the *Liberator* on December 24, 1852. Charles C. Foote (1811–1891) was a white abolitionist who worked closely alongside Henry Bibb and fundraised for the Refugee Home Society. Shadd Cary, Foote, and Bibb were embroiled in several public spats during the early 1850s. Shadd Cary openly accused the Refugees' Home Society of misusing the money they raised to support fugitives from slavery. She also disputed Foote's portrayals of newly-arrived Canadians, who, in Shadd Cary's view, were not as helpless as Foote described. In response, Foote and Bibb published several personal attacks on Shadd Cary in Bibb's newspaper, the *Voice of the Fugitive*. Foote also wrote to the American Missionary Association in what would prove to be a successful attempt to block their funding of Shadd Cary's school. For more, see Rhodes, *Mary Ann Shadd Cary*, 65–69.

The article in THE LIBERATOR of November 22 [*sic*], 1852, is truthful in every particular enumerated, and, moreover, Rev. C. C. Foote's letter does not disprove anything therein contained; but, with wonderful ingenuity, a strange medley of false statements, curious comparisons, stale recommendations of the Fugitives' Home by gentlemen who have never examined the scheme in working order, cant, and *Uncle Tom's Cabin*, is made to pass muster before an intelligent community.[6] Did Mr. Foote learn of the 'small faction of colored persons in and about Windsor, (most of whom have never been slaves,') from personal observation, or from the *Voice of the Fugitive*? The entire statement is *false*, as the author of it knows, if he knows anything of the population and state of things here; but as he speaks without qualification, he must take the award the public will give him. It would be a difficult matter to find twenty families originally free in this township; and at the meeting here, not five were represented; but there was a *crowd* of fugitives. The assertion that the resolutions express the voice of nine-tenths, could not be contradicted by a single meeting; if it could, will Rev. Mr. Foote please tell at what time it was contradicted, and where the meeting was held? Since the formation of the Refugees' Home Society, there has not been a meeting held in its favor in Canada.

How does Mr. Foote know that the 'new comers' are not, by their own industry, enabled in a short time to help others? Does he know any thing of the value of labor in this country, and the ease with which it may be had? If he is acquainted with the facts, then his attempt to make the truth appear ridiculous, is ridiculous enough, surely. It is well known here that the emigration of fugitives by families is the exception, not the rule, and, as a consequence, there are more persons able to work. But I will give authority on this point that, may be, Rev. C. C. Foote will not despise.

---

[6] Shadd Cary's mention of a November 22, 1852, letter is a reference to "Aid to Fugitives in Canada," which was dated November 23, 1852, and published on December 10, 1852. Foote wrote "The Colored People in Canada—Do They Need Help?" as a rebuttal to this article. "Aid to Fugitives in Canada" argued that refugees relied on each other, not on aid from benefactors in the United States. It asserted that free Black people in Canada were largely opposed to "begging," particularly that of the Refugee Home Society, which Shadd Cary frequently criticized. "Aid to Fugitives in Canada" accused the leaders of the Refugee Home Society of keeping monetary donations that were earmarked for fugitives and of collecting old, moldy clothes as charity. In addition, the letter criticized the *Voice of the Fugitive*, Henry Bibb's newspaper, for misrepresenting a meeting that recently took place among free Black people in Windsor (including Shadd Cary). Foote's retort disputed the findings presented in "Aid to Fugitives in Canada" and dismissed its opinions as those of a small minority of Windsor's Black population. It contended that African American refugees are not as wealthy or successful as "Aid to Fugitives in Canada" would suggest, and it presented testimonials to the contrary. Foote also alluded to Shadd Cary's repeated criticisms of Henry and Mary Bibb (1820–1877) as he mounted a defense of their character.

'Work *can be had* by all who are willing to work, and the lazy deserve not encouragement in their laziness.'—'*Globe of Toronto*'.

'I attended a large meeting, *** and was pleased to see and hear so many ministers and people express themselves very decidedly in detestation of the (begging) scheme. At a public meeting in New Canaan, there was a unanimous voice in condemnation of the whole system.'—*Rev G. Thompson*.

'I have travelled from New York to Florida, and I have seen no land where I can get a living as well as here. We cannot hope to have *union* among us here, until this begging system is stopped. It causes more ill-feeling and division than anything else. *Every time you beg, you curse God, who has given you this good land.* *** If you will do yourselves any good, buy your own land, settle down, and make homes for yourselves.'—*Reported by Rev. G. Thompson*.

Does it look reasonable that this speech would have been made, if these things cannot be done? Who helped that flourishing community of refugees? They distinctly say this begging has been 'a curse instead of a blessing.' 'Numbers of men have got rich on it, and above work.' The beggars did not help them—they were a curse; then they must have helped themselves, assisted at first by friends around them, and at times, too, when it was more difficult for fugitives to get employment than now. Fugitives, at one time, were known to go back to slavery from this country, because it was found difficult to get either shelter [or] work, at first; but who has heard of a recent case of the kind? At *this season*, as many passengers of the underground railroad as can come, can get, without difficulty, from seven shillings to one dollar a day, or from ten to fourteen dollars per month, along the entire frontier.

'Let us compare the following settlements with the whites: Colchester, New Canaan, Malden, Gosfield, Sandwich, Queen's Bush, Dawn, Chatham, and Raleigh, which is called the Elgin settlement. In all of the above, we know that our people are owners and tillers of the soil, many of whom possess from ten to two hundred acres of land, and whose money goes freely, every year, for the support of government, &c. In addition to this, they are supporting schools, churches[,] and temperance societies, quite as numerously as our 'decent white brethren'; and *nine-tenths* of these persons are refugees from Southern slavery, who commenced here in the forest, without a cent of capital with which to help themselves.'—*H. Bibb's review of the Larwill letter, Feb.* 25, 1851.

In commenting on the proceedings of a meeting held in Ann Arbor, Michigan, the *Voice* of May 20, 1852, says, among other things—

'The man (Wm. Lumney) [*sic*] has recently taken an agency under the latter, to help the *poor, starving fugitives* in Canada.[7] ****** All of the enlightened portion of the colored population of Canada West have uttered their protest against it, [the begging.] No people ever was or will be respected or elevated, who do not respect themselves more than to become public beggars, or who will even consent to *live on the charities of others*, sooner than work for their living. *** In cautioning the public against these men, we had occasion to say, that "there was no suffering among this people," or that all who would work could make a good living, and we now re-affirm the same thing,'—H. Bibb.

But to the inquiry, 'Does slavery better qualify people for successful labor than freedom?' the fugitives answer: [']No, sir; therefore, in refusing your homes, they prefer British Liberty to a degrading serfdom under the Refugees' Home Society.'

The comparison of the sufferers by fire in Montreal, and the allusion to hundreds of *white* families, seem like straining a point; the cause is in a sad plight that requires such a far-fetched effort. Mr. Bibb says—

'But these beggars, who, like drowning men, are ever ready to catch at straws, seized upon this part of the sentence, [referring to the absence of suffering,] and put a false construction upon it. Show us a community where there is a very considerable number of inhabitants, be they white or black, in this Province or the States, and we will show some of the number who have not all the necessaries of life, and yet they have generally too much self-respect to send out beggars.'

Then may the destitute and starving of the large cities of the United States not be deprived of comforts, or the cause of the Southern slave hindered, by the unnecessary and unrighteous diversion of thousands of dollars into the coffers of the Refugees' Home Society, as the foregoing testimony of its Corresponding Secretary conclusively shows they would be. Singular people are these begging 'brothers of ours, surely'!

Of the appeals made by almoners, it may be said that the 'doctors do not agree,' when at home, as to their necessity. The honesty of nearly every prominent almoner in Canada has been questioned by Henry Bibb and wife, when talking of them, among whom are Revd's Hiram Wilson, Wm. P. Newman, Isaac J. Rice, E. E. Kirkland, D. Hodgkiss, and a host of smaller names I do not remember. Mrs. Bibb gave *one* dollar for a copy of I. J. Rice's miserable circular, in order that what she designated his 'lies about destitution' might be

---

[7] The article that Shadd Cary referred to identified a "William Swaney." See "A Protest from the Colored People," *Voice of the Fugitive*, May 20, 1852.

exposed. That children have been sent a long distance for books and clothes, there is no doubt; persons who have lived in the country twenty years— owners of well-cultivated farms, have asked for clothes after having heard they *were here*, and should they send their little ones, the children would find the journey more comfortable and less dangerous, if made through the forest, than on an open road. However, persons who do know of our forests, doubt this new version of 'The Babes in the Woods.' Had Mr. Foote looked at the November letter carefully, he would see, that quotations he makes do not agree with the original exactly; but he can have the full benefit of his construction, for fugitives think that it is not that many almoners have not deserved the penitentiary, that they have not been sent there. The Rev. gentleman's testimony as to the money sent, and also to the *poor* fugitive boxes being sent away to this cold country in their own care only, is matter of especial thanks. He cannot find fugitives in this section of Canada, who ever got any of the money sent. Mr. Bibb says to them, he never received 'a cent' for them from the States; and of the boxes, our merchants say, that as the boxes come directed to him, they keep them in their storehouses until called for *by him*, except those he brings over. It is true that boxes consigned to almoners have been stopped by other almoners, but the result has been, they 'got by the ears;' hence quarrels among the missionaries. It is not true, however, that no one is at fault for 'the waste.' I will tell the story out now, and the Rev. C. C. Foote may disprove it, if he can. The mouldy clothes in this region are those kept in Henry Bibb's stable, consisting of new shirts, good coats, new caps, and other good and bad articles, for men, women, and children. The chickens have roosted on them, his horses have walked on them, and some are kept there wet and frozen in boxes. Is no one at fault?

Mr. Bibb says the friends give him full power to give or not. What greater power has a Commissioner?[8] Should he think a man applying is not a fugitive, though he be destitute,—should the fugitive say he drinks on his arrival, he need not give. As some destitute persons have the misfortune to have been born free, and as not one fugitive in twenty knew any thing about a Temperance Society before starting North, and as there is no inconvenience in having boxes of valuable clothing, etc., come—but, over all, as almoners of that class are irresponsible, the lower animals may use them, but 'poor humanity' may not. Mr. Thomas Henning, of Toronto, intimates, in a published

---

[8] Shadd Cary compared Bibb to federal commissioners who presided over hearings with slavecatchers and ruled on the question of whether alleged fugitives from slavery were free or enslaved.

letter, that 'persons of whatever complexion' need aid at times. That does not mean white and black, and the intermediate shades of complexion, by our almoners; does it mean horses and chickens?

If the Home Society cannot furnish homes faster than the people receive them, or can be persuaded into settling on their lots, the more need that Mr. Foote and the other gentlemen begging for it should stop their operations. I visited the Refugees' Home recently; I know who are settled thereon—how many there are, and what they think of it. From them I learned that the Constitution of the Society had been *read* to them by 'quite respectable people in Detroit' as it is not—or rather, was not read to them as it *is*. Had they understood it, the few men of good character connected with it would not have meddled with it. Where are the points of comparison between this abortion and Mr. King's settlement of *respectable* persons, promiscuously *free* and *slaves*?

Would the benevolent believe, that of the twenty-one months the Society has had authorized agents out on its mission, but *seven* families have settled on the land; and *so eager* are they to get lots, that the *Voice of the Fugitive* has actually advertised lots as ready, although but twelve persons have been cojoled [*sic*] into taking lots at all; and some of these have declared they will give them up!

I repeat, that at the public meeting which authorized this reply, fugitives from off the 'Home' and from different parts of the county were present, *all* of whom expressed themselves as opposed to the 'Home,' and as relieved from all doubts as to the evils inseparable from this begging, when such a resort may be had to further that object by such means as the letter under consideration. The most of those whose names appear below are but a small portion of those who attended the meeting, but who left before the proposition to take names was made.

Very respectfully, sir,
MARY A. SHADD.

WINDSOR, C.W., Jan. 12, 1853

———

MINUTES

A MASS meeting of the colored people was held in this place, (Windsor, C.W.) on the evening of January 11th, 1853, to express more fully their views of the Refugees' Home, and to consider, especially, the recent letter of Rev.

C. C. Foote, an agent of the Refugees' Home Society. Samuel Green, of the Refugees' Home, was appointed Chairman, George Williams, Assistant, and Wm. P. Francis, Secretary.

The object of the meeting having been stated, Messrs. Jacob Jones, Coleman Freeman, Samuel Green, George Wilson of the R. H. S., Robinson Bush, Rev.—Talcot of Amherstburg, D. Johnson, and others, expressed themselves, forcibly, against the Refugees' Home Scheme, and Mr. Foote's letter, and the following resolution and motions were carried without a dissenting voice:—

Whereas, the Rev. C. C. Foote, an agent of the Refugees' Home Society, has, in taking exception to an authorized statement made by persons here, uttered foul slanders against us, by representing us as in leading-strings to Henry Bibb and wife, and as eager to settle on the Refugees' Home; therefore,

Resolved, That as we have heretofore done, we will use all honest means to prevent our brethren from being deceived in regard to the Home, and ask that the friends of our 'race' will discountenance Mr. Foote's operations because not tending to our benefit, or wanted by us.

Voted, That Mary A. Shadd reply to said letter in behalf of the people.

Voted, That we hold meetings often, and otherwise be vigilant to prevent the success of the species of oppression shadowed forth in the Refugees' Home Scheme.

The most of the following names were then given as evidence that there was no 'clique' of free persons; and as it was a late stage of the meeting, many having retired, it was

Voted, to increase the list hereafter.

Samuel Green, R.H.S.	Wm. Willis,
George Williams	John Garner,
Thomas Dolston,	Leonard Strander,
Robinson Bush,	Wm. Nelson,
Davidson Johnson,	Thomas Jones,
Henry Blackstone,	Jacob Jones, *free*,
Ralph Carter	Delilah Jones,
Coleman Freeman, *free*,	Emeline Jones,
Oliver Thurston,	Amelia Gasaway,
Richard Bush,	J. T. Jackson,
James Tyner,	James Watson,
Thornton Smith,	Charles Elliott,
Peter Stokes,	Amistead Marshall,
John Hogan,	Lucy Ward,

Henry Keyes,   Wm. Walker,
Wm. Keyes,   Martha Smith,
Thomas Brown,   ·   John Woodson, ·
Louis Ford,   Jesse Rucker,
Peter Poyntz,   Peter Locke,
Elisha Robinson,   Wyley Reynolds, *free*,
John de Baptist,   Mr. Newman.
Anselm P. Wilburn,
   SAMUEL GREEN, *Chairman*
   GEORGE WILLIAMS, *Assistant Ch'n.*
Wm. P. Francis, *Sec'y.*

4. "A Good Boarding House Greatly Needed by the Colored Citizens of Canada," *Provincial Freeman*, December 6, 1856

It is very desirable that some one acquainted with managing properly a good Boarding House should open one in Chatham, at this time, both for the respectable entertainment of the public and the citizens of this place. A "house of all nations" wherein the essentials, good tables and lodging, excellent deportment from proprietors and visitors, could be insisted upon, and where the charges would be in keeping with the character of the place. A good *temperance house* of high tone, and fitted up properly and managed by competent persons, would pay well! At the present time, we do not know of a public boarding house that is not also a drinking house. A most unworthy state of morals! and yet such houses, not 'gin palaces' either, are blazoned forth as desirable places of resort. We regard them as degrading in their tendency—as calculated to not only corrupt and demoralize the young, but as dangerous to the physical health of the community as the small-pox or cholera. For it is not only that they hold out the temptation to beastly intoxication—a fact that cannot be denied,—the quality of their liquors is so inferior generally, as to facilitate disease and death with greater rapidity than ordinary. Some of our Chatham boarding houses *make* their own liquors and a "make" they may be supposed to be. While the character of houses here is indifferent so far as we have been informed, the rates for entertainment are enormous. The wants of the travelling community justify better provisions than have been made in this respect, and we sincerely hope some enterprising COLORED Canadian or American will take the matter in hand.—M.A.S.C.

5. "For the attention of all Temperance reformers, Legislators, Ministers of religion &c," *Provincial Freeman*, March 28, 1857[*]

(For the attention of all Temperance reformers, Legislators, Ministers of religion &c.)

———

(SHORTLY WILL BE PUBLISHED)
A Census List
Of
The Inhabitants of Stratford
C.W.

For 1857, shewing the religious denominations,—those who use intoxicating drinks and those who do not, with the religious Denominations appended,— also taverns and sellers of intoxicating drinks, with also such religious denomination appended—Lists of Distillers and Brewers, with the same—List of Ministers of the County of Perth—(Lists of members &c., of congregations may be added.) Names of the Teachers of Schools &c. &c.—As it is Stated that the Traffick and drinking habits, and the drunkenness of our land are confined to Presbyterians, Episcopalians, and Roman Catholics, such lists will practically show the truth or untruth of the statement.

"Have they not (the trafickers) got enough of our blood?"—Hon. M. Cameron—"the next best legacy and gift to every woman and child of our land, will be the *freedom* from the "traffick" L—

By "AMEN"!—

STRATFORD C.W.
March 1857

NOTE. The attention of all Temperance Associations Sons of Temperance, Legislators, Ministers of religion, and others favourable to

---

[*] Shadd Cary advocated for temperance throughout her lifetime as editor of the *Provincial Freeman*, in her own writing, and as a lecturer. Her involvement in the temperance movement tended to be in an individual rather than organizational capacity. For more, see Rhodes, *Mary Ann Shadd Cary*, 197–199, and Lorene Bridgen, "On Their Own Terms: Temperance in Southern Ontario's Black Community (1830–1860)," *Ontario History* 101, no. 1 (2019): 64–82.

the putting down of the "CURSE" and the "DISGRACE," of our and every Christian country—the *public Traffic* in *Intoxicating Drinks* (the savage, uncivilized and unchristian lands excepted)—that attention is called to the adopting of such a Plan as the above, to show STATISTICALLY and more EXACTLY those who in our several municipalities and communities, countenance the public evil and disgrace of our day, "the Traffic in Intoxicating drinks."—and also by said plan, to help to purify a British Colony which is the most foremost of Great Britain's possessions; and make it—Canada— more reliable as a home for the Emigrant, under a free, liberal; and loyal government.

To make the "Census" complete in its intention generally, a List should be subjoined of the names of those RESIDENT inhabitants, who publicly use Intoxicating drinks at our *Public* bars and "*Saloons*"—the latter commonly named as the "Hells" of our community—Sober farmers, mechanics, millers, carpenters, labour[r]s &c., are those, D.J. who realize a competence and prosperity in Canada and meet with ready employment.—All those connected with our Railways must be sober men.—Ask Mr. Bridges, the Railway manager at Hamilton C.W.—Is the same sobriety needed as we move through life?—

Will papers favourable to the cause please copy.

We take great pleasure in giving insertion and drawing attention to the above. Could a census list of the kind be taken for Chatham, it would no doubt subserve a great purpose. Many a profane man hereabouts, will find an inebriate['] s grave, because he has an excuse for his drinking practices, in the examples set him by Deacons, Elders, preachers and other professors of religion.

The church in Canada is the bulwark of the liquor traffic, as the same body in the United States is of the slave trade. It is a lamentable fact, that tippling by the pious prevails to an alarming extent among our Canadian churches, both white and colored.

That it[']s no bar to membership, one would suppose to be also true, as men making loud professions deal in the trade—and a rebuke by the church for personal indulgence in the use of intoxication drinks is a rare occurrence, and only then of ministers, and not then till profanity, or some other vice in connection, has served to give prominence to the besetting sin. Neither is the practice confined to the denominations above mentioned, here, we will not answer for other places. Methodists, Baptists and Radicals, should come in for their share of blame, in towns and country in this county. That there is enough whisky used in the rural districts, to clear up the lands, and more than enough by churches in town to pay off the church debts we believe to be within the bonds of truth. Let the church only take up this work, and we shall see a different and better aspect of society.—M.A.S.C.

6. "Meetings at Philadelphia," *Provincial Freeman*, April 18, 1857

We beg to call attention to the proceedings of a meeting held in Philadelphia lately, to express condemnation of the Dred Scott decision, &c. Mrs. Mott, Messrs. Still, Remon[d], Purvis, McKimm and many others, white and colored participated.[9]

The resolutions are strong and pointed, but why not go farther? This is not the time for strong words only; when all realize the yoke so forcibly as now why not act? Protests are well enough in their way, but to be of effect, they must point to determined action. Do the Purvises, Remonds, and others, who took part in the meeting intend to stay in the U. States? if so, the resolutions amount to nothing, if not why not say so friends? Your national ship is rotten sinking, why not leave it, and why not say so boldly, manfully?

Canada is a good country,—we have British freedom and an abundance of it,—equal political rights of course, and if you covet it, social intercourse with those in your position in life.[10] We here give you facts. If Canada should be distasteful, British Europe, or the Isles may be more to your mind; at all events, leave that slavery-cursed republic. Another meeting of respectable free and independent colored citizens was held previously, as they claim to believe in the United States Constitution, we shall wait with patience to see what it will do for them. We hope, however, that they too, will look at facts instead of everlastingly theorising.

– M.A.S.C.

[9] Shadd Cary referenced the 1857 *Dred Scott v. John F. A. Sanford* Supreme Court case. The Dred Scott decision determined that African Americans were ineligible for American citizenship. It also nullified the 1820 Missouri Compromise, thereby legalizing slavery in the western territories of the United States. Shadd Cary identifies some of the attendees at the meeting, including Lucretia Mott (1793–1880), William Still (1821–1902), Charles Lenox Remond (1810–1873), Robert Purvis (1810–1898), and James Miller McKim (1810–1874). The meeting minutes and resolutions were published approximately one week prior to Shadd Cary's article in "Spirited Meeting of the Colored Citizens of Philadelphia," *Liberator*, April 10, 1857.

[10] As Part 4 of this volume will explain in greater detail, Shadd Cary believed that the British Crown would guarantee African Americans racial equality in territories including Canada and the British West Indies.

7. "School for ALL!!," *Provincial Freeman*, June 13, 1857

The School taught by Mrs. Amelia Freema[n] Shadd, is still in operation in Stringer's buildings, wherein young people of both sexes are instructed thoroughly in the primary and higher branches necessary to a good practical English Education, at moderate charges, to those able to pay.[11] Music, Drawing, Painting, are also taught, on most reasonable terms.

Mrs. Shadd will afford Educational facilities, gratis, to the children of poor widows and other respectable, but destitute persons, really needing such aid, and to that end, competent assistance will be obtained. The enterprise is praiseworthy, and will, we sincerely hope, enlist public attention as the tact and qualifications of the principal, peculiarly fit her for the management of such a school; and an institution wherein those least cared for can have ample instruction side by side with those able to pay, must meet with general approval. No complexional distinctions will be made.—M. A. S. C.

8. "An Unmitigated Falsehood," *Weekly Anglo-African*, February 15, 1862

TO THE EDITOR OF THE ANGLO-AFRICAN,

SIR:—Permit me to call the attention of your readers to a publication which first appeared in the "Argus," then in the "Pine and Palm" of Jan. 30th., and also in the "Globe," under the caption, "Meeting of Colored Canadians."[12] I am constrained to take this step, because of the repeated and persistent attacks of a handful of mischievous persons, who find encouragement from the "Pine and Palm," and those papers in Canada, friendly to the removal from the Provinces of the colored people.

I cannot now go into the details in this matter, but permit me to say in brief, and for the information of a shamefully deceived public, that no such resolutions as those in the "Pine and Palm" ever passed at any meeting in Chatham. That the charges of deeding the Mission School property to I. D. Shadd as "private property," is a falsehood of the most infamous kind, because

---

[11] Amelia Freeman Shadd was Shadd Cary's sister-in-law. Shadd Cary's reference to the "good practical English Education" available at this school reiterated her belief that African American refugees should adopt British models of schooling, politics, and social relations in order to facilitate integration. For more, see "The Things Most Needed" in Part 3.

[12] "Meeting of Colored Canadians" is included in Part 4 of this book.

invented for a deliberate purpose by J. C. Brown, J. W. Menard—these in favor of the Haytian Scheme—S. Holden and others, principals in a church quarrel in Chatham—to prevent me from prosecuting the work confided to me by the Trustees of the school and church; the laudable much needed generally approbated work by the colored and white citizens of Chatham, of all classes, of securing a high school and Mission Church for the use of the colored people, refugees and others. This string of resolutions like the former charges from the same source, were not only never passed, but never offered at the meeting in question; resolutions were offered, in keeping in style and matter with the ignorance, jealousy and wickedness of the parties proposing them, but they were promptly voted down, and resolutions sustaining the Mission School, its agent Mary A. S. Cary, the action of its Trustees in securing their property, one of whom by regular appointment is I. D. Shadd, were unanimously adopted, and subsequently signed by seventy persons who were at the meeting.

But by your permission the real resolutions shall ere long speak for themselves.

The resolutions now in circulation were drawn up by a lawyer of Chatham, the next day after the meeting, and published in the "Argus" of Chatham, against the knowledge of, and in the absence of the editor, but were published by the "Globe"; after a true statement had been given. So complete has been the confusion of J. C. Brown and Menard at home since that time, that they have openly and frequently denied in Chatham, having signed or circulated such names.

A notorious falsehood, a series of falsehoods, are thus sent forth on the wings of the wind, which will no doubt as designed defect, and in the end may destroy the only Mission School ever established by the colored people among the fugitives. Should such be the case, one or two outrageously hypocritical and designing men in the United States and their colored associates and creatures in Canada, will no doubt enjoy a little triumph. However, believing fully that truth is mighty and will prevail, I shall by the help of God, prosecute the Mission School agency as heretofore,—shall as I now do, lecture against the Haytian Emigration Scheme,—Shall work with might and main for the establishment of the Mission High School [. . .], the work to which I have been [appointed]; I therefore would respectfully suggest those fugitive friends [and any] man Black or white, now in doubt, to visit Chatham for themselves, and there on the spot, learn for themselves; or otherwise communicate with gentlemen in Chatham, as A. McKellan Esq., M. P.

P.; Rev Geo. Cochrane; Rev. H. L. Simpson; R. Stephenson, Esq.; Ed. Plane, or the Trustees concerned, among of when and Dr. M. R. Delany now in New York City.

MARY A. SHADD CARY

9. "Editorial- by M. A. S. Cary (Editor)," *Provincial Freeman*, Spring Edition 1866[*]

Intemperance- A colored man passed under the windows of this office on Saturday, "full of strange oaths," and very indiscreet expressions, the promptings of the god to whom he had been pouring in his libations. We cannot tell whom he may have insulted or even hurt under this influence. There is a law against furnishing drink to Indians, and we cannot but think that a similar restriction applied to the "son of Ham" would be a wholesome protection both to themselves and others.—*Planet*[13]

The *Planet* gets worse, and worse! Something more than bare assertion of regard for colored people must take place to make the community believe it. We all heard a few days ago, of the Editors of anti-slavery tendencies, and yet, whenever it can put a word in edge-wise, which will bear injustly upon colored men it does so. The colored people are not *wild* Indians, neither do they drink more whiskey than their white friends and if he had not "hurt" somebody he might have done so, bah![14] They must be out of a subject to wirte [*sic*] about down at that office! Every colored man must be prohibited from drinking because one drank freely. Who patronize the saloons, taverns &c., in this place? Indians and colored women only? No! We believe in passing a strictly prohibitory law that will not only prevent Indians and colored men from getting drunk, but will stop white men from drinking as well and not

---

[*] This article is from the latest known issue of the *Provincial Freeman*. Unlike its earlier print runs, which attempted to conceal Shadd Cary's role in the production of the newspaper, the masthead on the front page of this issue identifies her as the sole editor. The title of this article further emphasizes her centrality to the paper. Shadd Cary's decision to lay claim to her editorship in this particular fashion is a significant departure from earlier iterations of the paper. It suggests that by this point in time, Shadd Cary was less concerned about shielding herself from gendered criticisms of her role in publishing the newspaper.

[13] The *Planet* was a newspaper in Chatham.

[14] Shadd Cary references a stereotypical depiction of indigenous people as she attempts to defend African Americans from charges of reckless drunkenness. It is unclear whether she did so sarcastically or in order to draw a sincere comparison of alcohol consumption across races. Shadd Cary sometimes struggled to consider Black and indigenous peoples' shared victimization by white supremacy.

only the "inferior" classes about Chatham, but a drunken Editor occasionally. But the Editor of the *Planet* must have too much good sense, must be too much of an abolitionist to propose a regulation of the sort in sober earnest, else he must have forgotten that while to see a drunken colored man is of so rare occurrence as to "call him out" on the subject. Drunken officers, "limbs of the law," a drunken M.P.P. or a drunken Editor of his class is quite common nowadays.

M.A.S. Cary

10. "Letter from Baltimore," *New National Era*, August 10, 1871

BALTIMORE, MD., Aug. 1, 1871

To the Editor of the New National Era:

In this centre of rabid Democrats, lukewarm Republicans, (very lukewarm,) and timid man-fearing thousands of colored people, a stranger has many things to learn, and much one would forget. To win white Republicans of Baltimore over to a healthy and hearty support of party measures, and the very best man and men for the occasion, would be, to express the sentiments of the management in a thriving institution here, to loosen the grasp upon federal purse-strings, and put Democrats out of power, where they prefer to keep them, rather than that the franchise in the hands of the freedmen, and its results to them, shall be an accomplished fact. Severe upon and from our party, if true!

From the same high authority I learn that the story of Ku-Klux outrages ia a "good["] electioneering card for "*our*" party. The charges of bad faith against some Republicans here I believe are "sustained by upright men["]— colored and white. The volunteer and very weak-tea character of Ku-Klux anti-faith I do not believe, and did not; but recall it as evidence of the satyr-like muddle of the situation *here*. If hot and cold both come from the friends of our party, I leave you to judge what of the opposition, and *what* of the poor people; the thirty-five thousand of this city, ground out of much honorable aspiration by these upper and nether mill stones; yet this party is the best we have, and it must be purified.[15]

---

[15] During the nineteenth century, the Republican Party supported African American rights and freedoms more than the Democratic Party, which was, at the time, known to be the party of white

A mission to Baltimore is in an eminent sense a mission to the State of Maryland. Seventeen thousand colored men are here invested with the franchise. Many thousands of colored women I here find anxious to learn about the requirements and duties of their prospective positions.[16] I feel encouraged just here; only lay the facts before the colored women of this and, and they will be a bulwark for the right, as they should, whether men wish it or otherwise. I have heard for the national organ—the NEW NATIONAL ERA—are from them; and except that they do not always hold a share in the purse-strings, I could have rolled up additional subscriptions in no mean number. But the "ring" creature, the hideous deformed body of which is so glaring in Washington as the national center, extends its disgusting feelers into this State, and how far beyond is not pleasant to contemplate. Some things have to be met—that is one—rings of colored men against colored men. In the most flourishing days of colonization rule, the fear that colored men and women would demonstrate their capacity was not greater than now, and here. Baltimoreans assure a stranger that then there was more to inspire the young, because they might "strive to try" in the dark and be-nighted fatherland. Then there were lyceums and other literary institutions, stock companies, etc., by managing which they could learn business routine. Then they had teachers among them, many educated abroad; now, although education is greatly encouraged among the most respectable classes,

supremacy. However, Shadd Cary calls into question the Republican Party's tepid commitment to antiracism. In the contemporary moment, progressive activists and social critics have argued that the Democratic Party is not sufficiently antiracist, even though it is more supportive of pro-Black legislation than the Republican Party. For example, in the midst of Black Lives Matter protests following the murder of George Floyd by a police officer, Rapper Ice-T stated on Twitter, "For the record. I am not a Democrat and I am not a Republican so you can miss me with all your Left-Right talk.. [sic] Both Wings are on the same Bird." Ice T (@FINALLEVEL), Twitter, June 1, 2020, 4:26 p.m., https://twitter.com/FINALLEVEL/status/1267553159364268032. Similarly, Shadd Cary argued that the Republican Party of the nineteenth century, although it ostensibly supported civil rights for African Americans, was not free from racism and was no better than the Democratic Party. For more on criticisms of the contemporary Democratic Party's approaches to racism, see Juliet Hooker, "How Can the Democratic Party Confront Racist Backlash? White Grievance in Hemispheric Perspective," *Polity* 52, no. 3 (2020): 355–369, and Malaika Jabali, "Pete Buttigieg Has a Race Problem. So Does the Democratic Party," *Guardian*, https://www.theguardian.com/commentisfree/2019/nov/22/pete-buttigieg-race-us-elections-2020-democrats, November 22, 2019. For more on similarities in racial attitudes between Republicans and Democrats, see Meghan Burke, "Racing Left and Right: Color-Blind Racism's Dominance across the U.S. Political Spectrum," *Sociological Quarterly* 58, no. 2 (2017): 277–294, and Nate Silver and Alison McCann, "Are White Republicans More Racist Than White Democrats?," *Five Thirty-Eight*, https://fivethirtyeight.com/features/are-white-republicans-more-racist-than-white-democrats/, April 30, 2014.

[16] Shadd Cary repeatedly framed voting as a duty, not as a right nor privilege. She reiterated this claim later in an unpublished essay, "A First Vote, Almost" (1871), and in her 1874 speech to the Judiciary Committee of the US House of Representatives, both reprinted in Part 2.

young people from here having been sent to New England, Philadelphia, and New York, and even to your own Howard University, when returned competent to take hold in the work of the education of any race, they are met by the Board of Education, before trial, with a flat refusal on the ground of incompetency, and *rebel* teachers, who by education and instinct, are opposed to giving them the most limited instruction, are placed in the schools. Accomplished colored teachers here, have been thus superseded, rebels of pronounced opinions placed over them; and Professor Rowan, the only true educator of the other race here, and whose flourishing institution is highly spoken of, has been insulted time and again, by teachers of colored schools and enemies of the people, for his impartiality. The illustration at Baltimore of rebel teachers of colored schools very decidedly conceals the point sought to be made by the report of colored schools South under rebel management. Jeff. Davis may well counsel patience when the Commissioner of Education reports such important agencies for our elevation, and turned over to the tender mercies of rebel grasp. Well, the colored man was always an item of interest on change, and whether the market be stock or greenbacks, what matter since they make such "sacrifices?" But wo! the poor negro! Buy him and sell him in slavery; manage him, educate independence and aspiration out of him in freedom! As results in Baltimore, in Maryland, and as human nature requires something upon which to center, we have "society" and "pleasure"—poor substitutes! Even family ties and affection, in notable and dangerous instances, are sought to be sacrificed to that most equivocal of all myths as yet, "colored society;" and the crowd looking on open up and rush through avenues of "pleasure."

Forty-eight thousand dollars receipts are the net exhibit of one single railway company of this city, where all compliment themselves on the gains in this behalf. But, after all, there are some here who are pledged to save this people. Dr. Willis Revels, Messrs. Lock, Gaines, Webb; Revs. Mr. Robinson, Cook, Bias, Wescott, Jaques, Myers, and others, are not dead, but active. These ministers, to their great credit, do a noble work for humanity in their respective denominations, and in the management of a financial success—the Dry-Dock Company. One pleasing feature of the semi-annual meeting of that company was the active participation of lady shareholders—household matters nicely cared for, and the ladies in season.

Women's suffrage here will have at least three circles of the best housekeepers in the city, and no interest injured. Irish, German, or American white women are not one whit ahead of our women in this city as housekeepers, carers for homes of the aged and institutions for the poor, without regard to color, as they should be. Mrs. A. Jourdan, now of Washington, has a brilliant record here as one not only famous in church, but in numerous good works by which both sexes are elevated. Her generosity to the NEW NATIONAL ERA, and subscription to the same, make no uncertain record here, and it is to be hoped representative women like her may multiply here and in your midst.

M. A. S. CARY

11. "Letter from Wilmington, DE," *New National Era,* August 31, 1871

Wilmington, Del., Aug. 24, 1871

To the Editor of the New National Era:

The same old route between Washington and Baltimore, but not quite the same railroad surroundings—the green car has taken a "new departure," and American citizens of doubtful descent now excite no more attention than others; and one is, at last, left comfortably alone.[17]

Arrived at Wilmington on the 12th instant, our old birth-place, and, after greetings from friends of long ago, we looked around as one into a new world. Such growth and enterprise on every hand! One is astonished at the general evidence of business success. The city will ere long extend to the Delaware river. Colored citizens are actively and energetically pushing their way everywhere—in the shops, in the market, opening up stores. Here Prof. Day and the *National Progress* flourish, doing much work in local politics, and to some purpose. The enemy is active here; the friends are more earnest than last year. The conservatives of the party have decided to work squarely in the interest of the organization. Fears were often expressed of again being "sold in the party," and very natural disgust at being compelled to help educate the children of white citizens indiscriminately, without their own having advantage of public school training.

It is safe to say, that more commodious brick dwellings are owned by the colored people of Wilmington than by equal numbers in any city of its size

[17] Shadd Cary traveled throughout the country during Reconstruction and frequently wrote letters evaluating how much progress has been made among Black communities in different cities. She commented on various aspects of Black life and racial uplift including politics, community institutions, social relationships, labor opportunities, and women's rights. This is one such letter.

in the country, besides three brick halls, neat and capacious churches, and other evidence of thrift and progress; and yet their petition for the very moderate sum of one thousand dollars per annum, in a population of seven thousand, as an initial experiment for them in free education, is met by the query whether or not some one's "temper has not soured upon too much breakfast." To be classed among friends, people must show themselves friendly.

I found the ministers of Zion, Union, and Radical churches and their stewards and people fast friends of the NEW NATOINAL [sic] ERA; and they propose to work for it when the dull season is past. To Messrs. Graves, Murray, and many others your agent is under obligations—they and their friends subscribed and otherwise aided.

The young men and women are an example; they have stock companies, a Christian association, and an Abraham Literary Society; besides which, the doors are thrown open to the active, sex being no barrier. Woman's suffrage finds no formidable opposition here. Camp-meetings, picnics, and other rural gatherings do not here absorb public attention, but find moderate countenance.[18] A female camp-meeting at Penn's Grove, in the vicinity, is only noticeable as showing the catholic spirit of the people and the hopeful aspect of the cause.

The colored people are a unit on Grant and the Republican party. It is safe to say that upon these points they "cannot be taught," or that any retrograde movement in the little State, which so confidently boasted, through its statesmen, of being able "to take care of Pennsylvania," must not be laid at the door of the colored voters. The Woman's Franchise question here finds much favor. Frederick Douglass as a leader is a favorite, and the importance of strengthening his hands by a better and a more perfect union of our leading men, is freely spoken of as a necessity of the situation. M. A. S. CARY

12. "Letters to the People—No. 1 Trade for Our Boys!," *New National Era*, March 21, 1872

To the Editor of the New National Era:
   I wish to call your attention to the importance of some movement whereby trades, &c., may be secured to our boys. There are hundreds of boys in the city alone who, after having exhausted every effort to secure employment, from

---

[18] Camp meetings were large, outdoor religious gatherings popularized during the nineteenth century.

the fact that paper-peddling, boot-blacking, driving, waiting and choosing, have more than their quota of employes [*sic*], resort to petty crimes; thence, through successive stages, to bolder schemes against the peace and security of society, and thus swell the number of criminals and vagrants, and prey upon the community, because an unrighteous public sentiment excludes them from the workshops, and religion, philanthropy, patriotism, have not a word to say in condemnation of the anti-American policy.

To the son of the German, the Irishman, the Canadian, Scotchman, the far off Pagan Japanese, the doors of your manufactories open wide, the next day after arrival; yes, before one word of the language has been mastered, while against the native-born colored youth, with the same aspirations as a white American, to appropriate and apply mechanical knowledge, and to improve upon it by application and invention, the doors are not only closed by individual bosses, but society combinations supplement the injustice by voting exclusion.

We have in this city colored mechanics whose work upon inspection equals the very best done by the fairest American or foreigner; these men take colored boys to be taught, but the hand of God is upon them in that He gave them a color which suited Him, so that the large numbers are so poorly patronized that but a limited number are now instructed.

The condition of colored youth in this city and District is true of them throughout the country. But the opposition by Americans is not the only cause of this sorry state of things, though mainly so; indifference on the part of leading colored men, and the death-like silence of colored women, contribute to it. A people whose leaders seek to learn the tortuous ways of speculation, and whose women are awed into silence upon vital questions, must for the time take back seats among the people. The white men of this and other countries deal vigorously now with every issue for the good of their youth, and white women are to the front with them in the work as having a common mission; they even unite in our exclusion and mutual congratulations, the result, are neither few nor whispered. Our women must speak out; the boys must have trades. What the crowned heads of Europe, and the poorest of white Americans do for their sons, we cannot afford to neglect.

I have a boy who must and shall have a trade, (D. V.,) and yet where may he learn it, or where exercise it when learned?

To begin at headquarters, not under Government patronage surely, for there, should a colored lad upon examination distance competitors, let but a persistent Southern rebel, a clamorous foreigner, or a Canadian rebel, seek the position also, and even after given, the well-known out-cry, "reduction of force" is made, which, by interpretation, means change of base, and down comes the headsman's axe upon apprentice, mechanic, clerk, and into his place goes the anti-Government aspirant.

Where then exercise it? The people exclude him. Clannish they worship their kind. As much as may be said about race ostracism by whites, and how much may not be, too much cannot be said against indifference among ourselves. I want our poor tongue-tied, hoppled, and "scart" colored women—"black ladies" as Faith Lichen had the bravery to call them, in her Mary-Clemmer-Ames-i-ades—to let the nation know how they stand.[19] White women are getting to be a power in the land, and the colored women cannot any longer afford to be neutrals. Never fear the ward-meetings; get the boys started properly in life, and the ward-meetings will come right.

I want to see the colored preacher canonized, who looking after the great interests of the Master's flock, will, Beecher-like, cry out on Sunday against this sin of keeping our boys from trades, to the fostering of iniquity and the ruin of their souls.

---

[19] Shadd Cary commended another writer, "Faith Lichen" (who likely wrote under a pseudonym) for her scathing response to a racist article written by a white journalist, Mary Clemmer Ames (1831–1884). Ames published "A Woman's Letter from Washington" in the *New York Independent* on January 25, 1872. The letter discussed the writer's displeasure at sitting next to well-dressed Black women on streetcars and, worse yet, being made to stand because Black women had already filled seats at a hearing for a civil rights bill put forth by Senator Charles Sumner. Ames was particularly offended that Black women had the audacity to think themselves equal to white women. Lichen's response, "That Woman's Letter from Washington," was published one month later in the *New National Era*. She affirmed Black women's right to occupy public space without showing deference to white women. Lichen also mobilized the politics of respectability by identifying Black women as "black ladies," which is the point Shadd Cary applauds. As several scholars have noted, during the late nineteenth century, African American women sought to embody middle-class notions of propriety in an attempt to combat derogatory stereotypes of Black people and avoid racist treatment. As Ames shows, however, respectability politics could not be an effective strategy if the prospect of respectable Black women was viewed as an affront in and of itself. Respectability politics represented an imperfect response to anti-Black racism. The same could be said of the contemporary moment, when the politics of respectability fails to protect Black people from state-sanctioned police violence. In the present day, the politics of respectability presents a flawed, individualized solution to structural problems. During the nineteenth century, however, respectability held promise as a strategy for Black women (and Black people more broadly) to avoid racial violence and discriminatory treatment. For more on Ames's and Lichen's comments, see Dorothy Sterling, *We Are Your Sisters: Black Women in the Nineteenth Century* (New York: Norton, 1997), 433–434, and Kate Masur, *An Example for All the Land: Emancipation and the Struggle over Equality in Washington* (Chapel Hill: University of North Carolina Press, 2010), 228–231. For more on Black women and the politics of respectability in the nineteenth century, see Evelyn Brooks Higginbotham, *Righteous Discontent: The Women's Movement in the Black Baptist Church, 1880–1920* (Cambridge: Harvard University Press, 1993); Jane E. Dabel, *A Respectable Woman: The Public Roles of African American Women in 19th-Century New York* (New York: Basic Books, 2010); Brittney Cooper, *Beyond Respectability: The Intellectual Thought of Race Women* (Urbana: University of Illinois Press, 2017); and Treva Lindsey, *Colored No More: Reinventing Black Womanhood in Washington* (Urbana: University of Illinois Press, 2017).

Four millions of "laborers" in the midst of thirty millions of active, energetic people with arts, science, and commerce in their hands, and the love of domination a cardinal point in their creed—four millions that chain to this dank and hoary "labor" carcass—are as certain of subjugation, ultimately, as were the Helots; and this should arouse to action the entire force among the people.[20] I know we have resolutions of conference and of conventions, and have had for a generation; and that each convention is the greatest ever held; but the people know comparatively little about them or their resolutions. We want then, an arousing of the people, and the pulpit must help in the work.

We have no theatres, beer-gardens, opera, nor grand lecture amphitheatres, wherein such questions may be discussed, reshapen, dramatized, made vital issues; the church—the pulpit stands to us in this stead; our preachers, as they should be, are politicians, and do use their churches often as places in which blessed white christians [sic] help them to adjust, arrange, and work party laws. No greater party work than this for our boys can they do.

I have not forgotten that we have a few live members of Congress, though I believe no one has as yet got around to trades; and although we must have Civil Rights, I look upon trades exclusion as meanly and wickedly beyond even the reach of that. In parenthesis, another of the many weak places in "your armor," so be it.

I know that we have members of State Legislatures and from whom more may be expected than from even Congress; also, attaches of the learned professions, and aspirants in the field of letters, all of which is enjoyably rose-tinted and gilded as compared with the past; but we, no more than others, can afford to build at the top of the house only.[21] Ill-timed and unseemly as it may appear, the craftsman, the architect, the civil engineer, the manufacturer, the thoroughly equipped citizen, must all come, though silently, surely through the door opened to us by the mechanic. So agitate for the boys!

MARY A. SHADD CARY

---

[20] Helots were an enslaved people in ancient Sparta.

[21] Shadd Cary's positions in "Letters to the People—No. 1 Trade for Our Boys!" predate Booker T. Washington's (1856–1915) racial uplift ideology and critique the notion of a "talented tenth" prior to W. E. B. Du Bois's coining of the term thirty years later. Similarly to Washington, Shadd Cary advocated for Black people to pursue trades and apprenticeships, although she did not prioritize the need for skilled laborers over the need for civil rights, protest, and political participation. Shadd Cary also rejected the view that African Americans should rely on the Black elite, or in Du Bois's words, the "talented tenth," to combat racism and secure equality for all African Americans.

13. "Letters to the People—No. 2 Trade for Our Boys!," *New National Era*, April 11, 1872

The more we examine this subject of trades exclusion, and others cognate thereto, the more intensely painful does the investigation become. A few, so few, favor the colored mechanic—fewer instruct the colored youth.

The history of our race is replete with efforts of workmen to become masters and contractors, but philanthropists boldly say: "*not one cent*" through your hands, to make opportunities for colored boys; "we would rather have a white aristocracy." As if aristocracy has anything to do with it. No, it is a determination to keep our people in the background by associate effort, the key to comprehensive and effective business success among others.

The manly and dignified demand of one of the Douglass Brothers for trades recognition, and the fierce, defiant, and powerful opposition through him to his race, all know.[22] When, however, a pitiful job is doled to a negro, he is very ungrateful not to prostrate himself in the dust and thank some one for permission to earn his daily bread; so that it comes to this that right to life is not inherent, but is by grace of, it may be, an enemy. I think that those who so loudly proclaim perfect freedom call out triumphantly before being out of the difficulty.

The lessons of slavery are not so readily unlearned by white Americans, and the serfs of European despotisms take to them like the Commodore's small-pox—in the natural way; but the depravity involved is amazing. To keep under foot a class, and that class, as is the colored Americans, largely allied through ties of blood relationship, shows a mean, uncertain, and cruel spirit. None but those of Saxon and Celtic combination, with iron eye and steel-cold heart have ever entered upon a task so clearly the greatest of outrages upon nature. A South African Hottentot, or a Dahoman cannibal never slaughters his own; but in America is the theatre, and here are the people who have traded in their own children, and, as if not enough, have, by a subtlety of iniquity almost incredible, arrayed colored men on against another—against his own kindred; then complacently, but in manner so deprecating, wonder that "your people are so divided." "You do not support one another." When should you insist upon the right to take initial steps in that direction, "friends" often combine and pronounce against your

---

[22] Shadd Cary referred to one of Frederick Douglass's sons, Louis Henry Douglass (1840–1908), Frederick Douglass Jr. (1842–1892), or Charles Remond Douglass (1844–1920).

"assurance" more loudly and effectually than known enemies. I recall the history of a colored mechanic of this city, and shall here let this branch of the case rest for the present.

A colored craftsman, admitted by slaveholders to be one of the best cabinet-makers in the District having been sold, (and at an unusually high price,) took the Underground Railroad and went to Canada. There he earned for successive years the first prize at exhibitions for his white employer. Since his return to the land of his birth he has received but little employment from white "friends" or colored "brethren;" the former having a Dutch friend or a cousin in Massachusetts, a Connecticut uncle, or family of relations to provide for; the latter, afraid of loss to "bread and cheese" don't like to risk it. Mr. White, or Green, or Gray, who gave a pair of boots, or a good-as-new old hat might get angry, or he don't know whether a colored man can do as well as a white one any how. This man, whom foreign ministers, cabinet officers, Senators, (men usually superior to so much worldly wisdom,) do patronize, went, armed with proper vouchers from men in high position to tender for a position in which instruction for colored boys, managing economically the details of a business to pay and be profitable, were included. Upon comparison of details, &c., so much was found to be unobjectionable; now to the test of skill.

When white men are upon trial, a specimen of best work upon best material is demanded. When a colored one, you must do the best upon inferior stuffs. He was told to furnish a set, such as is used in humble homes, strong, durable, but of his best workmanship, and give therewith, a statement of how much the actual cost of the raw material:—the set to be for exhibition, or as sample: all of which was done and upon inspection, was decided to be all that could be desired. Well, of course he got a contract! Not at all: he did not even get one cent for the time and labor taken to make them. The goods were not put on exhibition, but went to a private home. White men, one Yankee, one German got the business, the negro got the price of lumber, nails, varnish, etc., nothing more. The crowning point was that an abolitionist and a Christian developed this ingenious, but losing piece of kindness.

The mechanic works away, yet single handed, for notable ministers and Secretaries, but fails to understand why he should not only not aspire to management over even colored youth, made to pay white men, but should lose his labor beside.

Extremes are said to meet, and this perfect parallel to the slaveholding practice of taking a colored man and his time to the use of whites, suggests the query whether different principles like opposite policies, move in (rings) circles? These cases, when traced to their ultimate, show that whatever may have been, the name "friend" is fast losing its significance, and that we, who have always been the victims of policy, must in turn, and in the spirit of this era, make a policy.

Demand that a portion of patronage come to your shops, from both white men and colored, else withdraw your patronage from the corner grocery, and let it keep itself. We are told that prejudice against color is very wrong; all of which means prejudice against the white color. You must spend the last farthing in supporting white masters, mechanics, stores, and trades. See to it that colored men and women be encouraged to conduct business; and that they get more than whites give you, at least half of your support.

Give to colored tradesmen, at least, the favor you bestow upon an Irishman, an after-the-war Republican, or a rebel, all of whom make all they can out of you, and scheme to keep your boys, working in turn, to support their boys, and that without tolerating from any source, however high in a Republic, dictation. The three classes named, have no demand upon you; had no more at the start than you had: the last particularly you made, and altogether, as you give them material to "get up," strike you down, and through you cripple the Government. Nothing should make us forget class ties, and a common interest. A little quiet determination to be sustained by whites and negroes, or to stop buying from them; a little decisive action; a good deal of purpose among leading men to work some for your benefit, instead of helping white men and women, who never were able to own any body, up into places they know not how worthily to fill, and to use colored people for their benefit, would make a difference in the long run; and colored boys would have some rights that others were bound to respect.[23]

The poor of all countries make their money; their labor is needed; they spend it without tolerating dictation; your money, when earned, is yours, your labor is needed. The foreigner ships part of his wealth to Europe to keep up old dynasties, or to import others of his race, who aid in oppressing you. Yours remains in the country, and aids the white man to strengthen his hand, in the unrighteous fight against your people, and the exclusion of your sons.

Proclaim a policy and stick to it like grim death.

MARY A. SHADD CARY

---

[23] Shadd Cary alluded to Chief Justice Roger B. Taney's (1777–1864) majority opinion in the *Dred Scott* case, wherein he famously declared that African Americans "had no rights which the white man was bound to respect." See *Dred Scott v. John F. A. Sanford*, 60 U.S. 393 (1857).

14. "Should We Economise?," n.d.[*]

What is destiny as applied to colored Americans? I ask because in some respects we practically ignore duties, trials[,] tasks almost self-imposed by the people at large.

The days for croaking are past;—we need no longer to whimper and cry out at a pinch; bear in mind that pinches[,] cuffs, kicks, a stab now and then, are a part of the caresses with which white Americans greet us. So long did the people endure that it was said to be his normal condition to be abused— he could not be comfortable without it.

And the impression is very slow wearing. Thousands of colored men and women are whipped and murdered in the South—& sneers and incredulity meet one on every hand.[24] "It could not be so["]—white people ag[g]ress and only blacks are the sufferers: does a goaded negro turn[,] slay a murder[er] & whipper and the country is arouse[d] to suppress "negro["] "outlaws."[25]

[*] This document is an unpublished essay draft written at some point after 1865. Mary Ann Shadd Cary, "Should We Economise?" n.d., Mary Ann Shadd Cary Collection 13, Box 1, MSRC Division, Moorland-Spingarn Research Center, Washington, DC.

[24] From nineteenth-century lynchings to modern-day police brutality, conceptions of racial violence frequently center Black men. In her analysis of racial terror, however, Shadd Cary recognized that Black women, too, were targets of white supremacist violence during the mid- to late nineteenth century. Shadd Cary's inclusion of African American women in her framing of anti-Black violence runs counter to contemporary depictions of Black men as the primary, if not only, victims of racial violence, particularly during the Jim Crow era. See Orlando Patterson, *Rituals of Blood: The Consequences of American Slavery in Two Centuries* (New York: Basic Books, 1999). In the contemporary moment, Black women are infrequently seen as victims of racial or gender violence because of stereotypes that frame Black women as strong, promiscuous, or otherwise impervious to pain. This has the effect of obscuring the types of violence that Black women face, which prevents them from obtaining appropriate forms of protection or redress from harm. For more, see Saidiya V. Hartman, *Scenes of Subjection: Terror, Slavery, and Self-Making in Nineteenth Century America* (New York: Oxford University Press, 1997); Crystal N. Feimster, *Southern Horrors: Women and the Politics of Rape and Lynching* (Cambridge: Harvard University Press, 2011); Evelyn Simien, *Gender and Lynching: The Politics of Memory* (New York: Palgrave, 2011; Danielle McGuire, *At the Dark End of the Street: Black Women, Rape, and Resistance: A New History of the Civil Rights Movement from Rosa Parks to the Rise of Black Power* (New York: Vintage, 2011); and Andrea Ritchie, *Invisible No More: Police Violence against Black Women and Women of Color* (Boston: Beacon Press, 2017).

[25] Shadd Cary's commentary was prescient in many ways. Presently, as a result of racial bias, the criminal justice system continues to acquit perpetrators of anti-Black violence, such as George Zimmerman, while disparately punishing African Americans for similar and lesser offenses. See Cynthia Lee, "Making Race Salient: Trayvon Martin and Implicit Bias in a Not Yet Post-racial Society," *North Carolina Law Review* 91, no. 5 (2013): 1555–1612, and Christopher Ingraham, "Black Men Sentenced to More Time for Committing the Exact Same Crime as a White Person, Study Finds," *Washington Post*, November 16, 2017, https://www.washingtonpost.com/news/wonk/wp/2017/11/16/black-men-sentenced-to-more-time-for-committing-the-exact-same-crime-as-a-white-person-study-finds/.

Nameless outrages are committed upon colored women and children in the presence of bound and helpless fathers, sons & brothers and: "they say so, but it is absurd" say those not enemies, but "friends"(?) who cannot any sooner than in the slavery-times take a negroe's [sic] word, though he carry the scars. Formerly enemies only doubted, in obedience to a clanish [sic] instinct of defending their own, but the worst feature of the present situation friends doubt in the face of the facts.[26]

A foreign. A white child meets a colored one and the first greeting is likely a tweak of the nose or a "dig" to make him "squeal[."] The colored one retorts with a "face["]; well we gather up the little [white] one and send him to New England[,] Oberlin[,] or some other Heaven upon Earth to make them be good—because thoug[h] it is against the nature says my good white friend that they should be together;—it is convenient to have a little "colored person" to wait upon you and show his gratitude. Hence the buts, and scratches, & sneers, and wait and serve their way in school together for years to come out the white armed with the whip of "friendship["] to ply in the name of gratitude to his latest generation when the lion and lamb shall eat each other, the negro to demonstrate to the world how thoroughly a season of buffettings on equal terms can clean divert him of self-respect as a colored citizen, how important that he should cease to be colored as fast as possible and utterly incredulous of race success unless advised[,] managed[,] or lead [sic] solely by whites & for them. Mean time what benefit is he to his "race"? Why ten to one he will deny his race, or decry it.

---

[26] Shadd Cary alludes to concepts that Eduardo Bonilla-Silva would eventually refer to as two guiding principles of color-blind racism, "minimization of racism" and "abstract liberalism." See *Racism without Racists: Color-Blind Racism and the Persistence of Racial Inequality in America*, 5th ed. (New York: Rowman & Littlefield, 2017). Bonilla-Silva writes, "*Minimization of racism* is a frame that suggests discrimination is no longer a central factor affecting minorities' life chances ('It's better now than in the past' or 'There is discrimination, but there are plenty of jobs out there'). This frame allows whites to accept facts such as [racial violence and discrimination] and still accuse minorities of being 'hypersensitive,' of using race as an 'excuse,' or of 'playing the infamous race card' " (57). He also explains, "The frame of *abstract liberalism* involves using ideas associated with political liberalism (e.g., 'equal opportunity,' the idea that force should not be used to achieve social policy) and economic liberalism (e.g., choice, individualism) in an abstract manner to explain racial matters. By framing race-related issues in the language of liberalism, whites can appear 'reasonable' and even 'moral,' while opposing almost all practical approaches to deal with de facto racial inequality" (56). Similarly, Shadd Cary sarcastically expresses her frustration with "friends," who we might today refer to as "white allies," who downplay the severity of anti-Black racism and hesitate to remedy it despite their self-proclaimed distaste for racial inequality.

15. "Diversified Industries a ~~National~~ Necessity," n.d. [*]

Class or race sensitiveness and indecision ~~is~~ seems to have had a condition of all subordinated peoples intensified or [e]liminated in kind when located amidst[,] near[,] or more remote from each other and especially to be noted[,] as in our case[,] when equal political status is claimed. Indeed we are the only people except perhaps the Scotch in modern times where the apparent anomaly presents itself of theoretical political equality and apparent class or race domination, but with the separation by topographical limits. The special development of certain industries has been no less helpful to them that Englishmen not only claim for them. Equality, grace—but the Scotch are striving to turn the tables by floating equality of class and asserting superiority of race.

How then is this abnormal intellectual condition and collaterally physical diffidence to be changed? How relegate to indifference ~~and~~ or forgetfulness recurring phantoms or fantozies [sic] respecting individual and race capacity as compared with fellow citizens of the other and so-called dominant classes? How break the bonds of a morbid fearful self-hood[,] and with open eyes to the practical facts intercepting our foot-steps[,] seize upon the ways and means fast eluding our reach so that before too late we may demonstrate to a certainty that to us [,] as to men of every race[,] and as to the majority of the nation[,] abstract theories differing from those applying to others are wrong [?] [W]ould we realize the fruits of full citizenship? ~~What methods to the attainments of this object should we apply? The foregoing interrogatories seem to me suggested by the predicament if I am [. . .] so call it in which we find ourselves after years of "freedom." Another~~

Shall routine, inanity[,] infertility in a single groove of thought and action blend confidence[,] dependence[,] and servility as in the past and at present need and continue the advancing future[,] or shall we strike out into the illimitable field of enterprise and active national life, open to those who fear not ~~need~~ to en[g]age in the feats of competition with his fellows suggested by the increasing [. . .]

---

[*] This unpublished, handwritten essay draft by Shadd Cary is pictured in Figures 1.1 and 1.2. Although the surviving document is incomplete, it grants insight into how she experimented with and revised her ideas as they were in their early stages. Notably, this piece suggests that classism and racism amplify exploitation among people who are already oppressed. Shadd Cary also notes that despite the country's stated commitment to equality, classism and racism are rampant within the borders of the United States. She asks what steps African Americans can take to achieve "full citizenship," and begins to suggest that African Americans would benefit from entering various fields that would exhibit their intellect and capacity to contribute to American national life. "Diversified Industries a National Necessity," n.d., Mary Ann Shadd Cary Collection 13, Box 1, MSRC Division, Moorland-Spingarn Research Center, Washington, DC.

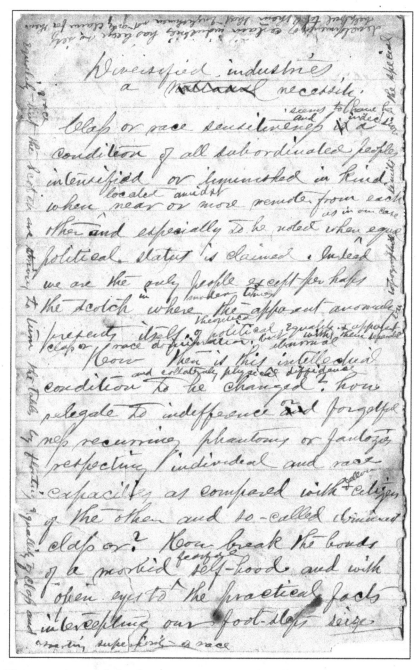

Figure 1.1 Diversified Industries a ~~National~~ Necessity." N.d. Mary Ann Shadd Cary Collection 13, Box 1, MSRC Division, Moorland-Spingarn Research Center, Washington, DC.

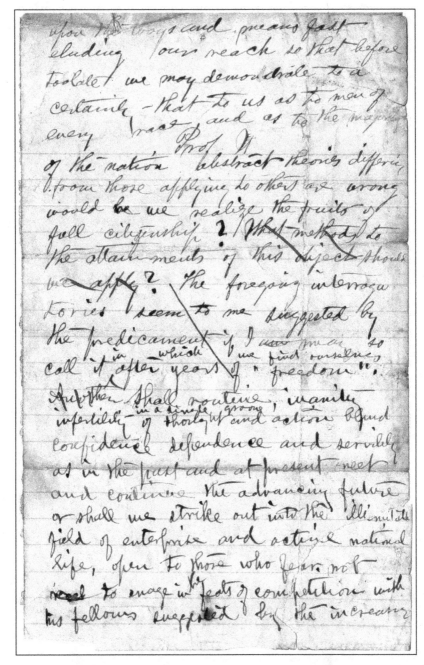

Figure 1.2 Diversified Industries a ~~National~~ Necessity." N.d., Mary Ann Shadd Cary Collection 13, Box 1, MSRC Division, Moorland-Spingarn Research Center, Washington, DC.

Part II

"Our Leaders Do Not Take the Women into Consideration"

Empowering Black Women

16. "Woman's Rights," *Provincial Freeman,* May 6, 1854[*]

In the N. Y. Assembly, the Committee to whom was referred the Woman's Rights memorial, have made a report. They assert that the education and elevation of women, are not the offspring of legislation, but of civilization and Christianity; and the more she is elevated the greater will be the difference between the sexes. On the subject of matrimony, the Committee are very conservative, maintaining that it is not a mere contract. Other points are referred to in the report, and the Committee finally recommended the passage of the following bill:—

> "1. Any married woman, whose husband, either from drunkenness, profligacy, or any other cause, shall neglect, or refuse to provide for her support and education, or for the support and education of her children, and any married woman who may be deserted by her husband, shall have the right, by her own name, to receive and collect her own earnings, and apply the same for her own support, and the support of her children, free from the control and interference of her husband, or of any person claiming to be released from the same, by or through her husband.["][1]

[*] This document is unsigned, but was likely written by Shadd Cary. Teresa Zackodnik also credits Shadd Cary with writing this editorial. See Teresa Zackodnik, *African American Feminisms, 1828–1923,* vol. 6: *Interracial and Black Feminist Organizing* (New York: Routledge, 2007).

[1] Shadd Cary referred to legislation that would have amended New York's Married Women's Property Law, but ultimately failed. Activists including Elizabeth Cady Stanton (1815–1902) delivered speeches to the New York General Assembly in favor of the proposed amendments. See "Women's Suffrage in New York State," New York Assembly, accessed May 31, 2020, https://nyassembly.gov/member_files/058/20090226/; and Norma Basch, *In the Eyes of the Law: Women, Marriage and Property in Nineteenth-Century New York* (Ithaca: Cornell University Press, 1982), 167, 186–193.

Mary Ann Shadd Cary. Nneka D. Dennie, Oxford University Press. © Oxford University Press 2024.
DOI: 10.1093/oso/9780197609460.003.0003

"2. Hereafter it shall be necessary to the validity of every indenture of app[r]enticeship executed by the father that the mother of such child if she be living, shall in writing consent to such indenture, nor shall any appointment of a general guardian of the person of a child by the father be valid, unless the mother of such child, if she be living, shall in writing consent to such appointment."

17. "To our Readers West," *Provincial Freeman,* June 9, 1855[2]

MR. ISAAC D. SHADD, an Agent of this paper, is now on a collecting tour West; he will also receive subscriptions.[3] We hope the patrons of the *Freeman* will do all in their power to facilitate his business, and use their influence among their friends and acquaintances, to increase our list of paying subscribers. That many persons do not like the *Freeman*, we know full well; but many do: so let those that do, be zealous to establish it permanently, and those that do not, cease to injure it, and all will go well. We cannot well afford to do without an organ in this country, at present, for our credit and interests; should it be cried down, as is attempted, the disgrace will not attach to the handful who labour for it, but immeasurably to the one who would "preach, lecture, edit for the blacks," and the people at large, who were eager to have it got up. The assertions of those interested in their own schemes, at your expense, as to a want of appreciation on your part, as a people, already too true in notable individual instances, will then tend too surely to consign you to an unenviable and subordinate position, as a class, and which can only be averted, or from which you can only be successfully rescued, by a press in your interest, well supported and well supplied with able managers; this

---

[2] Although this document is not signed, it was likely written by Shadd Cary. See Rhodes, *Mary Ann Shadd Cary*, 98; Rodger Streitmatter, *Raising Her Voice: African-American Women Journalists Who Changed History* (Lexington: University Press of Kentucky, 1994), 32. This editorial announced Shadd Cary's upcoming decision to step down as editor of the *Provincial Freeman*. She reflected on some of the difficulties she faced as editor, which she believed could be attributed, in part, to her gender. Shadd Cary's editorial illuminates her perspectives on Black women's right to participate in racial activism as well as her criticisms of other Black people, including Black women, who fail to support Black women leaders like herself.

[3] Isaac D. Shadd (1829–1896) was Shadd Cary's brother. He assisted in the publication of the *Provincial Freeman* by soliciting subscribers for the newspaper, serving as its partial owner, and managing its daily operations. Shadd was eventually elected to serve as the Speaker of the House of Representatives in Mississippi. Rhodes, *Mary Ann Shadd Cary*, 104, 108, 114–118.

latter, from the straightened circumstances under which the *Freeman* came into existence, it has not been able, as yet, to have. Without powerful friends at home, or abroad; opposed to begging, even to prolong its existence; no corps of devoted persons ready and willing, without pay, to make the "welkin' ring" with appeals in its behalf, beyond solicitations for subscriptions, advertising, and jobs; with Editors of the unfortunate sex, who never, in their most ambitious moments, aspired to the drudgery; with this chapter of difficulties at the outset, and attending it, it has had to struggle harder than the interests of any people require, if they too will not put their shoulder to the wheel.[4] But it must not be so; the *Freeman* must not be discontinued, because obnoxious persons have it in charge. You must not be suffered to fall into the error of starving, because you cannot get a "whole loaf" at once.

Arrangements are being made, which it is hoped will secure for the *Freeman* a gentleman Editor—one that *will* see to your interest—with a number of efficient canvassers; by that course, it is hoped, *your* business *will be attended to*.[5] The ladies will be pleased, and assist to sustain it, which they will not do while a *colored* female has the ugly duty to perform; then it is hoped, that the childish weakness, seen in some quarters, will disappear altogether.[6] Meanwhile, friends, do all you can to make the Agent's tour profitable, and the *Freeman* prosper. We had a severe winter: you all had; "dull times" was at this office, too; but you can keep him away in future, by paying up arrears, getting new names, and organizing tea-meetings among yourselves. Who will take the lead in the latter movement? It is at home; is

[4] Shadd Cary's mention of "editors of the unfortunate sex" referred to herself and her sister, Amelia Shadd (not to be confused with their brother Isaac Shadd's wife, Amelia Freeman Shadd). Amelia Shadd participated in publishing the *Provincial Freeman* by writing articles and occasionally editing the newspaper in Shadd Cary's absence (Rhodes, *Mary Ann Shadd Cary*, 96).

[5] Shadd Cary faced several obstacles as editor of the *Provincial Freeman*, including the newspaper's struggle for financial viability. Accordingly, by the summer of 1855, she resigned as editor and was succeeded by William P. Newman (1810–1866). As Rhodes explains, "Mary Ann's self-representation as the embattled reformer thwarted by gender prejudice was a self-serving strategy that allowed her to advance a political critique without taking responsibility for her own failings. Her harsh, often abrasive style of commentary had undoubtedly offended some readers who might otherwise have been more generous with their support" (Rhodes, *Mary Ann Shadd Cary*, 97). For more on the conditions that precipitated Shadd Cary's resignation, see Rhodes, 93–99.

[6] Shadd Cary intimated that some Black women in Canada were complicit in reproducing hegemonic, patriarchal ideals that sought to limit Black women's public race leadership. Over one hundred years later, bell hooks would echo Shadd Cary's criticisms, writing, "As with other forms of group oppression, sexism is perpetuated by institutional and social structures; by the individuals who dominate, exploit, or oppress; and by the victims themselves who are socialized to behave in ways that make them act in complicity with the status quo." See bell hooks, *Feminist Theory from Margin to Center* (Boston: South End Press, 1984), 43.

not begging, as some wiseacres have said; is for your paper, and they have heretofore been patronized by yourselves and a generous public. Those ready to stigmatise it as begging, do not know all they might, and are not of the class who help any good enterprise.

18. "Adieu," *Provincial Freeman*, June 30, 1855[*]

With this number of the paper we consign to other hands the literary department of the same, and in the course of a few weeks, shall pass over the keys of the business department also, and content ourself with active efforts to get subscribers for it. In taking leave of our readers, at this time, we do so for the best interests of the enterprise, and with the hope that our absence will be their gain. We want the *Freeman* to prosper, and shall labour to that end. When it was *not*, but was said to be needed, we travelled to arouse a sentiment in favor of it, and from then until now, have worked for it, how well others must say, but, through difficulties, and opposed to obstacles such as we feel confident few, if any, females have had to contend against in the same business, except the sister who shared our labors for awhile; and now after such a familiar acquaintanceship with difficulties, of many shapes, in trying with a few others to keep it alive for one year, as at first promised, we present it in its second year, afresh to the patronage of friends to truth and justice, and its Editor, the Rev. WM. P. NEWMAN, to their kind consideration. To its enemies, we would say, be less captious to him than to us; be more considerate, if you will; it is fit that you should deport your ugliest to a woman. To colored women, we have a word—we have "broken the Editorial ice," whether willingly or not, for your class in America; so go to Editing, as many of you as are willing, and able, and as soon as you may, if you think you are ready; and to those who will not, we say, help us when we visit you, to make brother Newman's burdens lighter, by subscribing to the paper, paying for it, and getting your neighbors, to do the same.

---

[*] This document is unsigned; however, it was likely written by Shadd Cary. See Streitmatter, *Raising Her Voice*, 32, and Rinaldo Walcott, "'Who Is She and What Is She to You?': Mary Ann Shadd Cary and the (Im)possibility of Black/Canadian Studies," *Atlantis: Critical Studies in Gender, Culture, and Social Justice* 24, no. 2 (2002), 145. This article was Shadd Cary's final editorial, wherein she reckoned with the disappointment of her resignation, her hopes for the *Freeman*, and the monumental significance of her editorial successes for Black women in Canada and the United States.

19. "Editorial Cor. for the Provincial Freeman," *Provincial Freeman*, April 26, 1856

Wheaton College and the friend in danger—Meetings on the Dixon Road— Depp & Co.—Woman's Rights—Friends at Sycamore, and Brush Point Anti-Slavery

Since I last wrote you, meetings have been held in a number of places, account of which Mr. Douglass has already sent to your readers. The weather, too, has assumed altogether a better character, so that travelling is comparatively pleasant. As my field of operations is not the same at present, as friend Douglass, your readers will be made acquainted with the state of the cause, &c., in two different sections almost at the same time.

At Wheaton, I found staunch friends of freedom, and the claims of the colored American were not presented in vain. Wheaton is the seat of a flourishing institution for ladies and gentlemen, in which no distinction of color exist[s], and yet, there have been but three colored persons among the students as yet I learn. In many respects, Wheaton should be preferred before Oberlin where prejudice of color is known to be so strong, although the latter is known only as an anti-slavery school.[7] The educational privileges of these Western States, are in many respects superior to the East for colored persons at present, how the case would be were colored people more numerous I am unable to say. You will get an idea of their numbers from the fact, that except when at Chicago and Milwaukie [*sic*], I have not seen one dozen all told, in the last month although incessantly changing place.

After attending meetings held at Batavia and Aurora, in company with H. F. Douglass, I journeyed towards the Dixon Road, and held meetings at St. Charles and Geneva, two pro slavery hamlets.[8] Deacon Ward and a few noble men and women keep the first named place from tumbling in; but the number of the faithful are yet fewer in the last named place. Held a very lean meeting at St. Charles indeed, the Congregationalists do not let their church for anti-slavery lectures—one at least, of the hotels is afraid to take colored female

[7] Wheaton College and Oberlin College were both founded as interracial, abolitionist institutions. They were also active stops on the Underground Railroad. For more, see "Underground Railroad," Wheaton History A to Z, accessed June 9, 2020, http://a2z.my.wheaton.edu/underground-railroad; and J. Brent Morris, *Oberlin, Hotbed of Abolitionism: College, Community, and the Fight for Freedom and Equality in Antebellum America* (Chapel Hill: University of North Carolina Press, 2014).

[8] Shadd Cary referred to Hezekiah Ford Douglas (1831–1865), a formerly enslaved activist who briefly emigrated to Canada. For more, see Robert L. Harris Jr., "H. Ford Douglas: Afro-American Antislavery Emigrationist," *Journal of African American History* 62, no. 3 (July 1977): 217–234.

travelers, and altogether the moral pulse throbs but feebly. The Unitarians at Geneva, are a deal more truly religious than the Evangelicals thereabouts, but the Episcopal Methodist pastor is a genuine anti-slavery man, whatever the dock may be. However there are numerous christians [*sic*], who dragging their dull lengths lazily behind the times, think and say by the aid of rum and slavery, that they have nothing to do with the peculiar institution.[9]

As those shabby representatives of their "race," Castus S. Depp and T. Clarkson have been the last on this route, and as they are noted for furnishing amusement as well as "humbug," the young people usually expect a "good time."[10] Cannot a good lock up be found for the graceless bores? [T]hey are ruining the cause of the oppressed by their trade. Their deception is the theme when colored lectures are referred to, so far as I have gone yet. The cause of "Women's Rights" does not flourish as it should do, and strange enough, the monkey tricks of such colored men are said to injure it. An honest and venerable abolitionist of Geneva, was free to express his fears for me and for women generally, because of the many "failures" of colored *men* in that region.[11] What absurdity next?

Left Geneva as soon as possible, and come by cars and stage to Sycamore. Thence to Brush Point through the kindness of Mr. Charles Townsend, with whose interesting family I spent a day, and talked in the school house on the 13th to a good audience.[12] Abolitionism flourishes at Brush Point, the *Freeman* was well cared for and its claims were further advanced by the kindness of the friends, at Vanderburg's school house four miles beyond.[13] The last named point is not so noted for anti-slavery sentiment as Brush Point;

[9] The "peculiar institution" is a euphemism for slavery that was popularized by proslavery South Carolina senator John C. Calhoun (1782–1850).

[10] Shadd Cary criticized Castus Depp because he was a former agent of the *Provincial Freeman*, but she suspected him of stealing money from the newspaper. An 1855 editorial publicly accused him of keeping a larger percentage of subscription fees than he agreed to and of failing to submit the names and payments he collected from the subscribers he solicited. See "To our Friends in the Western States," *Provincial Freeman*, February 17, 1855.

[11] Throughout her career, Shadd Cary criticized African American men who opposed women's rights. She believed that it was hypocritical for Black men to oppress Black women on the basis of their gender while challenging their own oppression on the basis of their race. The concerns she raised in this letter are reflective of her broader attention to how Black women's rights must be central to Black liberation.

[12] Charles Townsend and his family were white conductors on the Underground Railroad in Brush Point, Illinois. For more, see Nancy M. Beasley, *The Underground Railroad in DeKalb County, Illinois* (Jefferson, NC: McFarland, 2013), 118–121.

[13] Women's rights were not Shadd Cary's sole focus in this letter. She frequently addressed women's rights alongside other issues relevant to Black communities, such as abolition, in order to emphasize the connectedness between racial and gender oppression. For example, elsewhere, she couched a discussion of women's suffrage within a broader analysis of racism among Democrats and Republicans. See "Letter from Baltimore," *New National Era*, August 10, 1871, included in Part 1.

but the attendance was creditable, and except slight interruptions by the friends of slavery the meeting passed off nicely.

While thereabouts, I found a pleasant home in the family of Mr. Latin Nichols, and through the efforts of himself and lady, I was enabled to reach this place in time for an appointment on Tuesday night.[14] You can judge of the character of Brush Point anti-slavery, from the standing remarks of the *Black Democrats* of Sycamore, that they can smell a Brush Point Abolitionist as far as they can see him. So powerful was this odor at the last election, that Anti-Nebraska had an overwhelming majority at the polls. The pastor of the Congregational church at this place, the Rev. Mr. Gore, a christian [*sic*] gentleman had interested himself in circulating the notice of a meeting, and as a result, quite a large audience assembled in his church.[15]

After the meeting, a list of names which I herewith send, was through the exertions of friends [and particularly Mr. Brown, a merchant of this place,] added to your subscribers. Though rather indisposed from such incessant "going" when I came to this point, through the kindness of Mr. and Mrs. Gore, I hope to proceed on my journey today, and so keep your readers apprised from time to time my labors in these Western States.

M. A. SHADD.
Sycamore Illinois, April 16th, 1856

20. Sermon, April 6, 1858[16]

1st business of life, to love the Lord our God with heart and soul, and our neighbor as our self.—[17]

---

[14] For more on Latin Nichols (1820–1906) and his wife, Armena Jackman Nichols, see Beasley, *Underground Railroad*, 26, 43, 118. As Beasley has written, "In 1845 the antislavery advocate Armena supported freeing [Black] slaves, at a time when she did not even have the same rights as the men around her" (26). Shadd Cary's discussion of abolition in Brush Point acknowledged women's participation in antislavery movements, as she mentioned Armena Jackman Nichols and, shortly thereafter, Mrs. Gore, the wife of Reverend Darius Gore (1814–1873).

[15] Shadd Cary referred to Reverend Darius Gore of the Sycamore First Congregational Church. For more on Gore's antislavery work and his relationship with the American Missionary Association, see Beasley, *Underground Railroad*, 86–87 and 185.

[16] Sermon [Break Every Yoke], April 6, 1858, Mary Ann Shadd Cary fonds, F 14094-0-153, Archives of Ontario.

[17] Shadd Cary alludes to Luke 10:27, repeatedly invoking the biblical parable of the Good Samaritan in this sermon. The parable describes how a Samaritan passerby assisted a Levite who was attacked by robbers even though the Samaritan did not know the Levite. Luke 10:25–37.

We must then manifest love to God by obedience to his will—we must be cheerful workers in his cause at all times—on the Sabbath and other days[.] The more readiness we evince the more we manifest our love, and as our field is directly among those of his creatures made in his own image in acting as themself who is no respecter of persons we must have failed in our duty until we become decided to waive all prejudices of Education[,] birth nation or training and make the test of our obedience God's Equal command to love the neighbor as ourselves.—

These two great commandments, and upon which rest all the Law and the prophets, cannot be narrowed down to suit us but we must go up and conform to them. They proscribe neither nation nor sex—our neighbor may be either the oriental heathen the degraded European or the [en]slaved colored American.[18] Neither must we prefer sex[,] the slave mother as well as the slave-father. The oppress[ed], or nominally free woman of every nation or clime in whose soul is as evident by the image of God as in her more fortunate co[n]temporary of the male sex has a claim upon us by virtue of that irrevocable command equally as urgent. We cannot successfully evade duty because the suffering fellow woman be is only a <u>woman</u>! She too is a neighbor. The good samaritan of this generation must not take for their exemplars the priest and the Levite when a fellow wom[an] is among thieves—neither will they find their excuse in the <u>custom</u> as barbarous and anti-christian [*sic*] as any promulgated by pious Brahmin that they may be only females. The spirit of true philanthropy knows <u>no</u> sex. The true christian [*sic*] will not seek to exhume from the grave of the past its half developed customs and insist upon them as a substitute for the plain teachings of Jesus Christ, and the evident deductions of a more enlightened humanity.[19]

---

[18] Shadd Cary invoked a concept that Derrick Spires describes as "neighborly citizenship." See *The Practice of Citizenship: Black Politics and Print Culture in the Early United States* (Philadelphia: University of Pennsylvania Press, 2019). According to Spires, during the nineteenth century, "Black activists articulated an expansive, practice-based theory of citizenship, not as a common identity as such but rather as a set of common practices," one of which was being "neighborly" (3). Practicing neighborliness was a way for one to become a citizen by treating others well; as Spires states, "Pious citizens reach out to those in need according to an ethic of neighborliness. . . .The pious may be citizens of the world, but they demonstrate citizenship through concrete local, everyday interactions" (35). Shadd Cary connected the Christian charge to be neighborly with the imperative to abolish slavery. As she directed elements of her sermon towards women and addressed their gendered responsibility to confront oppression, Shadd Cary urged women to practice neighborly citizenship, thereby inviting African Americans into the citizenry as well.

[19] Shadd Cary, like other nineteenth-century Black women, used Christian teachings to advocate for abolition and for women's equality. For more on how nineteenth-century Black women deployed religious rhetoric to oppose slavery and lobby for Black women's rights, see Joycelyn Moody, *Sentimental Confessions: Spiritual Narratives of Nineteenth-Century African American Women* (Athens: University of Georgia Press, 2003); Carla Peterson, *"Doers of the Word": African-American*

There is too a fitness of time for any work for the benefit of God's human creatures. We are told to keep Holy the Sabbath day. In what manner? Not by following simply the injunctions of those who bind heavy burdens, to say nothing about the same but as a man is better than a sheep but combining with God, worship the most active vigilance for the resur[r]ector from degradation[,] violence[,] and sin his creatures. In these cases particularly was the Sabbath made for man and <u>woman</u> if you please as there may be those who will not accept the term man in a generic sense. Christ has told us as it is lawful to lift a sheep out of the ditch on the Sabbath day, if a man is much better than a sheep.

Those with whom I am identified, namely the colored people of this country—and the women of the land are in the pit[,] figuratively[,] are cast out. These were God[']s requirements during the Prophecy of Isaiah and they are in full force today.[20] God is the same yesterday[,] today[,] and forever. And upon this nation and to this people they come with all their significance[.] Within your grasp are three or four millions in chains in your southern territory and among and around about you are half a million allied to them by blood and to you by blood as were the Hebrew servants who realize the intensity of your <u>hatred and oppression</u>. You are <u>the</u> government[.] What it does to you enslaves the poor whites[,] [t]he free colored people[,] [t]he example of slave holders to accep[t] all.

What we aim to do is to put away this evil from among you and thereby pay a debt you now owe to humanity and to God[,] and so turn from their chan[n]el the bitter waters of a moral servitude that is about overwhelming yourselves.

I speak plainly because of a common origin and because were it not for the monster slavery we would have a common destiny here—in the land of

Women Speakers and Writers in the North (1830–1880) (New Brunswick: Rutgers University Press, 1998); Valerie C. Cooper, Word, Like Fire: Maria Stewart, the Bible, and the Rights of African Americans (Charlottesville: University of Virginia Press, 2011); Teresa Zackodnik, Press, Platform, Pulpit: Black Feminist Publics in the Era of Reform (Knoxville: University of Tennessee Press, 2011); and Kevin Pelletier, Apocalyptic Sentimentalism: Love and Fear in U.S. Antebellum Literature (Athens: University of Georgia Press, 2015).

[20] Shadd Cary appears to reference Isaiah 24, which prophesies the destruction of the Earth. It states, "Fear, and the pit, and the snare, are upon thee, O inhabitant of the earth. And it shall come to pass, that he who fleeth from the noise of the fear shall fall into the pit; and he that cometh up out of the midst of the pit shall be taken in the snare. . . . And they shall be gathered together, as prisoners are gathered in the pit, and shall be shut up in the prison" (Isaiah 24:17–22 [KJV]). Elsewhere, too, the Bible metaphorically frames "the pit" as a hellish or spiritually downtrodden place. Shadd Cary described Black people and women as being cast into "the pit" in order to highlight the severity of their subjugation in society.

our birth. And because the policy of the American government so singularly set aside al[l]ows to all free speech and free thought: As the law of God must be to us the higher law in spite of powers[,] principalities[,] selfish priests[,] or selfish people to whom the minister it is important that we assert boldly that no where does God look upon this the chief of crimes with the least degree of allowance nor are we justified in asserting that he will tolerate those who in any wise support or sustain it.

Slavery[,] American slavery[,] will not bear moral tests. It [exists] by striking down all the moral safeguards to society—[but] it is not then a moral institution. You are called upon as a man to deny and disobey the most noble impulses of manhood to aid a brother in distress—to refuse to strike from the limbs of those not bound for any crime the fetters by which his escape is obstructed. The milk of human kindness must be transformed into the bitter waters of hatred—you must return to his master he that hath escaped, no matter how every principle of manly independence revolts at the same. This feeling extends to every one allied by blood to the slave. And while we have in the North those who stand as guards to the institution the[y] must also volunteer as shippers away of the nominally free. You must drive from this home by a h[e]artless ostracism to the heathen shores when they fasted, bowed themselves, and spread sack cloth and ashes under them. Made long prayers &c[.] that they might be seen of men, but Isaiah told them God would not accept them. They must repent of their sins—put away iniquity from among them and then should their lights shine forth.

But we are or may be told that slavery is only an evil[,] not a sin, and that too by those who say it was allowed among the Jews and therefore ought to be endured. Isaiah sets that matter to rest[.] [H]e shows that it is a sin handling it less delicately than many prophets in this generation. These are the sins that we are to spare[,] not the sin of enslaving men—of keeping back the hire of the laborer. You are to loose the bands of wickedness, to undo the heavy burdens[,] to break every yoke and to let the oppressed go free. To deal out bread to the hungry and to bring the poor [. . .] speaking. Their cry has long been ascending to the Lord who then will assume the responsibility of prescribing times and seasons and for the pleading of their cause—[and of] righteous causes—and who shall overrule the voice of woman? Emphatically the greatest sufferer from chattel slavery or political proscription on this God's footstool? Say we have Christ's example who heal[e]d the sexes indiscriminately thereby implying an equal inheritance—who rebuffed the worldling Martha and approved innovator Mary.[21] The Him who respecteth not persons but who imposes Christian duties alike upon all sexes, and who in his wise providence metes out his retribution alike upon all.

So friends we suffer the oppressors of the age to lead us astray; instead of going to the source of truth for guidance we let the adversary guide us as to what is our duty and God[']s word. The Jews thought to[o] that they were doing [H]is requirements when they did only that which was but a small sacrifice.[22]

21. "Report on Woman's Labor," Proceedings of the Colored National Labor Convention, 1870[*]

The committee, to whom was referred the subject of Woman's Labor, beg leave to report that in their opinion no subject bearing upon the industrial relations of the colored people to community requires more earnest consideration.

The avocations of women hitherto, and particularly colored women, have been lamentably circumscribed, both as to diversity of employment and breadth of operation, seamstresses, laundresses, teachers, clerks, and domestic servants, constituting almost the entire complement of pursuits. In these departments of labor they work without system or organization, there not being, so far as we have been able to learn, but one association among them to promote labor interests, whether by guarding against monopoly or arresting extortion and oppression.

We are pleased, however, to be able to say that a quiet but manifest desire to widen the boundaries of manual and other pursuits, and to invoke aid in protecting the same and other interests, is apparent in examples of noble

[21] Shadd Cary referenced Jesus's visit to the home of two sisters, Martha and Mary. Martha attempted to be a good hostess by preparing the household, while Mary instead sat with Jesus to listen to his teachings. When Martha asked Jesus to instruct Mary to help her, Jesus replied that he supported Mary's decision to receive wisdom and that Martha need not be preoccupied with worldly things. See Luke 10:38–42.

[22] Shadd Cary alluded to the exodus of enslaved Jews out of Egypt, as recounted in the book of Exodus.

[*] This convention was organized by the Colored National Labor Union. Other labor organizers selected her to represent Detroit at the convention although she had already moved to Washington, DC, by this point in time. Rhodes, *Mary Ann Shadd Cary*, 168.

women of the more favored class who, in the face of a discouraging public opinion, though gradually awakening, now agitate the elective franchise for women, and of colored women who go forth into hitherto forbidden paths of duty or interest with distinguished success.

Miss Edmonia Lewis among sculptors, Mrs. S. M. Douglass and Miss Cole among physicians, Miss Ketchum among clerks, illustrate an aptitude and ability among colored women which, if cordially recognized and encouraged by colored men in their more matured experience in these directions, would be the beginning of an era of thought and effort among colored women creditable to them as a class, and highly promotive of the general well-being.[23]

With women as with the other sex, organized effort, whether in associations with men or in societies of their own, could not fail to be of benefit, as lifting them up from the plane of indifference, frivolity, and dependence, to the nobler sphere of systematized industries and intellectual effort so essential to the growth and prosperity of an enlightened people.

We would recommend to our women, therefore, a steady inculcation of habits of industry, economy, and frugality, to learn trades, to engage in whatever pursuits women of the most highly favored classes now pursue, and in whatever honorable calling besides their inclination or capacities qualify them for, and which will tend to enlarge their sphere and influence of labor.

In addition to present avocations, we would suggest that profitable and health-inspiring employment might be found at market-gardening, small fruit and berry culture, shop and storekeeping, upholstering, telegraphing, and insurance and other agencies, and to connect themselves with co-operative building societies whenever opportunity offers. No women have had a sadder and more varied experience than thousands who have labored in the fields of the South, and to such we would say, engage in agriculture. Bring to the pursuits of freedom the knowledge of husbandry learned when in bondage, and make it magnify and beautify your present improved condition.

---

[23] Shadd Cary referred to Sarah Mapps Douglass and Rebecca Cole. Douglass, who was an accomplished abolitionist speaker and writer, was the first Black woman to complete a medical program. For more on Douglass's and Cole's medical careers, see Gloria Moldow, *Women Doctors in Gilded-Age Washington: Race, Gender, and Professionalization* (Urbana: University of Illinois Press, 1987), 19–22. See also April R. Haynes, "Flesh and Bones," in Haynes, *Riotous Flesh: Women, Physiology, and the Solitary Vice in Nineteenth-Century America* (Chicago: University of Chicago Press, 2015), 132–162, for a discussion of Douglass's lectures on physiology and sex education. Shadd Cary also referenced Eleanor Ketchum, the first Black woman clerk to work for the US Treasury. See Jessica Ziparo, *This Grand Experiment: When Women Entered the Federal Workforce in Civil War–Era Washington, D.C.* (Chapel Hill: University of North Carolina Press, 2017), 31, 61.

An enlarged benevolence is eminently in keeping with the ever-widening sphere of activities into which woman can now enter, as well as with the highest dictates of humanity and religion. The vicissitudes of war, and the accidents inseparable from the great change many have undergone, have thrown to the surface thousands of cases of destitution which appeal to men and women for assistance and remedy. The formation, therefore, of associations, whence practical aid and direction can be extended to the thousands of infirm, aged, and poor, could not fail to impress upon the sterner sex the importance of removing all barriers to the full recognition and success of woman as an important industrial and moral agent in the great field of human activities and responsibilities.

All of which is respectfully submitted, M. A. S. CARY
CAROLINE E. G. COLBY,
JOSEPH P. EVANS.
BELVA A. LOCKWOOD,
J. S. GRIFFING.[24]

22. "A First Vote, Almost," 1871[*]

Many thousands, manly men, weak-kneed men, sick men[,] crippled men[,] white-faced—black complexioned, thronged the several election precincts in the memorable Thursday last past, but altogether they were not more heavily

---

[24] The list of Shadd Cary's coauthors illuminates how she participated in coed, interracial collaborations with other activists. Caroline E. G. Colby was a white widow of a Confederate soldier. Joseph P. Evans (1835–1889) was a formerly enslaved African American man who purchased his freedom and was elected to the House of Delegates and the Senate in Virginia. Belva A. Lockwood (1830–1917) was a white lawyer who eventually became the first woman to argue a Supreme Court case. Josephine Sophia White Griffing (1814–1872) was a white abolitionist and women's rights activist who was an agent for the Freedmen's Bureau. See Donal F. Lindsey, *Indians at Hampton Institute, 1877–1923* (Chicago: University of Illinois Press, 1995), 220; William Bland Whitley and the *Dictionary of Virginia Biography*, "Joseph P. Evans (1835–1889)," *Encyclopedia Virginia*, Virginia Humanities, last modified December 22, 2021, https://encyclopediavirginia.org/entries/evans-jos eph-p-1835-1889/; "About Belva Lockwood," George Washington University Law School, accessed June 13, 2020, https://www.law.gwu.edu/about-belva-lockwood; and Carol Faulkner and Laurie Olin, *Women's Radical Reconstruction: The Freedmen's Aid Movement* (Philadelphia: University of Pennsylvania Press, 2007).

[*] This document is an undated, handwritten essay. However, it was written in the days following Shadd Cary's 1871 unsuccessful attempt to register to vote alongside a large group of women. See Rhodes, *Mary Ann Shadd Cary*, 195. Mary Ann Shadd Cary, "A First Vote, Almost," 1871, Mary Ann Shadd Cary Collection 13, Box 1, MSRC Division, Moorland-Spingarn Research Center, Washington, DC.

weighted with the burden of the hour than the sixty three [*sic*] women citizens who voluntarily proposed to divide with them the onerous responsibility but who were so summarily refused. In truth the women showed by their course in this matter a juster appreciation of the situation. The jist of the election contest was constitutional republican rule as protested against by democratic interpretation & disfavor[.] The latter would do away with the 14th & 15th amendments to the Constitution because distasteful to them[;] the republicans would ignore them though of their own devising, thus practically conceding the argument to their opponents & weakening at every turn their own position. It is not merely a question whether the women shall vote by reason of their own established amendments[,] it is a virtual admission of the rebel claim that there is nothing in those amendments by which the people should be bound & is more potent as an element of future success to the democratic party than all else.

"I have done my duty," was singularly enough the uniform & literal remark of nearly every female applicant at the different precincts from the 2nd to the 21st inclusive. Under the amendments millions of men *and women had secured their freedom in citizens of the United States & without on [*sic*] a color of change in the record thousands of the same men had voted. [B]ut the thousands of women freed at the same time had been debarred the right & now sixty-three in addition were made to strengthen against their conviction to the democratic argument & rejoice the disloyal heart.[25]

The refusal was and is a bitter pill to swallow. And fortunate will this nation be if it should not thereby be dosed to death.

So much then for demagogy and its infallibility in political opp[ortun]ism—for the wire-working politicians not to the political salt of this nation must the condemnation be[.]

"I am sorry my wife is not along["] said an influential citizen after having learned of the result of application to register.

"Did they not let you register?—Very short sighted policy[,]" said one[.] ["]The election will be closely contested[,] want all the help we can get," another. ["]That's so[,]" all within a very few feet.

On polling day words of encouragement were given at every polling place by men who were standing around[.] "Let me compliment your bravery Madam," was said at one precinct with many other pleasant allusions and

---

[25] The passage beginning at the asterisk(*) and continuing to the end of this paragraph is crossed out in Shadd Cary's handwritten draft of this document, but is reproduced here in order to offer a holistic view of how Shadd grappled with how to most effectively articulate the gendered boundaries of Black people's citizenship.

approbative remarks & except occasional official "greetings" from some exalted male creature, upon whom impromptu stars had a sort of a moony effect, indications were many strong & [illegible]able that the rank & file are accessible to right & reason. Two or three ministers[,] God forgive them! Would like to be shocked because after having murdered Paul [illegible] this question the world yet moves—one of them pious—by voted the democratic ticket & thereupon walk off in "tall style.["]

Now for those really scandalized and who cannot and will not let it be done. Wise well Barracks are in hot water over the [document incomplete].

23. "Would Woman Suffrage Have a Tendency to Elevate the Moral Tone of Politics," n.d.[*]

Drunken women were not at the polls.

1 Morals of politics, money, consider duties of politics

Politicians are not minors. have [interest] to [subverse]—men have women have.

Buying votes. Women from principles. Men for money.

1[sic] Politics[,] science of government

2 Suffrage a voice given to deciding a question or choosing a man for an office

3 The theory of this form of government is the government derives its powers from the consent of the governed

4 The preamble to the constitution

5 Now as conducted not as intended [by the authors of the constitution]

6 [Now] corrupt party combinations of men by corrupt men[,] thieves[,] repeaters, plug uglies.[26] The dram shop. The vicious classes.

---

[*] This document, pictured in Figure 2.1, is a handwritten outline of the impact women may have on politics if granted the right to vote. There is no existing evidence that Shadd Cary completed or published an essay based on this early iteration. Mary Ann Shadd Cary, "Would Woman Suffrage Have a Tendency to Elevate the Moral Tone of Politics," n.d., Mary Ann Shadd Cary Collection 13, Box 1, MSRC Division, Moorland-Spingarn Research Center, Washington, DC.

[26] The Plug Uglies were a street gang in Baltimore, Maryland, that incited violent riots, intimidated voters, and rigged elections. For more, see Tracy Matthew Melton, *Hanging Henry Gambrill: The Violent Career of Baltimore's Plug Uglies, 1854–1860* (Baltimore: Maryland Historical Society, 2005).

7   The pioneer women & what they have done. Julia Ward Howe[.]
        Mrs Swisshelm[.] Women of Wyoming[27]

        Moral and Religious duties imperative for secular pursuits
        Matthew 5th and 13th
        Numbers 6th—3-4
        Isaiah 10th!
        Isaiah 9 –15th 16th
        Esdras 437
        Ecclesiasticus 11 and 8th
        [Ecclesiasticus] 19-1-2
        [Ecclesiasticus] 2921

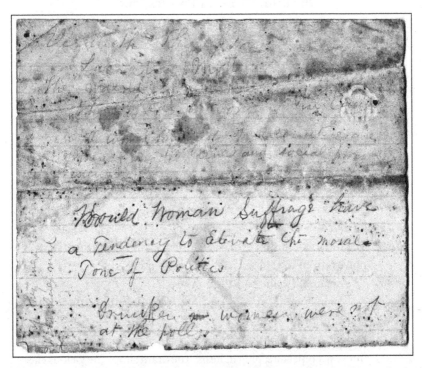

Figure 2.1 "Would Woman Suffrage Have a Tendency to Elevate the Moral
Tone of Politics." N.d. Mary Ann Shadd Cary Collection 13, Box 1, MSRC
Division, Moorland-Spingarn Research Center, Washington, DC.

[27] Shadd Cary referred to Julia Ward Howe (1819–1910) and Jane Swisshelm (1815–1884), who
were prominent white abolitionists and suffragists. Howe cofounded the American Woman Suffrage
Association and the Association for the Advancement of Women, while Swisshelm was a journalist.
Shadd Cary also alluded to women in Wyoming because, in 1869, it became the first territory to enact

24. "Speech to the Judiciary Committee Re: The Rights of Women to Vote," January 21, 1874*

Mr. Chairman, and gentlemen of the Judiciary Committee:—

In respectfully appearing before you, to solicit in concert with these ladies, your good offices, in securing to the women of the United States, and particularly, to the women of the District of Columbia, the right to vote,—a right exerc[ized] by a portion of American women, at one period, in the hi[story] of this country,—I am not vain enough to suppose, for [a] moment, that words of mine could add one iota of weight to the arguments from these learned and earnest women, nor that I could bring out material facts not heretofore used by them in one stage or another of this advocacy.[28] But, as a colored woman, a resident of this District, a tax-payer of the same;—as one of a class equal in point of numbers to the male colored voters herein; claiming affilliation [sic] with two and a half millions of the same sex, in the country at large,—included in the provisions of recent constitutional amendments,—and not least, by virtue of a decision of the Supreme Court of this District a citizen,—my presence, at this time, and on an errand so important, may not I trust be without slight significance.

The crowning glory of American citizenship is that it may be shared equally by people of every nationality, complexion[,] and sex, should they of foreign birth so desire; and, in the inscrutable rulings of an All-wise providence, millions of citizens of every complexion, and embracing both sexes, are born upon the soil and claim the honor.[29] I would be particularly clear

---

women's suffrage legislation. Early suffragists won this victory fifty-one years before the passage of the Nineteenth Amendment, which granted (white) women the right to vote, and nearly one hundred years before the Voting Rights Act of 1965, which extended the franchise to women of all races.

* The handwritten draft of Shadd Cary's speech is undated. However, Jane Rhodes identifies it as being delivered in 1874. As Rhodes writes, "In January 1874 a group of women petitioned the Judiciary Committee of the House [of Representatives] on behalf of 600 women in the District of Columbia who sought enfranchisement. Mary Ann prepared an address for presentation at the Committee hearing, but it was never recorded in the public transcript" (*Mary Ann Shadd Cary*, 194). This erasure highlights that congressional records are not free from the racial and gender biases that structure archival collections at large and create silences in the archive.

[28] All underlined emphasis in this document is original. Mary Ann Shadd Cary, "Speech to the Judiciary Committee Re: The Right of Women to Vote," Mary Ann Shadd Cary Collection 13, Box 1, MSRC Division, Moorland-Spingarn Research Center, Washington, DC.

[29] Shadd Cary's claim to birthright citizenship was not unique. As Martha S. Jones has shown, during the nineteenth century, African Americans deployed similar arguments that asserted their rights to citizenship not based on a single law or court case, but based on a sense of belonging and their generational relationship to the land. For more, see Martha S. Jones, *Birthright Citizens: A History of Race and Rights in Antebellum America* (New York: Cambridge University Press, 2018).

upon this point. By the provisions of the 14th & 15th amendments to the Constitution of the United States,—a logical sequence of which is the representation by colored men of time-honored commonwealths in both houses of Congress,—millions of <u>colored women</u>, to-day, share with colored men the responsibilities of freedom from chattel slavery. From the introduction of African slavery to its extinction, a period of more than two hundred years, <u>they, equally</u> with fathers, brothers, [were] denied the right to vote. This fact of their investiture with the privileges of free women of the same time and by the same amendments which disenthralled their kinsmen and conferred upon the latter the right of franchise, without so endowing themselves is one of the anomalies of a measure of legislation otherwise grand in conception and consequences beyond comparison. The colored women of this country though heretofore silent, in great measure upon this question of the right to vote by the women[,] so long and ardently the cry of the noblest of the land, have neither been indifferent to their own just claims under the amendments, in common with colored men, nor to the demand for political recognition so justly made by the women-suffragists of the country for women every where throughout the land.

The strength and glory of a free nation, is <u>not so much</u> in the size and equipments of its armies, as in the <u>loyal hearts</u> and willing hands of its <u>men</u> and <u>women</u>; and this fact has been illustrated in an eminent degree by well-known events in the history of the United States. To the women of the nation conjointly with the men, is it indebted for arduous and dangerous personal service, and generous expenditure of time, wealth and counsel, so indispensable to success in its hour of danger. The colored <u>women</u> though humble in sphere, and unendowed with worldly goods, yet, led as by inspiration,— not only fed, and sheltered, and guided in safety the prisoner soldiers of the Union when escaping from the enemy, or the soldier who was compelled to risk life <u>itself</u> in the struggle to break the back-bone of rebellion, but gave their <u>sons</u> and brothers to the armies of the nation and their prayers to high Heaven for the success of the Right.

The surges of fratricidal war have passed we hope never to return; the premonitions of the future, are peace and good will; these blessings, so greatly to be desired, can only be made permanent, in responsible governments, based as you affirm upon the consent of the governed,—by giving to both sexes practically the equal powers conferred in the provisions of the Constitution as amended. In the District of Columbia the women in common with the women of the states and territories, feel keenly the discrimination against them in the retention of the word <u>male</u> in the organic act for the same, and as by reason of its retention, all the evils incident to partial legislation are endured by them, they sincerely hope that the word <u>male</u> may be stricken out by Congress on your recommendation without delay. Taxed, and governed in other respects, without their consent, they respectfully demand, that the principles of the <u>founders</u> of the government may <u>not</u> be disregarded in their case; but, as there are <u>laws</u> by which they are tried, with penalties attached thereto, that they may be invested with the right to vote as do men, that thus as in all Republics <u>indeed</u>, they may in future, be governed by their own consent.

25. "The Last Day of the 43 Congress," circa March 1875[*]

Three facts combine to make a perpetual reminder in the District of Columbia. You are in the capital of the nation; you are accessible to the Capitol, the seat of legislative wisdom par excellence; you are within the gracious influence, or the scorching, withering, blighting, power of the concentrated national press.

Without political rights, the miles square has attained pre-eminence, in political and any other power, through the deft and wily manipulations of its migratory and local men and women residents; it would be a misnomer to say citizens yet. The capital of the United States is, then, a grand significant figure; or for that matter, twenty-three millions of figures comprised in one unit:—the other cities of the nation are political ciphers or figures less conspicuously obtrusive. The Capitol building is the greatest of meeting-houses. Like city like citizen workers for the press. Once converged to a focus the Capitol, and of it for the time being, they become of it unified and wo[e]fully significant men and women, to Presidential and other aspirants.

The men and women of the newspaper world—that most potential of dynasties—have become of late of especial wonder and admiration to the

---

[*] This is a handwritten short story wherein Shadd Cary described the anticipation surrounding women's rights legislation that would potentially be passed on the last day of the Forty-Third Session of Congress, March 4, 1875. She was perhaps inspired by the Civil Rights Act of 1875, which was enacted on March 1, 1875, five years after Senator Charles Sumner introduced it in 1870. The bill banned racial discrimination in public facilities and on public transportation. For more on the lengthy controversy surrounding the bill, see Masur, *An Example for All.* Mary Ann Shadd Cary, "The Last Day of the 43 Congress," c. 1875, Mary Ann Shadd Cary Collection 13, Box 1, MSRC Division, Moorland-Spingarn Research Center, Washington, DC.

uninitiated: from no perceptible beginnings, they seem to have come full-grown into the most satisfying completeness of permanence and power. At the extreme limits of every other legitimate pursuit the gentler sex has halted and hesitated, at most, plead to enter in deprecating protest—: "We would not seek admission but that we must have our daily bread[."] In this unique department of letters and labor she begs not place, but is confessedly an equal;—an honored member of the guild. By intuitive perception of their proper relations a unification of the sexes has been conceded, and so thoroughly accepted, as to demonstrate conclusively that the terms male and female are co-related:—if so in that department it should be in every other, concludes some enthusiastic pioneer for spoils and profits for women; and if not, why not? Very true! If not why not? Incredulity is almost a crime—facts are so prominent, so disagreeable,—so disenchanting; the hidden causes underlying these facts, are unattainable in reasonable time, because of the extent of outside territory; what better place, then, than Washington to solve the mystery? or than the last day of the session to give the needed zest to pursuit, and other indicating data in that direction?

Item. The thermometer ranged 97° Fa[h]renheit in the shade, on the magnificent lawn extending invitingly a few paces from the elevated west door entrance of the Capitol down towards its pleasant approaches at the Avenue entrance, and laterally, thence, through leafy shades and devious winding ways, grateful in the subdued shadow and wooing, breezy, stillness to the humble foot-sore and unaspiring, when and where golden high tone Sol. is, on less demonstrative days, on his best behavior in the moderate and mollifying 65°s and 70°s.

Item. 107° in third story front and back; in dormitory, saloon, or sky-parlor; up, up, under a vicious expanse of hybrid metallic roof and simmering tar. It was the last day of the session certain; but the final hour of adjournment was uncertain. The grateful shade of the nation's park would be in agreeable contrast to the sultry domicil[e] and seething resin over private lares and penates. The pageant of a final closing might supplement a discovered tiny clue, to the more than El[e]usinian [M]ysteries resulting in sex abnegation, and in the constantly increasing "pride, pomp and circumstance" of newspaper supremacy. Then, to thread numerous sultry avenues, to take the indispensable Avenue rail, or h[o]rse coach, and bump along like nicely packed pickled herring on end, was the post and route of duty for a brief hour, but safely made; and, to the infinite relief of two patient-long suffering and ancient beasts of burden, whose staggering endeavors to mount Capitol Hill caused sighs of pity and "lots of sweat" from feeling souls that would have done honor to Mr. Bergh. Once and safely atop and no time was lost in entering the quiet corridors and spacious lobbies of the Capitol.

The apparent want of continuity of purpose in the passing throng, the disjointed fragmentary manner of the well-organized and admirable corps of messengers, door-keepers, pages and attachees;—a supreme loosedness with unmistakable anxiety in the air and everywhere, made it plain that this was for other than a routine day. Back and forth swayed masses to and from the assembly chamber for either body.

Small companies and individual men and women went hurriedly, as if for further assurance that a particular measure was on its final and successful passage;—or aimlessly, as if doubt had driven hope from a last and lurking refuge.

One impolitic little woman, certainly educated; firm of nerve and brave of heart, one who in the path of duty[,] benevolence[,] and patriotism had scented war in the while, and din, and dust, and destruction of the enemy's cannon,—with a humane soul inside of a queer cut coat tunic or blouse, of true hygienic outline, it may be, but of abominable shape,—clearly a misfit as are all health inspiring costumes in this era of dyspepsia and grande toiletts [sic],—looked as if, by the inexorable law of compensation, unto her had been imposed the task of condemnation upon the male citizens[,] representatives of forty millions.

"Oblige me Mr. Messenger," handing a cord, "by taking this to" we will say "Mr. Moses and the prophets within[."]

"Certainly ma'am" replied the official servant of servants. And disappeared through an adjoining door. In a few moments he returned; and with a countenance as comical as if pushed to the utmost limit, consistent with the regulation gravity and dignity of an outside position: "Madame. The Honorable gentlemen are very much engaged, and must be excused for the remainder of the session[."] Without noticing the man, and eyes fixed intently on the eastern doorway she said, half aloud: "If you can wait gentlemen I can." "The mills of the Gods grind slowly" but they nevertheless grind surely, said the little woman in every lineament of face and poise and counterpoise of position.

If you can wait I can. I[,] outside of these doors at every session, to the confusion and vexation of ladies differently costumed, until the price of blood service be paid; you[,] outside of your comfortable seats after election. And with the men and women of the Press sounding her defeat through the land she took position outside: not silent by any means, though long-enduring; not calm but determined. "Who knows," said a still voice "but that there may be another side; and that therein may be the right side. Every thing worth-while has been ridiculed at sometime. Who knows?" But not there to endorse theories, but to make discoveries and note events, we passed along, a little "upset[."][30]

Taking the unwilling interview in its near and remote bearings, and the intensely hot day into account. Took a turn for breath of fresh air and a brief season of meditation down through the lower range of halls and thence towards the south entrance. The varied expanse of dense, quaintly built and promiscuously populated roadway, sheets, avenues, commons, bogs and fens, etcetera, etcetera known as South Washington, bounded by the quiet but withal grandly beautiful Potomac, acted instantly as a sedative to "mind diseased" or startled by impromptu indignation at legislative inhumanity to woman. Retraversing the hall-way, there in the "nick of time" and at a conven-ient angle and as if on purpose lay the lost clew. Leaning nonchalantly against a column there stood a 'an'some and potential lion of the Press discussing in jerky and sententious terms with two ladies of the force.

Glancing over what purported to be a memorandum or bill of items he remarked in tones slightly compounded of Yorkshire English, Knickerbaker vernacular, and Pennsylvania [Q]uaker "Impossible pou honor! $

" To letters against Bd P.k. Wks—		25.00
" " " [illegible] bill—		10.00
" " sundry letters against Civil Rts. Bill		
African reps in the House and		
Mandingoes in the galleries		30.00

"Pou honor Catharine, a fellow cant pay so much you know!["]

"Strike off a 'andsome percent, and hand in next mail." Looking hourly for stamps from the "Western sunset?—The name ours only.—["] "What have you there? A sensation telegram and a roll of items by one lady; and reaching forth—two envelopes of prepared articles by the other. Reads, "Capital— Saint George! Grant for a third item.—Butler on the moieties,—infamous

---

[30] Shadd Cary's comment that journalists like herself are "not there to endorse theories" is remi-niscent of her 1857 recommendation that African Americans who look to the nation-state to remedy racism should "look at facts rather than everlastingly theorizing." See "Meetings at Philadelphia," *Provincial Freeman*, April 18, 1857, included in Part 1.

legislation against the Press. The very thing! My gentle friend[!"] to lady no. 2. "Cheap at twenty dollars; set me down as constant customer with five percent bonus more than all others always.—Call at the Row for the cash["."] ["]But," Alfred or Agemon or like it, I do not remember quite which,—spoke up ["]no!["] with spirit. "Your discrimination is most unfair. The little firm of Kate & I compiled these papers simultaneously; we have fresh offers; some even, from dilettanti members of the corps; and unless you can manage to be the least bit prompt, Mathew, Johnadab and Boanarges—our names again,— will take all we furnish; indeed they want exclusive monopoly."

"Again; a half dozen of our lady itemizers, are demanding sums due; you see they hunt up for us at conventions on the promenade, in society &c[.]— you don't imagine we could, of ourselves, do this immense work? Why[,] they bring to us on slips, from an inch to entire correspondence; too retiring to face the world, yet they must have bread you know, and they do an immense amount of interviewing behind their vails. Their deman[d]s are most imperative! That bill covers quite a period altogether, we are quite set upon by the demands of business."

"Is that so?—Then that alters the case. Those fellows—I hold you to our original contract. To me first—! The eighty-five is yours before another sum. Count me as first customer for <u>telling hits</u>; short telegrams, and caustic criticism and correspondence! By by." And waving his dainty hand, disappeared towards Downings. "And now to the House" said Catharine; to the House said mental consciousness, from its involuntary halt in convenient side passage; and higher, higher, another corridor, and below, in the auditorium are the giants of the government doing battle (?) for the kings of the land.

In the ladies waiting room where we prefer to look at first, the appliances of comfort and elegance are so ample. The breezy air from the river so refreshing, after the involuntary experience, and almost cremating process in the streets and halls below, that one hesitates to leave for the theatre of confusion, the adjourning legislative hall; but, after a promenade, a survey of the inmates,—a chatty brace of dowagers in one recess, a colored member[']s voluble and rather prepossessing lady; a fair[,] gentle[,] and fascinating other half of a newspaper notability accompanied by sub-attache; a genuine female <u>principal</u> correspondent of Western papers and the colored person in charge, (who, by the way, is said to be by descent, and who is by right of both paternal and maternal service, a connexion of the Parkes, [B]astises, and the household of the father of his country,) nothing easier than to enter a lateral door, and lo! we are in the gallery on the "<u>last-day</u>.["]

The last is unlike any other day, in that more than the usual number of strangers and fewer residents are on hand; more members than usual leave their seats to pay respects to lady constituents in the galleries, and ladies' room[;] and over the head of the Speaker, horse, foot, and dragoons are the male-contents of the Press, for once, at their post including gentleman correspondent of lower hall interview. Just here arose a question anent rings, and the inconsistencies of those newspaper people who pose them, when they are so evidently just to the sexes and indispensable as managed by the profession.

But it was the last day in more respects than one, and instead of the usual: "Mr[.] Speaker! Mr. Speaker!["] of routine days, the clapping of a dozen hands from different parts of the House at once, for, and the skipping or hurrying to and from, of pages, the confusion and din attendant upon speech making, the hurrying hither and thither at the count, and the falling of the Speaker's mallet for silence, there was on every hand surroundings that bespoke the end.

The Republican members moved uneasily:—some, hitherto noticeable for stay-in-his-seatativeness and languor, making three or four calls at the desks of other members, before returning to the well-kept nest. General Butler the Nestor of the body, little the worse of recent illness, moved briskly about, seemingly intent upon final departure.

Twice, or thrice, the speaker announced a recess, intermitting which, came bills completed by the Senate; generally, a wiping out of the rebellion record of a repentant of the "lost cause," and conveying by implication, promise of a life of peace and patriotism in the future.

While anxiety, hope, and even fear were clearly shown by Republicans[,] on the Democratic side the scene was as different as if a distinct body.

There, members collected in twos and threes; when a vigorous handshaking would commence!—A lone member, as if by sudden impulsion, would reach across an intervening desk, and grasp, unexpectedly, an idle hand, and thereat a wonderfully affectionate mutual "squeeze["] would be the consequence. During the active congress, a supreme dignity and do-nothingness was characteristic of that side of the house, and on the last day, the religious joviality of the scene among the opposition, was marked apparently a series of bubbles of good fellowship, and subdued happiness;—a sort of right-hand of fellowship affair; meantime, taking in with benignant glances the ladies' gallery.

The Speaker, usually almost as much of a fixture at his post of duty, as the lock, moved restlessly in and out of his seat; yielded his well-proportioned self to the friendly embrace of some political confreré [*sic*], or, blandly and eagerly accepted the approving smile of some quondam friend of the lost cause, who thus showed his sense of obligation, for the rapidity with which some of the "vilest sinners[,"] were being regenerated and born again into the household of peace and fealty.

It was amusing to note, that though the Speaker might have yielded, so far as to take a turn in the lobby for a breath of air, that, at the half minute before the expiration of the recess, he would emerge through some convenient door, ascend the platform, and, when the hand on the dial pointed to the minute, down came the gavel. A few more bills from the Senate; mostly, prodigals praying to return, another recess; and off whisked the speaker; and galleries, and floor would lose their occupants until the next hour indicated.

Only one seeming objection was made to removing disabilities.[31] An unmistakably colored member smarting, doubtless, at the delay of the Civil Rights Bill, jumped like a flash to his feet, when a name from Alabama was presented, and as suddenly subsided by dropping down again, to the amusement of white and colored members around him.

A rapid glance was all the attention from the Chair;—the question was put, and another loyal citizen took rank.

During the recesses, the "Ladies Dressing Rooms" were invested with more than usual interest. There were members['] wines, lady lobbyists, reporters' wines, lady reporters, wish, at intervals, a member in close and confidential conversation with some fair one upon the critical points interfering with her little bill or casting a hopeful legislative horoscope for its future prospects; and thus giving happy thoughts and brightening hopes to the interviewer, as seen in age, and voice, and manner, though under wonderful control.

A lady lobbyist whose bill had passed, and another and ponderous lady, wholly devoted to public affairs, rotund and spectacled, displayed marvelous acquaintance with legislation, literature, politics, and the men and women of note and celebrity on the Press. A colored member's lady was strongly appealed to upon the most-approved method of training servants, and of restraining precocious young ladies, who dispose to

---

[31] Shadd Cary referred to "political disabilities." Following the Civil War, Congress created the Committee for the Removal of Political Disabilities. This committee was originally formulated to return voting rights to former Confederate rebels who rejoined the Union, but during the late 1870s and early 1880s, suffragists turned to the committee to submit petitions for women's right to vote. Shadd Cary herself submitted one such petition. See "Petition of Mary Shadd Cary, a citizen of Washington, District of Columbia, praying for the removal of her political disabilities," Petitions and Memorials, 45th Congress, c. 1879, included in this part.

monopolize parlor privileges to the detriment of the other domestic and social training; interpolated with recitals of ante-bellum and war experiences; all of which was curious, instructive, or amusing as you chose. To two ladies of the newspaper world the conversation afforded subject for amusement; and a slight derisive laugh from one to her companion, brought a stern rebuke from the successful lobby member, upon which they withdrew.

"Served them right![\"] said the fat lady, "to dare to sneer at the feelings of loyal women at that critical period in the country's history"; "I would have rebuked them if I had died for it" said lady lob;—"Such speeches and persons I consider beneath my notice" said colored member's lady.

An earnest eyed lady reporter, who meanwhile walked back and forth the length of the two rooms, and, half audibly half suppressed, made occasional and sundry ejaculations—in which, disappointment at failure of civil rights bill, and allusions to her profession, were prominent, aided in a sort of sympathetic way, to keep up the constant stream of rapid and entertaining conversation, and to call out a pointed diversion in favor of ladies of the Press: "So you report for the neutral financial section Miss Cath; In which gallery are you located?" "I have a seat in both" was the quiet reply. "I never see you.—Been here long?" "Several seasons." "Well I never! I've been here all winter; just got my bill through[.\"]

"Have you met Mrs[.] Scribbles"? said fat lady—"Read her new book? Wonderful woman!—Magnificent work! What a brain[!\"] "No dear," said Mrs. Lobby[. "]I have been so much engaged on my Revolutionary claims[.\"] The conversation continued to flow embracing an infinite variety of topics.—The fireside. Congress. The panic inflation civil rights, the recussant lady of the press; and with lesser chatty groups and her ambulatory media, might fairly, in comparison with the two Houses be called the outside chambers.

The termination of the first recess brought every lady to her feet; some to go to the House, some to the women room to interview the mirror; some to inspect the ice jug, or to gaze upon the glorious (?) south view, and "woo the balcony breeze[.\"] Through every avenue of the House hurried the members and thronged visitors;—more members to the ladies gallery than before. The same form of message from the Senate as before.—The Speaker of the identical moment brought down the hammer-members because all attention:— the reporters bristle; again a very tiara of gentlemen scorpions over the head of the Speaker and upon the brow of the devoted House.

A little orange girl with dark Italian eyes, a quiet but self-appointed rep-resentative of her sex moved in session time, cautiously but surely from seat to seat, and anon peered into cloak-room and closet cunningly without her basket, but with orange in hand, partly hid by the folds of her dress, success-fully winning custom and approving nods;—a foreign female competitor for the floor, with our native and foreign pages, and intensely suggestive to as-piring lady politicians. The wise heads of the nation, in a taste for the oranges overlooked the barriers taken down by the wee girl. Query. Was Eve's apple of Eden an orange after all?

A distinguished member Mr. Maynard, approached to deliver the final wishes of the President; the members visiting lady friends in the galleries, talked in tones more subdued and wooing, and were in turn fanned and coquetted to the verge of exalted friendship and tender sentiment. In a mo-ment of supreme silence, and with a compound curvilinear obeisance, made with right hand and arm, and a sympathetic sway of the head in an oppo-site direction, the member announced the determination of his Excellency to trouble that Congress no more forever. The mallet descended just as the hand on the dial-plate spoke the final minute, and the end of the 43 Congress was announced. A slight rustle of the west entrance of the House, and a troupe of Indians, warm spring braves, children and squaws, the reputed captors of Captain Jack, crossed the floor, scrutinizing with eager gaze and thence to the Rotunda, where, while the interpreter explained the pictures to them, their bedaubed faces, and striped blankets and breeches or leggins were the observed of all.

The 43 Congress had ended; the Indians come[,] interviewed[,] and gone; the male press whisked out almost before the end, but the heart and nerves of the force—the lady writer was as during the last recess of the House, reclining on a sofa in the interior parlor, pressing her forehead with clenched hands.

The dowagers, lobbyists, and several groups, were [in] full tide of suc-cessful colloquial point and counterpoint; and might have so continued, had not a deaf lady with huge mushroom umbrella of sandalwood, and accompanied by a mild but sad looking young person, entered and greeted the principal <u>members</u>: the younger passing to the inevitable looking glass in the interior, and to a confidential and sympathetic chat with the female press on the sofa, and alternately to the lady in the glass. These movements were harmless enough in themselves, but certain adjuncts were "too many" for the equanimity of the lobby, who were in confidential tones summing up the profits of success: "The special point I made was <u>three thousand</u>, if there was success—not a cent less—and there <u>is</u> success[!"] said angular lady. "Very moderate indeed my dear! The men demand from <u>five thousand to</u> fifty, and get it too[!"] said large lady.

"How do you do ladies[?"] said elderly deaf person: "House adjourned[?"] "Not yet dear[,"]—through a horn: "What an abominable odor" to lobby no. 2[.] "Yes dear! agreeable odor: it is real sandal wood, all the way from Asia[."] "Bless me[!"] said the angular lady rising. "Smells worse than an Injun camp[!"]: "Quite right,["] replied the owner smiling and approaching nearer, "it is in an excellent state of preservation.["] "Indeed" said the large lady "we must close this interview; else this Japanese nuisance will smother me[!"] and with furious glances at this abrupt termination of their session departed.

"What an interesting day it has been[!"] said lady before the glass to lady correspondent who then, lay gracefully on the sofa. "Do you know that in three years this is the second visit I have paid to this building?—sister is so mopy—never leaves her four walls." and, rattling on volubly "How do you manage? Your profession is so profitable; there is comfort in that[?"] "Well—yes—the compensation is fair[;] but oh dear[!"] with pressure of the two hands, "it is dreadfully tiresome—this itemizing[!"]

H[a]d the end of the chain been reached, with only such meager and unreliable data to guide in solving the mystery of the Press? After all, was this great power by which rings were ground to powder, in itself, a gigantic ring, all the stronger for the lithe but subtle and wiry female element permeating it? Was not the lobby with its generous compensation, at least a satisfying fact in some quarters? and what of strength does legislation lose at the hands of such adroit and executive bodies as the ladies just left?

There were vigor, and masculinity and success to believe them, which might alarm men, and frighten the timid of the other sex.

"Grand old ladies," said colored female of the department,

"They have been in every session, and keep the place lively."

"Abominable creatures[!"] replied a grave looking lady in quiet colors who had been almost stationary for hours.

"My sorrow! In intervals of their tiresome conversation, they were just backbiting every body; I never heard so much gossip in so short a time. Tut! Tut! What is the country coming to[!"] By that I knew that my riddle was yet unsolved, and that whether in politics, as lobby members, attaches of the

Press or whatsoever, so long as they could gossip they could not unsex themselves and that therefore the country was safe.[32]

26. "Petition of Mary Shadd Cary, a citizen of Washington, District of Columbia, praying for the removal of her political disabilities," Petitions and Memorials, 45th Congress, circa 1878

To THE SENATE AND HOUSE OF REPRESENTATIVES OF THE UNITED STATES, In Congress Assembled;

Mary Shadd Cary, a citizen of the United States and a resident of the District of Columbia, County of Washington, City of Washington, hereby respectfully petitions your honorable body for the removal of her political disabilities, and that she may be declared invested with full power to exercise her right of self-government at the ballot-box, all state constitutions or statute laws to the contrary notwithstanding.[33]

27. Colored Women's Progressive Franchise Association Minutes, February 9, 1880[34]

The 1st meeting of the Women's Progressive Committee was held in Pisgah Chapel[,] Rev[.] Nichols Pastor[,] Monday evening Feb[.] 9[,] 1880[.]

Pray[er] by Mrs. Williams[.] Rev J. Nicholas was called to preside and Mrs. M. Jennings was appointed Secretary[.] Mrs. Cary stated the object of the

---

[32] The beginning of the story critiqued women's exclusion from full political citizenship. The remainder offers a fictional account of the atmosphere on Capitol Hill on the last day of the Forty-Third Congress by imagining conversations between Black and white women journalists and lobbyists who await a vote on women's suffrage legislation. Her story sheds light on the nature of women's political participation despite their disfranchisement. Toward the end of the story, Shadd Cary offered a sarcastic criticism of women journalists who gossip. Its final lines contained a facetious retort to those who argued that women's suffrage would "unsex" women and make them less feminine. Shadd Cary contended that as long as women could gossip, they would always be feminine, and therefore, women's suffrage would not threaten to "unsex" them.

[33] This petition is not Shadd Cary's original writing, but a form that she completed that is identical to that of thousands of other petitioners across the country. The forms required petitioners to insert their name, state, city, and town.

[34] Mary Ann Shadd Cary, Colored Women's Progressive Franchise Association Minutes, February 9, 1880, Mary Ann Shadd Cary Collection 13, Box 1, MSRC Division, Moorland-Spingarn Research Center, Washington, DC.

movement to be the discussion of the franchise question and the practical extensions of privileges and measures for public good without sex discrimination[.] The need of a paper or papers unbiased by sex restrictions and jealousies—the need of institutions wherein the girls should enlarge their sphere of usefulness. The right of election to make perfect all progressive theories.

Mr[.] Wright in a neat speech gave in his adhesion to the demands of such an organization[.] Mr[.] I[.] Washington qualified his advocacy of women's demands—thought the ballot useless to her[.] Mrs. Ferris replied to him promptly and effectively.

Mr[.] Williams offered to give some views at the next meeting[.] [P]ersons subscribed for the Citizen and [a] number gave their names as favorable to franchise for women.

J. Nichols Chair
M. Jennings Secy.

Women's Progressive Committee
- A Franchise Organization

M. A. S. Cary	Mrs. Nichols
Anna Montgomery	Miss Jennings
Mrs. Robinson	Mrs. Ferris
Mrs. Monroe	

Our leaders do not take the women into consideration. The men furnish an example in that they have committees an[d] clubs to give information such as it is very few are permitted to know what is done[.] The women want light—The men need light. The uprising of whites and—The convention last week.

The disenfranchised District and how their government is just back by such displays [...]

The meeting of 2000 [...] 1/3 white women & but two colored women. Trades for girls and boys and the influence to demand them and determination to support them. Thirty or forty occupations for white women [,] half a dozen for colored ones. A sentiment must be created here that shall tell outside. If the local press are opposed we must support those that will agree with us. Colored women for educational work[.]

28. Colored Women's Progressive Franchise Association Statement of Purpose, circa February 1880[35]

The Colored Women[']s Progressive Franchise Association proposes[36]

1st To assert their demand of equal rights

2nd To take an aggressive stand against the assumption that men only may begin and conduct industrial and other things

3 The[y] seek to obtain the ballot—to look alive after the welfare of both girls & boys in the training of the youth [...] and to work promptly for the establishment of industries and to extend the number of occupations for women

---

[35] Mary Ann Shadd Cary, Colored Women's Progressive Franchise Association Statement of Purpose, c. 1880, Mary Ann Shadd Cary Collection 13, Box 1, MSRC Division, Moorland-Spingarn Research Center, Washington, DC.

[36] In the following list, the switch from ordinal to cardinal numbers, the misnumbering, and the inconsistent use of a period after the numbers are all present in the original document.

4 They propose Union & Co-operation to the colored people of the District.

5 They propose to establish and support newspapers controlled by those not opposed to equal rights for the sexes and to support a paper in this country which[,] conducted by colored women[,] shall set forth the capability of their class.

5 They recommend to the association a Banking institution[,] Co-operative stores[,] another printing establishment for instruction of both sexes.

6 A local Directory & Labor Bureau wherein trades[,] occupations[,] and business persons and laborers may enroll their names and so put themselves in communication with employers and patrons.

7. They would agitate for independence of thought and action—interdependence among members of organized bodies or committee working in harmony with this Guild, and less following of individual leaders.

8 Vigorous investigative freedom of thought and speech and prompt action as against demagogues or against wardship.

9 The vigilant and aggressive character of Home Missionary influence must be a distinctive feature to rescue the youth and direct them to right pursuits.

10 As an institution, neither Freedmen's Bank, Home of the Friendly[,] nor Banaker has been a success because selfishness[,] jealousy[,] and greed largely inspired the controllers[.] [T]his franchise association must act with determination but without such baleful motives.

11 As this is the new Gospel of freedom we hail the Exodus people as practical illustrators and must encourage the Exodus in every way.

12 As information is the great need of the men and women who oppose our movement we inaugurate a local and general Lecture Bureau to develop the home talent now discouraged by the selfish and egotistic two or three who would monopolize not only all places, but money, brain[,] and power possessed by the people. And who aim by coming in and out of season to the front to monopolize all advantages to themselves and thus keep the people in darkness[.]

13 Enlighten the people and there will be no need of long sentences nor vigilance committees.

Plan

A joint stock [c]ompany[,] the shares to be one dollar each[,] to be paid monthly. The funds to be invested in combination enterprises—to be loaned out on notes of small amounts on 30, 60 and ninety-days time without bonus but at reasonable interest and thus enable poor persons to get a start in business of either sex.

14 While no invidious distinctions may be made[,] women having the great interest at stake must be the controlling official power[.]
   15. Agriculture, and land interests must be a prominent interest & so all information upon the cheapness [of] location &c must be made.

16 The establishment of a Dry Goods Fancy & Millinery Store should be one feature & all women should be asked to patronize[.]

17 A gentlemen[']s new clothing place should be started & colored boys should be helped to work.

18 The system of credits should be discouraged. Cash payments [are] encourage[d].

19 At least three grocery & other places should be opened—but no tippling encouraged.

20 The local talent native & otherwise of both sexes should be brought out and it is the decided aim of this association [.]

29. "Advancement of Women," *New York Age,* November 11, 1887

MEETING OF THE ASSOCIATION IN NEW YORK.
Mrs. Mary Shadd Cary Appealed to the Women of
/ the Race to Join Work for the Welfare
/ of Humanity without Discrimination.
/ From the Chicago Conservator.

The Association for the Advancement of Woman, abbreviated A. A. W., Mrs. Julia Ward Howe, president, is called, after a lapse of fifteen years of peregrinating annual congresses in cities, East, West and South, whence they had assembled as was their wont, to receive reports of various clubs of woman, read papers and report progress, the child of Sorosis,—Sorosis, the preeminently leading society among American women, the objects of which are to promote scientific, artistic and philanthropic methods among women, planned and carried to success thus far through individual members of the A. A. W. and its most prominent and its influential members have been and are officers and directors. Mrs. Howe, Prof. Maria Mitchell, Miss Frances Willard and others are or have been officers and members.[37]

Leading women in art, letters and society, and in the various plans for women's work and help, MesDames Demorest, Holmes, Thomas, Hoffman, Eastman, Wolcott, Dr. Smith and others, being active members of both, so that justly the A. A. W. can be called the daughter of an illustrious parent. The statistics relating to clubs, to literary, scientific and practical methods for women's help included every species of work and every device for the welfare of humanity without race of sex discrimination, as fearlessly asserted and approbated and were the words of forceful import that commended themselves to the colored members of the congress.

And just here the colored woman in the limits of your broadening horizon and the far-reaching beyond I beg through you to say to them, inquire of the methods of these great workers of the universal race, and let us form clubs, embracing the various means for a broader and more worthy citizenship, and as means to develop a higher moral and economic excellence for us, by concert of purpose and the practical methods so successfully tried by fifteen years experience of those eminent workers; that we may broaden our lives and make less the divergence and conditions, whether heretofore voluntary or involuntary, between the colored people as a class and other native or adopted Americans.

The present congress, after a vast amount of excellent work, endorsed without stint, the best work for woman's advancement, though reserving its right to accept or not methods specified. Various institutions and societies and private citizens extended invitations which were kindly received. Delegations from Sorosis, from W. C. T. U., from scientific institutions, from the national museum, and not least from the Woman's Suffrage Association came to them, and two delegates will be sent from the A. A. W., to meet a conference of women suggested by the suffragists next January at the Opera House in Washington, D. C.

---

[37] Maria Mitchell (1818–1889) was a white astronomer who cofounded the Association for the Advancement of Women and served as its president from 1875 to 1877. Frances Willard (1839–1898) was a white cofounder and president of the Woman's Christian Temperance Union.

The young and vigorous and aggressive element of women workers in the congress is a mighty, growing force, sustaining the hands of the older and original workers in the congress, and augur lively but peaceful conflict with whatever stands opposed to the advanced thought respecting woman's work and methods.

Now to our special household, (colored women). I a member and witness for several years of the, to me, marvelous results by the more favored members, [in] consideration of the plans of this great organization and hope clubs may be formed everywhere among us, covering all worthy means of success.

It should not be this woman or the other but the world of the earnest everywhere. A thousand capable colored women are on hand, not one or two only. Theory and methods in the abstract are widely known to educated colored women, North and South. Apply them practically and it is safe to say that no better methods than those so well used by the A. A. W. need be adopted to work good results among the six millions of which we form at least the half. Mrs. F. E. W. Harper and daughter, members of the A. A. W., were conspicuous for quiet conscious force and effectiveness, and with yours truly make the complement of our side of the American race in the A. A. W.[38]

[38] Shadd Cary referred to poet, novelist, lecturer, abolitionist, and suffragist Frances Ellen Watkins Harper (1825–1911). During the *Provincial Freeman*'s run, Shadd Cary repeatedly published Harper's poetry and William Still's (1821–1902) praise for her writing. See W. S., "Letter to the Editor," *Provincial Freeman*, September 2, 1854; Frances Ellen Watkins, "The Burial of Moses," *Provincial Freeman*, May 24, 1856; Watkins, "Died of Starvation," *Provincial Freeman*, March 7, 1857; and W. S., "Letter to the Editor," *Provincial Freeman*, March 7, 1857.

Part III

"The Men Who Love Liberty Too Well to Remain in the States"

Enabling Emigration

30. Letter to Isaac Shadd, September 16, 1851[*]

1851
Toronto Canada West Sept 16

Dear Brother[:]

I heard you were in Buffalo. I have not time to say much to you for I leave here for Sandwich[,] Canada West today. I have been here more than a week and like Canada[.] Do not feel prejudice and repeat if you were to come here or go west of this where shoemaking pays well and work at it and buy land as fast as you make any money, you would do well. If you come be particular about company—be polite to every body [*sic*]—go to Church, every body [*sic*] does to be <u>respected</u>—but [though] you would occasionally visit cold ones[,] select the English Chapel or some [other] <u>respectable</u> one to attend regular and [you] would get along well.[1] Storekeeping is a first rate business. You could attend to some business and take lessons from masters and discard [swearing] company. If [. . .] at boarding go where whites & cold board. Every man is respected and patronised according to his ability <u>and</u> capacity and the respectable stand be taken.[2] I would like much to see you, but cannot

---

[*] This document is pictured in Figure 3.1. Isaac Shadd (1829–1896) was Shadd Cary's brother. He emigrated to Canada in the fall of 1851 and edited the *Provincial Freeman* with her. For more, see Rhodes, *Mary Ann Shadd Cary*, 97, 101–104, 108, 114–128, 133.

[1] In this letter, "cold" appears to be Shadd Cary's shorthand for "colored." M. A. Shadd to Isaac Shadd, September 16, 1851, Mary Ann Shadd Cary fonds, F 1409-1-0-001, Archives of Ontario.

[2] The year after writing this letter, Shadd Cary published *A Plea for Emigration*, her best-known publication. "A Plea for Emigration" reproduced some of the ideas that she first expressed in this letter, including her beliefs that there is no prejudice in Canada, there are ample work opportunities for African Americans who emigrate, and that all people are treated fairly.

Mary Ann Shadd Cary. Nneka D. Dennie, Oxford University Press. © Oxford University Press 2024.
DOI: 10.1093/oso/9780197609460.003.0004

write more. All were well at home when I left. If you see Rev. Mr. Campbell in Buffalo tell him to write to me at Sandwich about the school. Yours dear brother.

M. A. Shadd

Figure 3.1 M. A. Shadd to Isaac Shadd. September 16, 1851. Mary Ann Shadd Cary fonds, F 1409-1-0-001, Archives of Ontario.

31. *A Plea for Emigration; or, Notes of Canada West, in its Moral, Social, and Political Aspect: with Suggestions Respecting Mexico, West Indies, and Vancouver's Island, for the Information of Colored Emigrants*[*]

INTRODUCTORY REMARKS

—

THE increasing desire on the part of the colored people, to become thoroughly informed respecting the Canadas, and particularly that part of the province called Canada West—to learn of the climate, soil and productions, and of the inducements offered generally to emigrants, and to them particularly, since that the passage of the odious Fugitive Slave Law has made a residence in the United States to many of them dangerous in the extreme,—this consideration, and the absence of condensed information accessible to all, is my excuse for offering this tract to the notice of the public.[3] The people are in a strait,—on the one hand, a pro-slavery administration, with its entire controllable force, is bearing upon them with fatal effect: on the other, the Colonization Society, in the garb of *Christianity* and *Philanthropy*, is seconding the efforts of the first named power, by bringing into the lists a vast social and immoral influence, this making more effective the agencies employed. Information is needed.— Tropical Africa, the land of promise of the colonizationists, teeming as she is with the breath of pestilence, a burning sun and fearful maladies, bids

---

[*] Shadd Cary published *A Plea for Emigration* in order to offer African Americans practical guidance about emigrating to Canada, like information on the environment and weather, and to argue that emigration could improve Black people's quality of life in their ongoing struggle for freedom. When this pamphlet was published in 1852, Canada was still a British colony. It did not become an independent country until 1867. Shadd Cary writes specifically about a region called "Canada West," which is present-day Ontario. Many of Shadd Cary's comments pertain not simply to Canada West as a geographical area, but also to British governance and customs. She also shares observations about why Canada West would be superior to other parts of Canada, other British territories including the West Indies, and other parts of North America including Mexico. All footnotes in this part are Shadd Cary's original footnotes, not editorial commentary, which is instead located in endnotes. All emphasis in this document is original, including italicizations, capitalizations, etc. Some words in the surviving copy of *A Plea for Emigration* are illegible due to wear and tear on the original document, which has resulted in some discoloration. In those instances, I offer an approximation of the unclear words in brackets. At times, these bracketed phrases are drawn from two prior scholarly editions of *A Plea for Emigration*, edited by Richard Almonte (1996) and Phanuel Antwi (2016). At other times, the bracketed phrases correct typographical errors or misspellings.

[3] When Shadd Cary states "the Canadas," she is speaking of two colonies: Canada West and Canada East (present-day Québec.)

them welcome;—she feelingly invited to moral and physical death, under a voluntary escort of their most bitter enemies at home.[4] Again, many look with dreadful forebodings to the probability of worse than inquisitorial inhumanity in the Southern States from the operation of the Fugitive Laws. Certain that neither a home in Africa, nor in the Southern States, is desirable under present circumstances, inquiry is made respecting Canada. I have endeavored to furnish information to a certain extent, to that end, and believing that more reliance would be placed upon a statement of facts obtained in the country, from reliable sources and from observation, than upon a repetition of current statements made elsewhere, however honestly made, I determined to visit Canada, and to there collect such information as most persons desire. These pages contain the result of much inquiry— matter obtained both from individuals and from documents and papers of unquestionable character in the Province.

M. A. S.

A PLEA FOR EMIGRATION, &C.

—

BRITISH AMERICA.
BRITISH AMERICA, it is well known, is a country equal in extent, at least, to the United States, extending on the north to the Arctic Ocean, from the

---

[4] Shadd Cary's remarks about the drawbacks of going to Africa are reminiscent of those by Maria W. Stewart (1803–1879), a Black abolitionist who was also the first woman to publicly lecture to interracial and coed audiences in the United States. Twenty years prior, Stewart wrote, "Why sit ye here and die? If we say we will go to a foreign land, the famine and the pestilence are there, and there we shall die." Marilyn Richardson, ed., *Maria W. Stewart, America's First Black Woman Political Writer: Essays and Speeches* (Bloomington: Indiana University Press, 1987), 48. Throughout the nineteenth century, Black activists questioned whether African Americans should remain in the United States or go to Canada, Haiti, or Liberia in search of a better life. Some were opposed to the notion that Black people should go to Africa—a movement that was referred to as "African colonization." Shadd Cary—and indeed, Stewart, before her—thought that that illness in Africa made it an unsuitable destination for African Americans. Despite her opposition to African colonization, Shadd Cary supported Canadian emigration, which she discusses throughout this pamphlet. For more on the distinctions that Black people drew between colonization and emigration, see Ousmane K. Power-Greene, *Against Wind and Tide: The African American Struggle against the Colonization Movement* (New York: New York University Press, 2014) and Beverly C. Tomek, *Colonization and Its Discontents: Emancipation, Emigration, and Antislavery in Antebellum Pennsylvania* (New York: New York University Press, 2011).

Atlantic on the east, to the Pacific on the west, and the southern boundary of which is subject to the inequalities in latitude of the several Northern States and Territories belonging to the United States government. This vast country includes within its limits, some of the most beautiful lakes and rivers on the Western Continent. The climate, in the higher latitudes, is extremely severe, but for a considerable distance north of the settled districts, particularly in the western part, the climate is healthy and temperate: epidemics are not of such frequency as in the United States, owing to a more equable temperature, and local diseases are unknown. The province claiming especial attention, as presenting features most desirable in a residence, is Canada, divided into East and West; and of these Canada West is to be preferred.

THE CANADAS—CLIMATE, ETC.

Canada East, from geographical position and natural characteristics, is not so well suited to a variety of pursuits, as the more western part of the province. The surface is generally uneven, and in many parts mountainous; its more northern location subjects the inhabitants to extremely cold, cheerless winters, and short but warm summers. The land is of good quality, and vegetation is of rapid growth, but the general healthiness of the country is inferior to some of the other districts. The State of Maine presents a fair sample of Lower Canada in the general.[5] Population (which is principally French) is confined chiefly to the valley of the St. Lawrence, and the country contiguous. In Canada West, the variation from a salubrious and eminently healthy climate, is nowhere sufficient to cause the least solicitude; on the contrary, exempt from the steady and enfeebling warmth of southern latitudes, and the equally injurious characteristics of polar countries, it is highly conducive to mental and physical energy. Persons living in the vicinity of the Great Lakes, and the neighboring districts, say that their winters are much less severe than when, in past years, vast forests covered that region—that very deep snows are less frequent than they were, and that owing to the great body of ice that accumulates in the Lakes, the people living in the States bordering, suffer

[5] "Lower Canada" was the name of Canada East and "Upper Canada" was the name of Canada West prior to 1841, at which point the two separate colonies were unified into one province. See James Maurice Stockford Careless, "Province of Canada (1841–67)," *The Canadian Encyclopedia*, Historica Canada, https://www.thecanadianencyclopedia.ca/en/article/province-of-canada-1841-67.
   Catechism of Information Intended Emigrants of all Clandestine Upper Canada

more severely from the cold than Canadians,—the ice making more intense the north winds sweeping over it. If these statements admit of a doubt, we well know that many flourishing towns in Canada are farther south than a large portion of Maine, New Hampshire, Vermont, New York, Michigan and Oregon, and should in considering this fact, have the full benefit of geographical position. I have thought proper to allude to the cold, at first, for the reason that it is the feature in the climate most dwelt upon—the solicitude of friends, ignorant on this point, and of persons less disinterested, often appealing to fears having no foundation whatever, when the facts are fairly set forth.

The products of a country make an important item, in all cases in which this question is being considered; so in the present instance. In Canada we find the vegetation of as rank growth as in the middle and northern United States. In order to promote a luxuriance in the products of a country equally with another, the conditions necessary to that end must be equal,—if by reference to facts, an approach to similarity can be made, that part of the subject will be settled for the present. As early as March there are indications of permanent Spring weather, and in June and July, the summer will compare with the same season south of the line. In January and February there are always cold spells and warm alternating, as is our experience; but when the warm season commences, the heat is intense, and the growth of vegetation is rapid, so that whatever deficiency may be attributed to a brief period, may be fully compensated for in the steady and equal temperature after the warm season has fairly set in; though it is late beginning, it is prolonged into what is the autumn with us, and farmers harvest their crops of wheat, hay, &c., at a later period than in the Middle States, generally,—August and September being the months in which hay, wheat, and some other crops are gathered in. Taking this circumstance in connection with the regularity of the seasons, and uniform heat or cold when they have such weather, the superiority of many products, as wheat, fruit, &c., may be accounted for. I say superiority, because, in its place, I hope to give such evidence as will substantiate the assertion. Annexed is a table setting forth the greatest degree of cold and heat,—in the years mentioned, as indicated by Fahrenheit's Thermometer, together with the highest and lowest range indicated in the months of September and December of 1851, which last has been said to be unusual, (the lowest is twenty years) by the "oldest inhabitant."

GREATEST DEG. OF HEAT.				LOWEST DEG. OF COLD.					
1840	-	-	-	82°4'	-	-	-	-	-	18°6'
1841	-	-	-	93°1'	-	-	-	-	-	6°7'
1842	-	-	-	91°	-	-	-	-	-	1°9'
1843	-	-	-	89°	-	-	-	-	-	9°4'
1844	-	-	-	86°8'	-	-	-	-	-	7°2'
1845	-	-	-	95°	-	-	-	-	-	4°2'
1846	-	-	-	94°6'	-	-	-	-	-	16°7'
1847	-	-	-	87°	-	-	-	-	-	2°9'

"These are the extreme ranges of cold and heat indicated at the Observatory, on one day during the seasons, but which do not last beyond a few hours; the mean temperature of the four months of summer and four winter for the last eight years have been respectively: Summer 75°6'; Winter 26°7', Fahrenheit."* In addition to the usual state of the weather of the last year, as contrasted with former periods, the last summer and first autumn months were very warm, and in the month of September indicated 95° Fahrenheit, in the shade, without eliciting remarks other than a similar state of weather at that season, would have in the United States. In short, from much conversation with persons of many years residence, I believe that climate opposes no obstacle to emigration, but that it is the most desirable known in so high a latitude, for emigrants generally, and colored people particularly. In other parts of British America, as, for instance, Lower Canada, Nova Scotia, and New Britain, the cold is more intense, but when we think of the extent of Upper Canada, there would be no more reason for ascribing severe cold to the whole, than there would be to class the climate of the United States with that of the torrid zone, because of the great heat in the lower latitudes. In this province the regularity of the seasons promote health in a greater degree than in those countries subject to frequent changes, as in many of the United States, where cold and warm weather alternate in quick succession; and in the upper province especially, universal testimony to the healthiness of the climate obtains.

SOIL,—TIMBER,—CLEARING LANDS.
The quality and different kinds of soil must form the second subject for consideration, because, in connection with climate, it enters largely into all our ideas of comfort and pecuniary independence; again, because so far as

colored people are interested in the subject of emigration to any country, their welfare, in a pecuniary view, is promoted by attention to the quality of the soil. Lands out of the United States, on this continent, should have no local value, if the questions of personal freedom and political rights were left out of the subject, but as they are paramount, too much may not be said on this point. I mean to be understood, that a description of lands in Mexico would probably be as desirable as lands in Canada, if the idea were simply to get lands and settle thereof; but it is important to know if by this investigation we only agitate, and leave the public mind in an unsettled state, or if a permanent nationality is included in the prospect of becoming purchasers and settlers.

The question, does the soil of Canada offer inducements sufficient to determine prospective emigrants in its favor? may be answered by every one for himself, after having properly weighed the following facts. Persons who have been engaged in agriculture the greater part of their lives,—practical and competent farmers, and judges of the capacity of different soils,—say, that the soil is unsurpassed by that of Kentucky and States farther south, and naturally superior to the adjoining northern States. It is not only indicated by the rich, dark and heavy appearance, and the depth of the soil, which is seldom reached by plows of the greatest capacity, but by the character of the products, and the unequalled growth and size of timber on uncleared lands. Wheat, the staple product of the country, averages sixty pounds to the bushel—often actually exceeding that; fifty-six is the standard weight in the United States; and leaving out Delaware, that is seldom reached. The forest consists of walnut, hickory, white and burr oak, basswood, ash, pine, poplar—all of the largest size, and other inferior kinds of wood with which we are not familiar in our northern woods. There is a greater variety in them, and larger size and knowing that the size of vegetables depends mainly upon the quantity of nutriment afforded by the soil, we are led in this instance to infer its superiority. Besides the well known wheat, oats, buckwheat, Indian corn, and other grains, are raised of good quality, and with profit, and more to the acre than is usually obtained in the States, except on the application of fertilizing materials—a mode not much practised in Canada hitherto, the land not having been exhausted sufficiently to require such appliances to further its productiveness. The varieties of soil, are a black loam, sandy loam, clay, and sand, but a black loam is the predominating kind. I speak now of the cultivated districts and those in process of clearing, as far north as Lord Selkirk's settlement, for the country beyond the present limits of civilization, I do not feel warranted in speaking, nor to give in other general terms, the testimony of those acquainted with that region.[6] It is said to be equally fertile, but the products not so varied, because of its more northern situation. The general appearance of the province is undulating, though there is much level country. Numerous and beautiful rivers, and smaller streams, run through the country, in all directions, so that there is no lack of water power. "The plains," a term applied to level country, "are generally sandy, and yield regular average and certain crops, without reference to the seasons."* They are all similar to the western prairies, but more capital is necessary to cultivate them than for timber lands. The advantage of timbered land, to purchasers of small capital, over plains, is considerable. On cultivated, or plain lands, on which timber is thinly scattered, the earliest return for labor spent is deferred to the growth of a crop; besides the mode of tillage is different. Not so on the timbered lands; wood ever meets a ready and cash sale, and more may be realized from firewood than to three times pay the cost of a farm. Wood land will average seventy cords to the acre, every cord of which can be readily disposed of at two and two [sic] and a half dollars, cash, in the towns. The regularity of the seasons tends, also, to increase the farmer's security, so that of all other men, he is least apprehensive of want. "If the fall wheat fails," says the little book referred to, "he replaces it with spring wheat; and our seasons are so peculiar that some crops are always certain to be productive." * * * Those whose capital invested in it is their own, are sure to increase their means and wealth. * * * If a farmer determines to keep out of debt, and be satisfied with what his farm yields, independence in a few years will be the result." The above extracts are intended for the benefit of the emigrants in general,—men of small means, or with no capital,—and show what may be expected by generally the least wealthy who settle in a new country.[7] From the many instances of success under my observation,

---

[6] Shadd Cary references Thomas Douglas, 5th Earl of Selkirk (1771–1820). Douglas was a Scottish man who, similarly to Shadd Cary, was of the view that emigrating to British North America could improve the quality of life for displaced Scots. See J. M. Bumsted, "Thomas Douglas, 5th Earl of Selkirk," The Canadian Encyclopedia, Historica Canada, https://www.thecanadianencyclopedia.ca/en/article/thomas-douglas-5th-earl-of-selkirk.

[7] It was common parlance among abolitionists and Black activists to use the term "emigrants" to refer to African Americans who migrated to Canada. Shadd Cary's description of a typical emigrant highlights whom she envisions as her audience for A Plea for Emigration. Shadd Cary assumes that emigrants will be fugitives from slavery as well as free Black people who would arrive with little to no financial resources. As a result, much of her pamphlet attempts to provide newcomers with information that would aid them in living and working in Canada. Free African Americans pursued a range of different occupations during the nineteenth century and established thriving communities

(particularly of formerly totally destitute colored persons,) I firmly believe that with an axe and a little energy, an independent position would result in a short period. The cost of clearing wild lands, is also an important item; by that is meant putting land in a state to receive a crop,—it includes clearing of trees, fencing, &c. This can be done at less cost near the settled districts. "In moderately timbered" lands, ten dollars the acre is the least for which it can be done,—more remote, the price varies from that to twenty dollars. Though the prevalent opinion in the province, is, that the soil is second to none for agricultural, purposes, yet it is hardly possible to state the actual productiveness of the soil, as the attention has not been given to farming that the land admits. There are, and must be for a great time, few experimental and scientific farmers, as it is more as a means of present subsistence, than to test the capacity of different soils, that the farmer labors to procure a crop; though the conviction is irresistible that indigence and moderate competence must at no distant day, give place to wealth, intelligence, and their concomitants.

GRAINS, POTATOES, TURNIPS, &C.

The accompanying table exhibits the average yield to the acre, of the several grains mentioned, in fallow land:

ARTICLES.	NO. BUSH.	ARTICLES.	NO. BUSH.
Wheat,——————30		Oats,—————————70	
Buckwheat,————15		Barley—————————40	
Rye,——————————35		Indian Corn,————50	

Other products yielding a profitable return, and that form a part of the crop in well cultivated farms generally, in the United States, are potatoes—white

for themselves. White supremacy and employment discrimination did, however, restrict their opportunities to earn an income, build wealth, and own property. Shadd Cary wrote *A Plea for Emigration* with these factors in mind. For more on the lives of free African Americans during the antebellum era, see Warren Eugene Milteer Jr., *Beyond Slavery's Shadow: Free People of Color in the South* (Chapel Hill: University of North Carolina Press, 2021); James Oliver Horton and Lois E. Horton, *In Hope of Liberty: Culture, Community, and Protest among Northern Free Blacks, 1700–1860* (New York: Oxford University Press, 1997); and Ira Berlin, *Slaves without Masters: The Free Negro in the Antebellum South* (New York: Pantheon Books, 1976).

* Catechism.

or Irish or sweet,—carrots, turnips, pumpkins, (several kinds, and the best I ever saw,) squashes and tobacco. These vegetables grow very large, and are not included in what we term garden plants. I have never seen in the large markets of our northern cities, vegetables of the class here mentioned, to equal them in the general, except the sweet potato. The Irish potato grows much larger, and is in every respect superior; so of the others. Tobacco grows finely, and meets with ready sale as what would be called a high price with us. These articles, I repeat, are of the finest description, and have not, of course, the pithy and stringy characteristics so general in the same kind with us. It is difficult to get at the average yield of such things, except potatoes and turnips, but a full crop will convey the idea.

GARDEN VEGETABLES, &C.
The most abundant are tomatoes, cucumbers, onions, beets, cabbage and cauliflower, egg-plants, beans, peas, leeks, celery, lettuce, asparagus, melons, (water-melons and musk-melons,) cantelopes and spinage. There are other vegetables, but they have been mentioned elsewhere. These articles, ex-cepting water-melons and cantelopes, are cultivated with as great success, at least, as in the United States, and the specimens generally seen in the gardens and market-places are decidedly superior.

FRUITS—VINES—BERRIES.
Canada is emphatically a fruit country. The fruits of New York, Michigan and New Jersey, have long been famous: but if comparison is fairly instituted, pre-eminence will be the award to the Province. Apples grow in abundance, wild and cultivated, from the diminutive crab to the highly flavored bell-flower and pippin; and pears, plums and cherries, in many varieties. The extent to which fruit is cultivated, and the yield, are incredible. Egg and blue plums are raised with ease, and strawberries, raspberries, grapes, whortleberries, and in fact all of the fruits seen in our markets, are plentiful. Other ideas than those of a barren soil, and scarcity of products, are induced when visiting the market-places of Toronto, Hamilton and other large towns. At Toronto, may be seen one of the best markets in America in every way—the supplies furnished by the farmers of their own agricultural districts. At the State Fair, held in Detroit, Michigan, 1851, the first prizes, for fruits, fowls, and cattle, were awarded to Canada farmers; so of the Fair held in Western New York during the same year.

DOMESTIC ANIMALS—FOWLS—GAME.

In the general, the horses are not of that large size found in the Middle and Western States, but are of medium size, particularly those used by the French; yet occasionally, one may see large horses among them, and cattle, sheep, etc., also. The size of cattle seems not to affect their market value as beef and mutton, it being thought by epicures to be of the best quality. I speak of the French in this connection, because it is well known, they form no inconsiderable part of the population. Among English, and other farmers, more attention is paid to improving stock—competition is as spiritedly carried on as in the States, consequently cattle and horses of the finest kinds, as to size and repute, are owned by them. The Canadian pony, with them, gives place to the fine English draft and carriage horse, and Durham and other kine of celebrity are justly appreciated. The pride of Canadian farmers, as shown in a fine selection of such animals, is not at all less than that of their "American" neighbors: as before said, the highest premiums given for superior cattle and sheep at Rochester and Detroit, in 1851, were received by Canada farmers. To understand fully the resources of the Canadas in this particular, both as to quantity and quality, for labor or other purposes, a view of the well stocked farms, with their swarms of horses, oxen, cows, sheep and hogs, would well repay a visit to the country, to those skeptical on these points, or to see the excellent beef, mutton, veal and pork, exposed for sale—unsurpassed any where for quality and abundance. Prices vary as elsewhere, according to demand, but ordinarily they are:

[a] Beef,	4 and 5 cts.	Per pound.
Mutton	5 "	"
Veal,	4 "	"
Pork,	5 and 6 "	"

[a] Prices of meat are not uniform, as before said, and owing to the increased demand prices have risen very recently, to the ordinary price in the States. That, of course, will not be the rate henceforth, but will be determined by the supply.

Again, the butter and cheese, derived directly from these animals, must be, and are, superior, from the nature of the pasture and other food eaten; though, from the circumstance of recent settlement, means of disposal and abundance, matter in the housewife's department are not generally so thoroughly conducted as in more populous and older settled countries, where a competition of tastes and judgment, in managing these articles and arranging for the market, is freely indulged. The comparative cost of keeping stock is little, the summer pastures affording ample for that season; in winter, many mark their horses, and turn them out in the woodlands and open country, where they never fail of a supply of roots and grasses. Numbers are seen in mid-winter, looking as well as those housed and fed. The snows protect the grasses, and from their peculiar length and frequency, animals subsist well on the matter they are thus enabled to get by removing them, and from the early growth of shrubs in the woods. The farms generally, have chickens, turkeys, geese, and other fowls, in great numbers; and they meet with a ready sale— prices are generally for poultry two shillings and two and six-pence the pair, when in great plenty; eggs 10 cents and 12 ½ cents the dozen, and may be disposed of in any quantity to the traders without leaving the farm: numerous hucksters go in all directions through the country to purchase, to sell again in the large cities. In the winter, these articles, in common with vegetables and other commodities, are often sold at a rate that in the United States would be called high, the rapidly increasing population making the ordinary supply insufficient. Geese uniformly command two shillings; turkeys one dollar, domesticated or wild. There is an abundance of game, and turkeys meet with ready sale. Hunting is much the custom of all classes, and ducks, squirrels, (black,) pigeons, deer, hares, quails, pheasants, and other game, are brought down in great numbers. Wild animals are not troublesome, though in remote districts, an occasional bear or wolf is seen; foxes also make depredations at times, but not frequently.

PRICES OF LAND IN THE COUNTRY—CITY PROPERTY, &C.

The country in the vicinity of Toronto and to the eastward, being thickly settled, (farms being advertised "thirty miles on Yonge street,") the price of property is, of course, very much higher than in the western districts. City property varies according to location—two hundred dollars the foot, is the value of lots in good position in Toronto: in the suburbs very fine lots may be had at reasonable rates. Farms, at a few miles distant, range from thirty to fifty dollars the acre—fifty dollars being thought a fair price for the best quality of land with improvements; but in the western districts, farms may be bought for one thousand dollars, superior in every way, to farms near the city of Toronto, that are held at five thousand. Improved lands near Chatham, London, Hamilton, and other towns west, may be bought at prices varying from ten up to one hundred: at a few miles distant, uncleared lands, belonging to Government, may be had by paying one dollar sixty-two cents, two, and two fifty, according to locality—well timbered and watered, near cultivated farms on the river and lake shore. Thousands of acres, of the very best lands in the Province, are now in the market at the above prices, and either in the interior, or well situated as to prospect from the lakes, and near excellent markets. The land is laid out in what are called concessions, these concessions, or blocks, being sub-divided into lots. There is, therefore, a uniformity of appearance throughout in the farms, and no contest about roads on individual property can result—the roads being designed to benefit equally contiguous property, and under jurisdiction of Government. One hundred acres is the smallest quantity to be had of Government, but individual holders sell in quantities to suit purchasers. Large quantities of land are held by individuals, though at a higher rate generally than that held by Government; and their titles are said to be often defective. In every respect, the preference should be for purchases of Government—land is cheaper, as well situated, and below a specified number of acres, may not be bought; a prohibition of advantage to many who would buy, as there is induced a spirit of enterprise and competition, and a sense of responsibility. Too many are now *independently* dragging along miserably, on the few acres, ten, twenty, or such a matter, bought at the high rates of individual holders, in a country in which the prices must, for a long time, require more land in process of culture, to afford a comfortable support. There is every inducement to buy, near or in towns, as well as in the country, as land is cheap, business increasing, with the steady increase of population, no lack of employment at fair prices, and complexional or other qualification in existence.

LABOR—TRADES.

In Canada, as in other recently settled countries, there is much to do, and comparatively few for the work. The numerous towns and villages springing up, and the great demand for timber and agricultural products, make labor of every kind plenty: all trades that are practiced in the United States, are there patronized by whomsoever carried on—no man's complexion affecting his business. If a colored man understands his business, he receives the public patronage the same as a white man. He is not obliged to work a little better, and at a lower rate—there is no degraded class to identify him with, therefore every man's work stands or falls according to merit, not as is his color. Builders, and other tradesmen, of different complexions, work together on the same building and in the same shop, with perfect harmony, and often the proprietor of an establishment is colored, and the majority of all of the men employed are white. Businesses that in older communities have ceased to remunerate, yield a large percentage to the money invested.[8]

The mineral resources of the Canadas not being developed, to any extent, for fuel wood is generally used, and a profitable trade in that commodity is carried on; and besides lumber for buildings, the getting out of materials for staves, coopers' stuff, and various purposes, affords steady employment and at fair prices, for cash. This state of things must increase, and assume more importance in Canada markets, as the increasing population of the western United States burn and otherwise appropriate their timber. Railroads are in process of construction—steamboats now ply between Toronto and the several towns on the lakes; and in process of time, iron and other works will be in operation, it is said, all requiring their quota, and of course keeping up the demand. Boards for home and foreign markets, are successfully manufactured, and numerous mill-sites are fast being appropriated to saw and grist mils. In some sections, colored men are engaged in saw mills on their own account. At Dawn, a settlement on the Sudydenham [River], (of which hereafter,) and at other points, this trade prosecuted with profit to them.[9] To enumerate the different occupations in which colored persons are engaged, even in detail, would but fatigue, and would not further the end in view, namely: To set forth the advantage of a residence in a country, in which chattel slavery is not tolerated, and prejudice of *color* has no existence whatever—the adaptation of that country, by climate, soil, and political character, to their physical and political necessities; and the superiority of a residence there over their present position at *home*.[10] It will suffice, that colored men prosecute all the different trades; are store keepers, farmers, clerks, and laborers; and are not

[8] As I have written elsewhere, Shadd Cary "frequently argued that emigrating would empower Black people to control their labor and achieve economic independence." Nneka D. Dennie, "Leave That Slavery-Cursed Republic: Mary Ann Shadd Cary and Black Feminist Nationalism, 1852–1874," *Atlantic Studies: Global Currents* 18, no. 4 (2021): 487. In her view, mobility offered a number of advantages, some of which were financial. As Shadd Cary indicates here, emigration was attractive in part because it would shield Black people from racial discrimination without restricting their labor or compensation.

[9] Shadd Cary is referring to the Dawn Settlement, which she discusses in greater detail later in *A Plea for Emigration*. The Dawn Settlement was a community established for fugitives from slavery by Reverend Josiah Henson (1789–1883), who escaped slavery in 1830. See Josiah Henson, *The Life of Josiah Henson, Formerly a Slave, Now an Inhabitant of Canada, as Narrated by Himself* (Boston: A. D. Phelps, 1849); Marie Carter, "Reimagining the Dawn Settlement," in *The Promised Land: Historiography of the Black Experience in Chatham-Kent's Settlements and Beyond*, ed. Boulou Ebanda de B'béri et al. (Toronto: University of Toronto Press, 2014).

[10] Shadd Cary is insistent that there is no racism in Canada. For more on histories of race and slavery in Canada, see Maynard, *Policing Black Lives*; Walker, *Race on Trial*; and Afua Cooper, *The Hanging of Angélique: The Untold Story of Canadian Slavery and the Burning of Old Montréal* (Athens: University of Georgia Press, 2007).

only unmolested, but sustained and encouraged in any business for which their qualifications and means fit them; and as the resources of the country develop, new fields of enterprise will be opened to them, and consequently new motives to honorable effort.

CHURCHES—SCHOOLS.

In the large towns and cities, as in similar communities in other Christian countries, the means for religious instruction are ample. There are costly churches in which all classes and complexions worship, and no "negro pew," or other seat for colored persons, especially. I was forcibly struck, when at Toronto, with the contrast the religious community there presented, to our own large body of American Christians. In the churches, originally built by the white Canadians, the presence of colored persons, promiscuously seated, elicited no comment whatever.[11] They are members, and visitors, and as such have their pews according to their inclination, near the door, or remote, or central, as best suits them. The number of colored persons, attending the churches with whites, constitutes a minority, I think. They have their "own churches." That that is the feature in their policy, which is productive of mischief to the entire body, is evident enough; and the opinion of the best informed and most influential among them, in Toronto and the large towns, is decided and universal. I have heard men of many years residence, and who have, in a measure, been moulded by the better sentiment of society, express deep sorrow at the course of colored persons, in pertinaciously refusing overtures of religious fellowship from the whites; and in the face of all experience to the contrary, erecting Colored Methodist, and Baptist, and other Churches. This opinion obtains amongst many who, when in the United States, were connected with colored churches. Aside from their caste character, their influence on the colored people is fatal. The character of the exclusive church in Canada tends to perpetuate ignorance, both of their true position as British subjects, and of the Christian religion in its purity.[12] It [is

---

[11] During the nineteenth century, "promiscuous" was sometimes used to describe men and women occupying the same space together. In this instance, Shadd Cary means that men and women were seated together.

[12] Shadd Cary was critical of Black people who chose to create their own, separate Black institutions in Canada. In her view, to do so was to perpetuate American ways of being and what she described elsewhere as the "spirit of caste." Mary A. Shadd to George Whipple, November 27, 1851, American Missionary Association Archive, Amistad Research Center, New Orleans, LA (included in Part 1). Shadd Cary believed that racial separatism in Canada was not simply unnecessary, but also detrimental to Black people. For more on Shadd Cary's support for integration, see Conaway, "Mary Ann Shadd Cary."

impossible] to observe thoughtfully the workings of that incipient Zion, (the Canadian African Church, of whatever denomination,) in its present imperfect state, without seriously regretting that it should have been thought necessary to call it into existence.[13] In her bosom is nurtured the long standing and rankling prejudices, and hatred against whites, without exception, that had their origin in American oppression, and that should have been left in the country in which they originated—'tis that species of animosity that is not bounded by geographical lines, nor suffers discrimination.

A goodly portion of the people in the western part of the Province, (for there are but few in the eastern,) are enjoying superior religious opportunities, but the majority greatly need active missionary effort: first, to teach them love to their neighbor: and again, to give them an intelligent and correct understanding of the Sacred Scriptures. The missionary strength, at present, consists of but six preachers—active and efficient gentlemen, all of them, and self-sacrificing in the last degree; and several women engaged in teaching, under the same auspices. Much privation, suffering, opposition, and sorrow await the missionary in that field. If it were possible for him to foresee what is in store for him there, a mission to India, or the South Sea Islands, would be preferable; for, in that case, the sympathy of the entire community is enlisted, and his sojourn is made as pleasant as possible—the people to whom he is sent, are either as little children, simple and confiding, or out-right savages; and in that case, deadly enemies.[14] In this less remote field—almost in speaking distance—neglect from friends, suspicion, abuse, misrepresentation, and a degrading surveillance, often of serious and abiding consequences, await him. Not directly from the fugitives—those designated primarily to be benefitted—may assaults be looked for, at first. They possess a desire for the light, and incline to cluster around the missionary invariably. There are those who pretend to have been enlightened, and to have at heart the common good, whose influence and operations, he [will find] designedly counteracting his conscientious efforts, the [more effectively] appealing to a common origin and kindred suffer[ings secretly] striking behind, and bringing his character as a missiononary [sic], and his operations, into discredit in the eyes of a sympathizing Christian community.[15] This, and more,

[13] Almonte, ed., *A Plea for Emigration*, 62; Antwi, ed., *A Plea for Emigration*, 36.

[14] Despite her criticisms of slavery and white supremacy in the United States, Shadd Cary sometimes struggled to extend her worldview to include other forms of global domination. Her description of the other peoples across the world as "simple" and "savages" highlights that she was not entirely free of popular nineteenth-century biases against indigenous and colonized peoples.

[15] Almonte, ed., *A Plea for Emigration*, 63; Antwi, ed., *A Plea for Emigration*, 37.

awaits those who may be called to the field; but the case is not a hopeless one. The native food sense [of the fugitives, backed by proper schools, will eventually develop the real character of their operations and sacrifices. They and their families, of all others, should have the support of Christians.

The refugees express a strong desire for intellectual culture, and persons often begin their education at a time of life when many in other countries think they are too old. There are no separate schools: at Toronto and in many other places, as in the churches, the colored people avail themselves of existing schools; but in the western country, in some sections, there is a tendency to "exclusiveness."[16] The colored people of that section petitioned, when the School Law was under revision, that they might have separate schools: there were counter petitions by those opposed, and to satisfy all parties, twelve freeholders among *them*, can, by following a prescribed form, demand a school for their children; but if other schools, under patronage of Government, exist, (as Catholic or Protestant,) they can demand admission into them, if they have not one. They are not compelled to have a colored school. The following is that portion of the school law that directly relates to them:

"And be it enacted, That it shall be the duty of the municipal Council of any township, and of the Board of School Trustees of any city, town or incorporated village, on the application in writing of twelve or more resident heads of families, to authorize the establishment of one or more separate schools for Protestants, Roman Catholics or colored people, and, in such case, it shall prescribe the limits of the divisions or sections for such school, and shall make the same provisions for the holding of the first meeting for the election of Trustees of each such separate school or schools, as is provided in the fourth section of this Act for holding the first school meeting in a new school section: Provided always, that each separate school shall go into operation at the same time with alterations in school sections, and shall be under the same regulations in respect to the persons for whom such school is permitted to be established, as are [common] schools generally: Provided, secondly, that none but colored people shall be allowed to vote for the election of Trustees of the separate school for their children, and none but the

---

[16] Shadd Cary's use of "separate" and "exclusiveness" refers to voluntary racial separatism among the newly arrived refugees. Black people were not universally interested in attending integrated schools. Some wanted to build strong intraracial community ties rather than forcibly enter environments that may be hostile toward them, as increased interracial contact could sometimes lead to increased risks of encountering racism.

parties petitioning for the establishment of, or sending children to a separate Protestant or Roman Catholic school shall vote at the election of Trustees of such schools: Provided, thirdly, that each separate Protestant, or Roman Catholic, or colored school, shall be entitled to share in the school fund according to the average attendance of pupils attending each such separate school, (the mean attendance of pupils for both summer and winter being taken,) as compared with the average attendance of pupils attending the common schools in such city, town, village or township: Provided, fourthly, that no Protestant separate school shall be allowed in any school division, except when the teacher of the common school is a Roman Catholic, nor shall any Roman Catholic separate school be allowed except when the teacher of the common school is a Protestant."[17]

As before said, the facilities for obtaining a liberal education, are ample in the large towns and cities. In Toronto, students of all complexions associate together, in the better class schools and colleges. The operations of missionaries being chiefly among colored people, they have established several schools in connection with their labors, yet they are open to children without exception. The colored common schools have more of a complexional character than the private, which, with no exception that I have heard of, are open to all. The Act of Parliament above referred to, was designed to afford the fullest and more equable facilities for instruction to all, and that particular clause was inserted with the view to satisfy them, though less objectionable to the body of them, than what they asked for.

The fugitives, in some instances, settled on Government land before it came into market, cleared away and improved it. Their friends established schools which were flourishing, when they were obliged to break up, and the people to disperse, because of inability to purchase and other persons buying. This cause has, in a measure, retarded the spread of general information amongst them.

[Again], twenty or more families are often settled near one another, or interspersed among the French, Dutch, Scotch, Irish and Indians, in the woodland districts: often, English is not spoken.[18] There may not be an English school, and all revel together in happy ignorance. Nothing but the sound of the axe, and their own crude ideas of independence, to inspire them, unless it be an Indian camp fire occasionally. This may be rather an

[17] Almonte, ed., *A Plea for Emigration*, 65; Antwi, ed., *A Plea for Emigration*, 38.
[18] Almonte, ed., *A Plea for Emigration*, 66; Antwi, ed., *A Plea for Emigration*, 39.

uninviting state of affairs to those living in crowded cities, but it is true there are numerous grown up families, of white and colored, who do not know. But as uninteresting as is the detail, in this particular aspect of these affairs, the signs are encouraging. If they went to labor honestly, in a region semi-barbarous, they have cut their way out, and are now able to make themselves heard in a demand for religious instructors of the right kind, and schools. Many efficient persons have devoted their time and talents to their instruction, but there has not been anything like an equal number to the work: neither are they often found to have materials to work with. Individuals in the United States often send books to those most needy yet they are usually of such a character as to be utterly useless. I have often thought, if it is really a benevolent act to send old almanacs, old novels, and all manner of obsolete books to them, what good purpose was accomplished, or even what sort of vanity was gratified, by emptying the useless contents of old libraries on destitute fugitives? It would be infinitely better not to give, it seems, though probably persons sending them think differently. The case is aggravated from the fact of a real desire, on the part of the recipients, to learn, and their former want of opportunity. Probably the propensity to give is gratified; but why not give, when gifts are *needed*, of that which is useful? But the question, if it is answering any good purpose to give such things as books even, has not been satisfactorily answered in the affirmative, to persons who have seen the fugitives in their Canadian homes.

SETTLEMENTS,—DAWN,—ELGIN,—INSTITUTION,—
FUGITIVE HOME.
Much has been said of the Canada colored settlement, and fears have been expressed by many, that by encouraging exclusive settlements, the attempt to identify colored men with degraded men of like color in the States would result, and as a consequence, estrangement, suspicion, and distrust would be induced.[19] Such would inevitably be the result, and will be, shall they determine to have entirely proscriptive settlements. Those in existence, so far as I have been able to get at facts, do not exclude whites from their vicinity; but that settlements may not be established of that character, is not so certain. Dawn, on the Suydenham [R]iver, Elgin, or King's Settlement, as it is called,

---

[19] Shadd Cary repeatedly warns that African Americans should not seek to reproduce the United States' racial dynamics in Canada. In her view, creating racially separate institutions like Black churches, Black schools, and Black settlements would have a detrimental impact by once more relegating Black people to second-class citizens.

situated about ten miles from Chatham, are settlements in which there are regulations in regard to morals, the purchase of lands, etc., bearing only on the colored people; but whites are not excluded because of dislike. When purchase was made of the lands, many white families were residents,—at least, locations were not selected in which none resided. At first, a few sold out, fearing that such neighbors might not be agreeable; others, and they the majority, concluded to remain, and the result attests their superior judgment. Instead of an increase of vice, prejudice, improvidence, laziness, or a lack of energy, that many feared would characterize them, the infrequency of violations of law among so many, is unprecedented; due attention to moral and intellectual culture has been given; the former prejudices on the part of the whites, has given place to a perfect reciprocity of religious and social intercommunication. Schools are patronized equally; the gospel is common, and hospitality is shared alike by all. The school for the settlers, at Elgin, is so far superior to the one established for white children, that the latter was discontinued, and, as before said, all send together, and visit in common the Presbyterian church, there established. So of Dawn; that settlement is exceedingly flourishing, and the moral influence it exerts is good, though, owing to some recent arrangements, regulations designed to further promote its importance are being made. Land has increased in value in those settlements. Property that was worth but little, from the superior culture given by colored persons over the method before practiced, and the increasing desires for country homes, is held much higher. Another fact that is worth a passing notice, is, that a spirit of competition is active in their vicinity. Efforts are not put forth to produce more to the acre, and to have the land and tenements present a tidy appearance. That others than those designed to be benefitted by the organization, should be, is not reasonable, else might persons, not members of a society justly claim equal benefits with members. If Irishmen should subscribe to certain regulations on purchasing land, no neighboring landholders could rightfully share with them in the result of that organization. But prejudice would not be the cause of exclusion. So it is of those two settlements; it cannot be said of them, that they are caste institutions, so long as they do not express hostility to the whites; but the question of their necessity in the premises may be raised, and often is, by the settlers in Canada as well as in the States. The "Institution" is a settlement under the direction of the A.M.E. Church; it contains, at present, two hundred acres, and is sold out in ten acre farms, at one dollar and fifty cents per acre, or one shilling less than cost. They have recently opened a school, and there is a log meeting house in an unfinished state, also a burying ground. There are about fifteen families settled on the land, most of whom have cleared away a few trees, but it is not in a very prosperous condition, owing, it is said, to bad management of agents—a result to be looked for when a want of knowledge characterize them. This "Institution" bids fair to be one nucleus around which caste settlements will cluster in Canada.

The Refugees' Home is the last of the settlements of which I may speak in this place.[20] How many others are in contemplation I do not know, though I heard of at least two others. This Society is designed to appropriate fifty thousand acres of land for fugitives from slavery, *only*, but at present the agents have in possession two hundred acres, situated about eight miles from Windsor, in the western district. The plan is to sell farms of twenty-five acres, that is to give five acres to actual settlers, with the privilege of buying the adjoining twenty acres, at the market value—one third of the purchase money constitutes a fund for school and other purposes; and ten years are given to pay for the twenty acres, but no interest may accumulate. This society may now be considered in operation, as they have made a purchase, though, as yet, no one has settled thereon, and the results to be looked for from it, from the extent of the field of operations, will have an important bearing on the colored people who are now settled in Canada, or who may emigrate thither. The friends of the society, actuated by benevolent feelings towards victims of American oppression and the odious Fugitive Law, are sanguine as to the success of the measure, but not so universal is the opinion in its favor, even among those designed to be benefitted; in fact, all the objections raised against previously existing settlements, hold good against these, with the additional ones of greater magnitude. It is well known that the Fugitive Bill makes insecure every northern colored man,—those *free* are alike at the risk of being sent south,—consequently, many persons, always free, will leave the United States, and settle in Canada, and other countries, who would have remained had not that law been enacted. In pro-slavery communities, or where colonization influence prevails, they would leave at a sacrifice; they arrive in Canada destitute, in consequence, but may not settle on the land of the Refugees' Home, from the accident of nominal freedom, when it is well known that even slaves south, from the disgrace attending manual labor

---

[20] The Refugee Home Society was established by Henry Bibb. For more on Shadd Cary's criticisms of Bibb, see Almonte, ed., *A Plea for Emigration*, 112, 116, and Rhodes, *Mary Ann Shadd Cary*, 42–48, 53–69.

* Scobies' Canadian Almanac for 1852.

when performed by whites, have opportunities, in a pecuniary way, that colored men have not in some sections north. Again, the policy of slaveholders has been to create a contempt for *free* people in the bosom of their slaves, and pretty effectually have they succeeded. Their journey to Canada for liberty has not rooted out that prejudice, quite, and reference to a man's birth, as free or slave, is generally made by colored persons, should he not be as prosperous as his better helped fugitive brethren. Thus, discord among members of the same family, is engendered; a breach made, that the exclusive use by fugitives of the society lands is not likely to mend. Again, the society, with its funds is looked upon in the light of a powerful rival, standing in the way of poor *free* men, with its ready cash, for its lands will not all be government purchases; neither does it contemplate large blocks, exclusively, but, as in the first purchase, land, wherever found, and in small parcels also. From the exclusive nature of the many settlements, (as fugitive homes,) when it shall be known for what use it is wanted, individual holders will not sell but for more than the real value, thus embarrassing poor men who would have bought on time, and as an able purchaser from government, the society must have a first choice. The objections in common with other settlements, are: individual supervision of resident agents, and the premium indirectly offered for good behavior. "We are free men," say they who advocate independent effort, "we; as other subjects, are amenable to British laws; we wish to observe and appropriate to ourselves, *ourselves*, whatever of good there is in the society around us, and by our individual efforts, to attain to a respectable position, as do the many foreigners who land on the Canada shores, as poor in purse we were; and we do not want agents to beg for us." The accompanying are articles in the Constitution [of the Refugee Home Society]:

> *Article 2.* The object of this society shall be to obtain permanent homes for the refugees in Canada, and to promote their moral, social, physical, intellectual, and political elevation.
> *Article 11.* This society shall not deed lands to any but actual settlers, who are refugees from southern slavery, and who are the owners of no land.
> *Article 12.* All lands purchased by this society, shall be divided into twenty-five acre lots, or as near as possible, and at least one-tenth of the purchase price of which shall be paid down by actual settlers before possession is given, and the balance to be paid in equal annual instalments.
> *Article 13.* One-third of all money paid in for land by settlers, shall be used for educational purposes, for the benefit of said settlers' children, and

the other two-thirds for the purchase of more lands for the same object, while chattel slavery exists in the United States.

BY-LAWS.

No person shall receive more than five acres of land from this society, at less than cost.

Article 4. No person shall be allowed to remove any timber from said land until they have first made payment thereon.

These are the articles of more importance, and, as will be seen, they contemplate more than fifty thousand acres continual purchases, till slavery shall cease; and other terms, as will be seen by Art. 13 of Con., and Art. 4, By-Laws, than most fugitives just from slavery can comply with, (as destitute women with families, old men, and single women,) until after partial familiarity with their adopted country. This, say many colored Canadians, begins not to benefit until a man has proven his ability to act without aid, and is fit for political equality by his own industry, that money will get for him at any time.

POLITICAL RIGHTS—ELECTION LAW—OATH—CURRENCY.

There is no legal discrimination whatever effecting [*sic*] colored emigrants in Canada, nor from any cause whatever are their privileges sought to be abridged. On taking proper measures, the most ample redress can be obtained. The following "abstracts of acts," bearing equally on all, and observed fully by colored men qualified, will give an idea of the measures given them:*

"The qualifications of voters at municipal elections in townships, are freeholders and householders of the township or ward, entered on the roll for rateable real property, in their own right or that of their wives, as proprietors or tenants, and resident at the time in the township or ward."

"In towns, freeholders and householders for rateable real property in their own names or that of their wives, as proprietors or tenants to the amount of £5 per annum or upwards, resident at the time in the ward. The property qualification of town voters may consist partly of freehold and partly of leasehold."

In villages it is £3 and upwards, with freehold or leasehold; in cities £8.

The laws regulating elections, and relating to electors, are not similar in the two Canadas; but colored persons are not affected by them more than others.

"No person shall be entitled to vote at county elections, who has not vested in him, by legal title, real property in said country of the clear yearly value of forty-four shillings and five pence and one farthing, currency. Title to be in fee simple or freehold under tenure of free and common soccage [*sic*], or in *fief* in *rature*, or in *franc allen*, or derived from the Governor and Council of the late Province of Quebec, or Act of Parliament. Qualificatiori, to be effective, requires actual and uninterrupted possession on the part of the elector, or that he should have been in receipt of the rents and profits of said property for his use and benefit at least six months before the date of the writ of election. But the title will be good without such anterior possession, if the property shall have come by inheritance, devise, marriage or contract of marriage, and also if the deed or patent from the Crown on which he holds to claim such estate in Upper Canada, have been registered three calendar months before the date of the writ of election. In Lower Canada, possession of the property under a written promise of sale registered, if not a notarial deed, for twelve months before the election, to be sufficient title to vote. In Upper Canada, a conveyance to wife after marriage must have been registered three calendar months, or husband have been in possession of property six months before election."[21]

"Only British subjects of the full age of twenty-one are allowed to vote. Electors may remove objection by producing certificate, or by taking the oath."

These contain no proscriptive provisions, and there are none. Colored men comply with these provisions and vote in the administration of affairs. There is no difference made whatever; and even in the slight matter of taking the census it is impossible to get at the exact number of whites or colored; as they are not designated as such.[22] There is, it is true, petty jealousy manifested at times by individuals, which is made use of by the designing; but impartiality and strict justice characterise proceedings at law, and the bearing of the laws. The oath, as prescribed by law, is as follows:

"I, A. B., do sincerely promise and swear, that I will bear faithful and true allegiance to Her Majesty Queen Victoria, as lawful Sovereign of

---

[21] For a discussion of these legal terms, see Almonte, ed., *A Plea for Emigration*, 113–114.

[22] As Almonte has written, "Shadd is not quite correct in maintaining that no designation was made in the census between Black and white. In fact, people were asked in the 1851 census (as well as in earlier and later censuses) to choose a 'national origin.' One of the twenty-eight choices was 'Negro.'" Almonte, ed., *A Plea for Emigration*, 114.

the United Kingdom of Great Britain and Ireland, and of this Province of Canada, dependent on and belonging to the said United Kingdom, and that I will defend her to the uttermost of my power against all traitors, conspiracies and attempts whatever which shall be made against Her Person, Crown and Dignity, and that I will do my utmost endeavor to disclose and make known to Her Majesty, Her Heirs and Successors all treasons and traitorous conspiracies and attempts which I shall know to be against Her or any of them, and all this I do swear without any equivocation, mental evasion, or secret reservation, and, renouncing all pardons and dispensations from persons whatever, to the contrary. So help me God."

"The Deputy Returning Officer may administer oath of allegiance to persons who, according to provisions of any Act of Parliament, shall become, on taking such oath, entitled to the privileges of British birth in the Province."

"Persons knowing themselves not to be qualified, voting at elections, incur penalty of £10; and on action brought, the burden of proof shall be on the defendant. Such votes null and void."

"The qualifications of Municipal Councillors are as follows:—Township Councillor must be a freeholder or householder of the township or ward, * * * as proprietor or tenant rated on the roll in case of a freeholder for £100 or upwards; householder for £200 or upwards: Village Councillor, in case of a freeholder, for £10 or upwards; a householder for £20 and upwards: Town Councillor, in case of a freeholder £20 per annum; if a householder to the amount of £40 and upwards. The property qualification of Town Councillors may be partly freehold and partly leasehold. A tenant voter in town or city must have occupied by actual residence, as a separate tenant, a dwelling house or houses for twelve months, of the yearly value of £11 2s. 1½ d. currency, and have paid a year's rent, or that amount of money for the twelve months immediately preceding the date of election writ. A person holding only a shop or place of business, but not actually residing therein, is not entitled to vote. And a voter having changed his residence within, the town during the year does not affect his right to vote, but must vote in the ward in which he resides on the day.

ARTICLES EXEMPT FROM DUTY.

The following are some of the articles exempt from duty on importation.

"Models of machinery and other inventions and improvements in the arts. Horses and carriages of travelers; and horses, cattle and carriages and other vehicles when employed in carrying merchandize, together with the neces-sary harness and tackle, so long as the same shall be *bona fide* in use for that purpose, except the horses, cattle, carriages and harness of persons hawking goods, wares and merchandize through the Province for the purpose of retailing the same, and the horses, cattle, carriages and harness of any circus or equestrian troop for exhibition; the horses, cattle, carriages and harness of any to be free."

"Donations of clothing specially imported for the use of or to be distrib-uted gratuitously by any charitable society in this Province."

"Seeds of all kinds, farming utensils and implements of husbandry, when specially imported in good faith by any society incorporated or established for the encouragement of agriculture."

"Wearing apparel in actual use, and other personal effects not merchandize; horses and cattle; implements and tools of trade of handicraftsment."

*** "Trees, shrubs, bulbs and roots; wheat and indian [*sic*] corn; animals specially imported for the improvement of stock; paintings, drawings, maps, busts, printed books, (not foreign reprints of British copy-right works,) ashes, pot and pearl, and soda."

CURRENCY OF CANADA.

GOLD.		CURRENCY.	
The British Sovereign when of full weight,		£1 4s 4d.	
U.S. Eagle, coined before 1st July 1834,		£1 13s 4d	
U.S. Eagle, between 1st of July, 1834, and 1st of July 1851,		£2 10 s 0d	

SILVER.		SILVER.	
British Crown,	6s 1d	Other eighth silver dollar,	0s 6d
Half crown,	3 0	U.S. sixteenth dollar,	0 3½
Shilling,	1 2	Other " "	0 3
Sixpence,	0 7 ¼	Five franc piece,	4 8
The dollar,	5 1	COPPER.	
Half "	2 6½	British penny,	0 1
U.S. quarter dollar,	1 3	" half penny,	0 0½
Other " "	1 0	" farthing,	0 0 ¼
U.S. eighth. "	0 7 ½		

*ABSTRACT OF LAW OF SUCCESSION IN UPPER CANADA.
* * * "Be it therefore enacted, &c., That whenever, on or after the first day of January, which will be in the year of our Lord one thousand eight hundred and fifty-two, any person shall die seized in fee simple or for the life of another of any real estate in Upper Canada, without having lawfully devised the same, such real estate shall descend or pass by way of succession in manner following, that is to say:

Firstly—to his lineal descendants, and those claiming by or under them, *per stirpes.*
Secondly—To his father.
Thirdly—To his mother: and
Fourthly—To his collateral relatives.

Subject in all cases to the rules and regulations hereinafter prescribed.

2. "That if the intestate shall leave several descendants in the direct line of lineal descent, and all of equal degree of consanguinity to such intestate, the inheritance shall descend to such persons in equal parts, however remote from the intestate the common degree of consanguinity may be.

3. "That if any of the children of such intestate be living, and any be dead, the inheritance shall descend to the children who are living, and to the descendants of such children as shall have died, so that each child who shall be living shall inherit such share as would have descended to him if all the children of the intestate who shall have died, leaving issue, had been living, and so that the descendants of each child who shall be dead shall inherit the share which their parents would have received, if living, in equal shares.

"18. That children and relatives who are illegitimate shall not be entitled to inherit under any of the provisions of this Act."

THE THIRTY THOUSAND COLORED FREEMEN OF CANADA.
The colored subjects of her Majesty in the Canadas are, in the general, in good circumstances, that is, there are few cases of positive destitution to be found among those permanently settled. They are settled promiscuously in cities, towns, villages, and the farming districts, and to equal number of colored men in the States, north or south, can produce more freeholders. They are settled

* 14 and Vic. Cap. 6—1851. Scobie.

on, and own portions of the best farming lands in the province, and own much valuable property in the several cities, etc. There is, of course, a difference in the relative prosperity and deportment in different section, but a respect for, and observance of the laws, is conceded to them by all; indeed, much indifference on the part of whites has given place to genuine sympathy for the *free* man is not misplaced, as more than compensation for their own exertions for those yet in bonds. I have said, there is but little actual poverty among them. They are engaged in the different trades and other manual occupations. They have a paper conducted by the Rev. Henry Bibb, and other able men, white and colored, are laboring among them, and in view of the protection afforded, there is no good reason why they should not prosper. After the passage of the fugitive law, the sudden emigration of several thousand in a few months, destitute as they necessarily were, from having, in many instances, to leave behind them all they possessed, made not a little suffering for a brief period, (only among them,) and the report of *their* condition had an injurious bearing upon all the colored settlers. Clothing, provisions, and other articles were sent them, but often so disposed of, or appropriated, as not to benefit those for whom intended. Distrust of agents, indiscriminately, and altogether but little real good has followed from the charity. The sensible men among them, seeing the bad results from a general character poverty and degradation, have not been slow to express their disapprobation in the social circle, in meetings, and through the public papers. The following extracts express fully the sentiments of nine-tenths of the colored men of Canada; they think they are fully able to live without begging. There are others (very ignorant people,) who think differently, as there will be in all communities, though they are in the minority. There are those, also, and they are a respectable minority, (in point of numbers,) who are in favor of distinctive churches and schools, and of being entirely to themselves; they will come in for especial [*sic*] notice, but first, let us hear the people of Buxton and other places:

"If facts would bear out the statements made, the fugitives would have little to choose between slavery on one side of the line, and starvation on the other; but we rejoice that he is not reduced to the alternative. The man who is willing to work need not suffer, and unless a man supports himself he will neither be independent nor respectable in any country." * * * "The cry that has been often raised, that we could not support ourselves, is a foul slander, got up by our enemies, and circulated both on this and the other side of the line, to our prejudice. Having lived many years in Canada, we hesitate not

to say that all who are able and willing to work, can make a good living."
* * * It is time the truth should be known concerning the relief that has been
sent to the "suffering fugitives in Canada," and to what extent it has been applied. The boxes of clothing and barrels of provisions which have been sent
in, from time to time, by the praiseworthy, but misguided zeal of friends in
the United States, has been employed to support the idle, who are too lazy
to work, and who form but a small portion of the colored population in
Canada. There are upwards of thirty thousand colored persons in Canada
West, and not more than three thousand of them have ever received aid, and
not more than half of them required it had they been willing to work. We
do not think it right that twenty-seven thousand colored persons, who are
supporting themselves by their own industry, should lie under the disgrace
of being called public beggars, when they receive nothing, and don't want
anything. * * We wish the people of the United States to know that there is
one portion of Canada West where the colored people are self-supporting,
and they wish them to send neither petticoat not pantaloons to the county
of Kent. * * * The few cases of real want which arise from sickness or old age,
can, with a trifling effort, be relieved here, without making it a pretext for a
system of wholesale begging in the United States."

     EDWARD R. GRANTS,
     SAMUEL WICKHAM,   }   COMMITTEE
     ROBERT HARRIS

"As to the state of things in Toronto and in Hamilton, I can say, from actual observation, that extreme suffering is scarcely known among the black
people, while some who are far from being as industrious and deserving as
they ought to be, receive aid to which they would hardly seem entitled."—
S.R. Ward's Letter to the Voice of the Fugitive.[23]

Notwithstanding the prosperity and liberal sentiment of the majority,
there is yet a great deal of ignorance, bigotry, prejudice, and idleness. There
are those who are only interested in education so far as the establishment of
separate schools, churches, &c., tend to make broad the line of separation
they wish to make between them and the whites; and they are active to increase their numbers, and to perpetuate, in the minds of the newly arrived

---

[23] S. R. Ward is Samuel Ringgold Ward, a Black newspaper editor and activist who escaped slavery.
See Samuel Ringgold Ward, *Autobiography of a Fugitive Negro: His Anti-slavery Labours in the United
States, Canada, & England* (London: John Snow, 1855); R. J. M. Blackett, *Samuel Ringgold Ward: A
Life of Struggle* (New Haven: Yale University Press, 2023).

emigrant or refugee, prejudices, originating in slavery, and as strong and objectionable in their manifestation as those entertained by whites towards them. Every casual remark by whites is tortured into a decided and effective negro hate. The expressions of an individual are made to infer the existence of prejudice on the part of the whites, and partiality by the administrators of public affairs. The recently arrived [fugitive], unacquainted with the true state of things, is "*completely convinced* by the noisy philippic against all the "white folks," and all colored ones who think differently from them, and he is thus prepared to aid demagogues in preventing the adoption of proper measures for the spread of education and general intelligence, to maintain an ascendency over the inferior minds around them, and to make the way of the missionary a path of thorns.[24] Among that portion, generally, may those be found, who by their indolent habits, tend to give point to what of prejudice is lingering in the minds of the whites; and it is to be feared that they may take some misguided step now, the consequences of which will entail evil on the many who will hereafter settle in Canada. The only ground of hope is in the native good sense of those who are now making use of the same instrumentalities for improvement as are the whites around them.

THE FRENCH AND FOREIGN POPULATION.
The population of Canada consists of English, Scotch, French, Irish and Americans; and, including colored persons, numbers about 1,582,000. Of the whites, the French are in the majority, but the increasing emigration of Irish, Scotch, English and other Europeans, is fast bringing about an equality in point of numbers that will be felt in political circles. In Canada West the French are in the minority.

The disposition of the people generally towards colored emigrants, that is, so far as the opinions of old settlers may be taken, and my own observation may be allowed, is as friendly as could be looked for under the circumstances. The Yankees, in the country and in the States adjoining, leave no opportunity unimproved to embitter their minds against them. The result is, in some

[24] Once again, Shadd Cary advocates for African Americans and newly arrived Black Canadians to reject what she sees as distinctly American thought patterns. She is critical of Black people who are suspicious of white Canadians. Presumably, some Black people who held these views intended to protect themselves from the types of racism they had previously experienced at the hands of white Americans. However, Shadd Cary differentiates between white Canadians and white Americans. In her view, whiteness in and of itself did not produce racism. Rather, she understood racial discrimination as a byproduct of the specific interplay between race, nationality, slavery, and the law in the United States. Shadd Cary was an ardent supporter of racial integration, which she did not think could be achieved if Black people assumed that white people in Canada were racist.

sections, a contemptible sort of prejudice, which, among English, is powerless beyond the individual entertaining—not even affecting *his circle*. This grows out of the constitution of English society, in which people are not obliged to think as others do. There is more independent thought and free expression than among Americans. The affinity between the Yankees and French is strong; said to grow out of similar intentions with respect to political affairs: and they express most hostility, but it is not of a complexional character only, as that serves as a mark to identify men of a different policy. Leaving out Yankees—having but little practical experience of colored people—they, (the French,) are predisposed, from the influence alluded to, to deal roughly with them; but in the main benevolence and a sense of justice are elements in their character. They are not averse to truth. There is a prevailing hostility to chattel slavery, and an honest representation of the colored people: their aims and progressive character, backed by uniform good conduct on their part, would in a very short time destroy every vestige of prejudice in the Province.

"The public mind literally thirsts for the truth, and honest listeners, and anxious inquirers will travel many miles, crowd our country chapels, and remain for hours eagerly and patiently seeking the light. * * * * Let the ignorance now prevalent on the subject of slavery be met by fair and full discussion, and open and thorough in-vestigation, and the apathy and prejudice now existing will soon dis-appear."—*S.R. Ward.*

Colored persons have been refused entertainment in taverns, (invariably of an inferior class,) and on some boats distinction is made; but in all cases, it is that kind of distinction that is made between poor foreigners and other passengers, on the cars and steamboats of the Northern States. There are the emigrant train and the forward deck in the United States. In Canada, colored persons, holding the same relation to the Canadians, are in some cases treated similarly. It is an easy matter to make out a case of prejudice in any country. We naturally look for it, and the conduct of many is calculated to cause unpleasant treatment, and to make it difficult for well-mannered persons to get comfortable accommodations. There is a medium between servility and presumption, that recommends itself to all persons of common sense, of whatever rank of complexion; and if colored people would avoid the two extremes, there would be but few cases of prejudices to complain of in Canada.[25] In cases in which tavern keepers and other public characters

[25] Although Shadd Cary is adamant that racial discrimination is nearly nonexistent in Canada, here, she makes some concessions to acknowledge the possibility that there may, in rare instances, be some measure of mistreatment of Black people. However, she determines that class, not race, is the primary driver of any social divisions in Canada, unlike in the United States.

persist in refusing to entertain them, they can, in common with the traveling public generally, get redress at law.

Persons emigrating to Canada, need not hope to find the general state of society as it is in the States. There is as in the old country, a strong class feeling—lines are as completely drawn between the different classes, and aristocracy in the Canadas is the same in its manifestations as aristocracy in England, Scotland and elsewhere. There is no approach to Southern chivalry, not the sensitive democracy prevalent at the North; but there is an aristocracy of birth, not of skin, as with Americans. In the ordinary arrangements of society from wealthy and titled immigrants and visitors from the mother country, down through the intermediate circles to Yankees and Canadians, it appears to have been settled by common consent, that [one] class should not "see any trouble over another;" but the common ground on which all honest and respectable men meet, is that of innate hatred of American Slavery.[26]

RECAPITULATION.

The conclusion arrived at in respect to Canada, by an impartial person, is, that no settled country in America offers stronger inducements to colored people. The climate is healthy, and they enjoy as good health as other settlers, or as the natives; the soil is of the first quality; the laws of the country give to them, at first, the same protection and privileges as to other persons not born subjects; and after compliance with Acts of Parliament affecting them, as taking oath, &c., they may enjoy full "privileges of British birth in the Province." The general tone of society is healthy; vice is discountenanced, and infractions of the law promptly punished; and, added to this, there is an increasing anti-slavery sentiment, and a progressive system of religion.

—

[26] Almonte, ed., *A Plea for Emigration*, 88; Antwi, ed., *A Plea for Emigration*, 55.

THE BRITISH WEST INDIES—MEXICO—SOUTH AMERICA—AFRICA.

Inducements have been held out by planters to colored men, to settle in the British West Indies, and agents have been sent particularly from Jamaica and Trinidad, from time to time, to confer with them on the subject. The most prominent feature in their efforts, has been the direct advantage to the planter from such emigration. The advantages to be derived by settlers, in a pecuniary point, from any system of emigration originating with proprietors of estates, will be doubtful, so long as the present mode of planting, managing and involving estates, continues, if the emigrants consent to be mere laborers instead of owners of the soil.[27] But from a system of voluntary emigration to those islands, different results may be looked for. The former method would but degrade them, the latter materially elevate them. The vicinity of those islands to the southern United States [makes] it necessary that they should be peopled by colored men, and *under British protection;* in short, that they should be British subjects. The policy of the dominant party in the United States, is to drive *free* colored people out of the country, and to send them to Africa, only, and at the s[a]me time, to give the fullest guaranty to slaveholders, for the continuance of their system. To fulfil[l], to the letter, this latter, they make large calculations of a future interest in the West indies, Honduras, and ultimately South America. They wish to consecrate to slavery and to slave power that portion of this continent; at the same time they deprecate the vicinity of freeman. To preserve those countries from the ravages of slavery, should be the motive to their settlement by colored men.[28] Jamaica, with its fine climate and rich soil, is the key to the gulf of Mexico.

[27] Shadd Cary's use of "planters" refers to those who owned plantations in the Caribbean, many of which produced sugar cane. She argues that emigration will primarily benefit those own property (most likely white Europeans), not the Black emigrants who would work for the planters. This distinction between the possibility for Black people to become landowners in Canada and the likelihood that would only become laborers in the West Indies was one of the reasons why Shadd Cary believed that Canada would be a preferable destination for emigrants. Shadd Cary does not use Marxist language to describe bourgeoisie ownership of the means of production in the Caribbean nor proletarian labor on plantations. However, her analysis of the potential limitations to emigrating to the British West Indies resonate with *The Communist Manifesto*, which was published four years prior to *A Plea for Emigration*. See Karl Marx, *The Communist Manifesto*, ed. Frederic L. Bender (New York: Norton, 1988). Nineteenth-century Black women did not ordinarily articulate their analyses of labor, class, and race in explicitly Marxist terms, as many Black radicals later would in the twentieth century. They were nevertheless critical of class exploitation, particularly as it was informed by the history of transatlantic slavery.

[28] Throughout her writings and speeches, Shadd Cary argued that emigration was an abolitionist strategy. In this instance, she suggests that greater numbers of Black people in the West Indies could prevent the expansion of US slavery into the region.

It is not distant from the United States, Cuba, nor Hayti; but, as if providentially, is just so positioned that, if properly garrisoned by colored free men, may, under Britain, promptly and effectually check "foreign interference in its own policy,["] and any mischievous designs now in contemplation toward Cuba and Hayti. So of that portion of the Isthmus now under the protection of Great Britain. In view of the ultimate destiny of the southern portion of North America, it is of the first importance that colored men strengthen that and similar positions in that region.[29] They are the natural protectors of the Isthmus and the contiguous country: it is said by medical men, that those of the human family, physically capable of resisting the influences of great heat, are also capable of enduring severe cold; and the varied experience of colored persons in America, proves that they live to as great age as whiter [persons], whether as whalemen in the northern seas, and settlers in the British provinces, (far north of the United States,) or in the West Indies. The question of availability, can never be raised, for at this time there are those who conduct with great ability the business of the Islands. Colored men [are] greatly in the majority, not more than one-sixth are whites. [They] are legislators, lawyers, physicians, ministers, planters, editors, merchants, and laborers; and they demonstrate clearly their [capacity] for self-government, and the various departments of civil [life], by the great change in their condition since emancipation. [The story] of loss from the emancipation act, is a gross misrepresentation, gotten up by interested parties for the benefit of slavery.[30] Thus there may not be so much exported as formerly, for the very good reason that there are more purchasers at home. The miserably fed slave of former days, is now the independent *free* man, with the ability to buy whatever his judgment prompts him to. Neither is the demand for laborers for large estates evidence that the peasantry are idle. There are more small famers and cultivators on their own account, more store-keepers and traders, and they of the emancipated class. More attention is, of course, paid to education, and the children are thus relieved, in a measure, from out door [*sic*] duties. Much has been done by the colored people of those islands to improve their condition, and much more may be done conjointly with emigrants from the States, to perfect society, strengthen the British in that quarter, and this keep up "the

---

[29] As I have noted elsewhere, "Although Shadd Cary did not offer an in-depth analysis of Black people's shared oppression in the United States and the British West Indies, she nevertheless embraced a transatlantic understanding of racial solidarity as she proposed that African Americans align themselves with Afro-Caribbean peoples." Dennie, "Leave That Slavery-Cursed Republic," 486.

[30] Almonte, ed., *A Plea for Emigration*, 91; Antwi, ed., *A Plea for Emigration*, 57.

balance of power." It needs no prophet to foretell the establishment of an em-
pire formed out of the southern United States and Mexico. The settlement
by colored people of those countries, with their many sympathizers, is but
a preparatory step: that step has been taken, slavery and republican rapacity
will do the rest. Under what more favorable auspices could emigration to the
West Indies be made than the present, now that a general welcome would
be extended by the people to those who would like a milder climate than
the States? What government so powerful and so thoroughly impartial, as
Her Majesty's; so practically anti-slavery, and so protective? None. The objection that "we wish our own government, to demonstrate our capacity for self-
government,["] is done away with at once, for there are colonies controlled,
so far as their immediate affairs extend, by colored men. The assertion that
white men universally degrade colored, is disproved by the facts. There is
no aristocracy of skin; every [incentive] to honorable effort is kept before
them.[31] It is of the first importance, then, that the government of those islands should be anti-slavery and that only governments, anti-slavery in spirit
and tendency[, and] having a liberal religious policy, should be sought out by
[colored] people from the United States. They, of all others on this continent,
have drank plentifully of the cup of degradation, made more bitter from the
never ending parade about freedom. They would be powerful auxiliaries of
the present inhabitants, in forming a wall of defense, or available for offensive
operations, as a *decided protest*, for instance, as the best interests and policy of
the British government might demand. Those who oppose emigration from
the United States, say, "you (colored people,) will not desire to be the laborers
in other countries; to dig the canals, work on rail roads, ditch, and the like, but
you will prefer to engage in trade, and that others will forestall you." Men who
are honest in their desire for a change, who love liberty better than slavery,
or who are unwilling to await the tedious process by which, in the United
States, their rights will be given, if ever, will not be fastidious on emigrating
to a country. Emigrants to any country, who should aim at a monopoly of the
so called respectable occupations, exclusively, would be looked upon with
distrust, as well as contempt, and the result to the emigrant would not be far
different from a monopoly of menial employments. There will be no scarcity

[31] Almonte, ed., *A Plea for Emigration*, 92; Antwi, ed., *A Plea for Emigration*, 58. Shadd Cary was
optimistic about the true state of affairs in the British West Indies following the abolition of slavery in
1834. Despite the Black majority in the Caribbean, the effects of slavery and colonialism continued to
jeopardize its Black population in the following centuries. For more see Hilary Beckles, *How Britain
Underdeveloped the Caribbean: A Reparation Response to Europe's Legacy of Plunder and Poverty*
(Mona: University of the West Indies Press, 2021).

of land, and a medium, between the extensive operations of capitalists, and the degrading occupations of colored people, generally, in the crowded cities of the United States, thus opens to them a certain road to future eminence, in every way preferable to the sudden changes and chances of trade, exclusively.

Allusion is at times made to South America, and plans for a grant of territory from governments in that country, in which to form an "independent government," have been proposed. Others say, "unite with existing governments." Neither plan can recommend itself to prospective emigrants generally. In the first place, there is no precedent on record of a grant, similar to the one sought, and the policy of independent governments, with respect to each other, would always be opposed to unqualified grants. The great object[ion to] uniting with those governments at present, would be their [want of] toleration in matters of religion; so long as the intimate [connection] of the State with the Romish Church exists, those countries [must be] but a poor asylum for the oppressed. The liberals, with [them form] a minority, struggling for life against the exactions of popery, and the ambition of military chiefs.[32] Would colored men be prepared to adopt the religion of the country? That with them would be the only guaranty of protection, such "protection as vultures give to lambs." "Let us seize upon Africa, or some other, unappreciated terri[tory] while we may," say others, "and establish our own governments." But Africa has already been seized upon; the English, French, Portuguese, Spanish and Turks, have long since shared her out among themselves, and little Liberia may yet revert to some heir-at-law, who has purposely been unmindful of her. There is yet Mexico, to be spoken of hereafter, and a southern continent, but that belongs to the United States, it may be by right of discovery; so there seems to be no safe alternative left but to be satisfied with that government now existing that is most reliable and most powerful. That government is Great Britain; her dependencies for a *secure* home for the American slave, and the disgraced *free* man. The last of her possessions to which I shall call attention in this place, is Vancouver's Island.

MEXICO.
The vicinity of Mexico to the United States, and the known hostility of Mexicans to the institution of slavery, weigh strongly with some persons in favor of emigration to that country; but on careful consideration, it will be seen that the country does not present the features, in the main, that the States

[32] Almonte, ed., *A Plea for Emigration*, 94; Antwi, ed., *A Plea for Emigration*, 58.

of South America do. The hankering of the old Castilians after lost power, is much greater in Mexico than farther south; and to regain that there would not be scruples about a coalition with American Slaveholders, even.[33] The spirit of democracy has never so thoroughly pervaded that country, as those under the shadow of Simon Bolivar [sic].[34] Mexico was called New Spain. In her was remodelled the prominent features of Spanish policy in Europe. There was the grand centre point of Spanish [dignity], religious intolerance, and regal domination, for the New World. In the States of South America, a change of policy was a [necessity] growing out of the relations of the Church of Rome to [society] generally.[35] In Mexico, it was an earnest demand of the majority to throw off the Spanish yoke. This is shown in the relative position of the Church in those countries. In Mexico the Roman Catholic church is in undisputed supremacy, and the pope is to them the ultimatum. In the [S]tates of South America, though that religion prevails, yet concession has been made, by Rome, in the person of a dignitary of equal powers there with the pope elsewhere. With them the pope is but little more respected than the Greek Patriarch. In those States, except Peru, (in which there is but one idea generally among Natives and Spanish,) there was no previously civilized class, continually brooding over Spanish wrongs: the natives came to terms, and they and Creoles combined to destroy Spanish tyranny backed by Rome; consequently, after victory over Spain was achieved by them, their remaining enemy was and is the Church in its modified form. It yet has, as before said, sufficient influence to make those countries undesirable for colored people from the United States in the present phase of things. We want a strong position; Mexico does not offer that, even though the majority are anti-slavery. The Southern United States have "marked her for their prey," which she will be for a time; and combining with the minority, the probability is a contest for the supremacy of slavery for a long time. If it were certain that slavery would not be tolerated but for a short period, still the move would be inexpedient, as direct contact with revolutionary movements, or other plans of progress, in her present state affecting it, would be inevitable. The position of colored Americans must be a conservative one, for a time, in any foreign

---

[33] Shadd Cary expresses fear that Spain's efforts to retain control over its colonies in Mexico and South America might prompt it to turn to slaveholders in the United States as allies. She was attentive to how various struggles for national independence throughout South America could negatively impact African American emigrants.

[34] Simón Bolívar (1783–1830) was a Venezuelan revolutionary who fought for several countries' independence from Spain. See Gerhard Straussmann Masur, "Simón Bolívar," *Encyclopedia Britannica*, July 20, 1998; last modified December 13, 2022, https://www.britannica.com/biography/Simon-Bolivar.

[35] Almonte, ed., *A Plea for Emigration*, 95; Antwi, ed., *A Plea for Emigration*, 60.

country, (from the very nature of their relations to foreign nations,) as well as for themselves in the United States; and it were folly in them to voluntarily enter the breach between any two hostile nations until stronger in position; their efforts, to be rational, should be to gain strength. People who love liberty do not emigrate to weak governments to embroil themselves in their quarrels with stronger ones, but to strong ones, to [add] to their strength and better their own condition, and [f]oreigners fighting for others, are, generally, either hirelings, or isolated adventurers striving after fame. Whatever people go to Mexico and adopt [her] institutions, must calculate before hand, to set aside the habits of independent civil life—must for a long time repudiate the plough, the arts, and trade, with their concomitants, in a great country, or make them but secondary in importance to the, there, paramount idea of military life, and the certainty of frequent attacks from abroad and at home.[36] The weakness, or rather the internal feuds of Mexico, invite attack from unscrupulous parties, is it meet then that emigrants of any nation should make haste to "settle there?" We look in vain for the precedent of emigration to a country, distracted even to bloodshed, with internal feuds, by any people; and we may look in vain for prosperity. In advocating this, we would leave out of sight, the check that a fortifying of the West indies with our emigrants would give to depredations on the contiguous countries, and only gratify the love to fight, without immediate advantage. Let Mexico, at present, take care of herself, by the efforts of her own mixed population rightly directed, and let our emigrants so *abolitionized* and strengthen neighboring positions as to promote the prosperity and harmony of the whole. This can be done without compromising away honor; in fact, the sentiment "liberty or death," is never realized but by so proceeding as to secure the first permanently, and only courting the latter when life is no longer of utility. I know that the recollection of innumerable wrongs, makes the desire for payment in like coin the necessity of some men's natures, but no real end is attained after all: the Indians have learned sense from frequent defeat, the consequence of going to war before they were prepared, and whole tribes now cultivate the arts of peace and progress. Let us learn even of savages! We can get up a fight at any time, but who is the wiser for the sight?[37] No one, honest men would but try

---

[36] Almonte, ed., *A Plea for Emigration*, 96; Antwi, ed., *A Plea for Emigration*, 61.

[37] Shadd Cary does not explicitly endorse Black armed resistance to slavery; however, her decision to recruit Black soldiers to the Union army during the Civil War appears to offer tacit support to Black self-defense approximately a decade after the publication of *A Plea for Emigration*.

to suppress it; so would a coalition with any nation, and especially a weak one, to carry out retaliatory measures, result.

The pro-slavery party of the United States is the aggressive party [on] this continent. It is the serpent that aims to swallow all others. [To] meet then to make strongholds, and if need be, defend them; [that] will be the most effective check to greediness of land and [negroes].

VANCOUVER'S ISLAND—CONCLUDING REMARKS.

This island is situated between 49° and 51° north latitude, or on the southern boundary of British America; and between 122° and 127° west longitude. It is about three hundred miles long, and between ninety and one hundred miles broad, and contains about twenty-eight thousand square miles. Though remotely situated, and comparatively uninhabited, (there being not more than twenty thousand persons on it,) it will, it is said, be the first island in importance on the globe. It has a fine climate, being in the same latitude as the south of England, Germany, and the north of France: the soil is also of the best description. But it is not as an agricultural island that it will surpass all others. The Western Continent, and particularly the northern part, say "wise men of the east," must eventually leave the eastern far in the distance, (a fact that should not be lost sight of by colored men,) and that over the Pacific will trade with eastern nations be prosecuted. It is important now as a stopping place for whale ships visiting the Northern Seas, and is directly in the route to the East Indies, Japan Isles, and China, from Oregon and British America. The overland route to the Pacific terminating near that point, the great Atlantic trade of Western Europe and America will find there the most practicable outlet and the shortest distance to Eastern Asia; consequently the people there settled, of whatever complexion, will be the "merchant princes of the world," and under the protection of Great Britain. Now, there are two weighty reasons why the people settled there should be colored principally; the first, because by that means they would become more fully involved in the destiny of this Continent; any eastern move of magnitude, as for instance to Africa, if *possible*, would appear a retrograde step, now that the current of affairs is so clearly setting west: and, secondly, in no more effectual way could a check be given to the encroachments of slavery on free soil. The purely American sympathy for "kith and kin" only, would experience unmistakable obstacles to its free exercise, in the event of a contemplated annexation of that delightful Western country.

It will be seen, that the possibility of a pretty extensive emigration to those countries has been the prominent feature throughout this tract, and for that reason direct reference has been made to other points, under British jurisdiction, than Canada. The preference given to these, (Canada, West Indies, and Vancouver's Island,) over British Colonies elsewhere, has been because of their strong position and availability in every way. There would not be as in Africa, Mexico, or South America, hostile tribes to annoy the settler, or destroy at will towns and villages with their inhabitants: the strong arm of British power would summarily punish depredations made, of whatever character, and the emigrants would naturally assume the responsibility of British freemen.

The question whether or not an extensive emigration by the free colored people of the United States would affect the institution of slavery, would then be answered. I have here taken the affirmative of that question, because that view of the case seems to me most clear. The free colored people have steadily discountenanced any rational scheme of emigration, in the hope that by remaining in the States, a powerful miracle for the overthrow of slavery would be wrought. What are the facts. More territory has been given up to slavery, the Fugitive Law has passed, and a concert of measures, seriously affecting their personal liberty, has been entered into by several of the Free states; so subtle, unseen and effective have been their movements, that, were it not that we remember there is a Great Britain, we would be overwhelmed, powerless, from the force of such successive shocks; and the end may not be yet, if we persist in remaining targets, while they are strengthening themselves in the Northwest, and in the Gulf. There would be more of the right spirit, and infinitely more of real manliness, in a peaceful but decided demand for freedom to the slave from the Gulf of Mexico, than in a miserable scampering from state to state, in a vain endeavor to gather the crumbs of freedom that a proslavery besom may sweep away at any moment. May a selection for the best be made, now that there are countries between which and the United States a com[parison] may be instituted. A little folding of the hands, and there [may be no] retreat from the clutches of the slave power.[38]

32. "Our Free Colored Emigrants," *Provincial Freeman*, May 20, 1854

We have alluded before to the emigration of large numbers of free colored people from the U.S. to Canada; but we would call the attention of our

[38] Almonte, ed., *A Plea for Emigration*, 100; Antwi, ed., *A Plea for Emigration*, 64.

readers to a few particulars connected with them, not of general currency hereabouts.

The free colored people, North, are at this time in a state of revolution—a condition of things directly traceable to Slavery, as is nearly every event or commotion which is connected with them. They are divided and sub-divided into as many factions in proportion to numbers, as are their more highly favored fellow-citizens.

There are the Anti-Emigrationists, on the one hand,—the men who think nothing, say nothing, do nothing, in affinity with the Anti-Emagrationists [sic]. The Emigrationists, who wish to set up a nation of their own, and the men who love liberty too well to remain in the States, but would not agree to an exclusive nationality, those are in sympathy with Emigrationists No. 1, so far as they admit the propriety of leaving the States.—Animated by a similar spirit with Hungarians, Poles, German and other people who settle in America from a love of liberty, these latter make up the class constantly arriving on our shores.

Staid, sober, industrious, and "long-headed" men, many of them previously of those chosen to act as deliberators for their people, they have surveyed the entire fields, and now, after the years of opinion they settle down practically upon their first thought, "Canada." The prevailing ignorance in this country, on the condition of Northern free colored people, is often subject of amusement to us. A colored man from Scotland or the isles of the sea, is a man, and falls into the ranks at once. In some instances, we have heard that the *penchant* for a foreign birth by this class, is so strong, growing out of the supposed character gained, that men last from Egypt or Guinea, boldly assert a Scotch or West Indian origin, though natives of the "sunny South." This to our mind should hardly be allowed, as it is clearly underestimating Yankee notions. When fugitives come, (and thanks to the Under-ground Railroad, that is very often in large numbers,) they at once get a place: they are known as "hunted" and "panting" and destitute in every way, and a position is taken accordingly: but to what place belongs the free man from the States, who knows the value of pounds, shillings and pence—he who has attended to his business without the "anxious care" of a master? is a question not often solved at first sight.

How he will deport himself—what will be the result of his indiscriminate settlement, are wonders that have their origin in the many slanderous reports gratuitously circulated of colored people, by prejudiced Americans; but those must cease.

The people of whom we, write, are a little more energetic than any to be found among those who will not occupy a more desirable field. Their determination to leave, settles that point.—They are fully equal to those among whom they are now living—whose farms and other property, they buy and *improve*; which last is the proof of that too.

Having come at last to the sensible conclusion, that it is better to grow up with, and prosper in this noble country, than to remain in the States, where the mephitic air of Slavery is poisoning white and colored, in a greater or less degree, they are here not only buying lands and cultivating the same, but they enter largely into other profitable pursuits in a manner and on a scale equal to their white brother Yankees, who come as they do, to better their condition, and in a way vastly superior in the general, to that which those in the States who opposed emigration, think of doing. We hear much of the work to be done, but to our mind, these emigrants give evidence that they at least, are doing their share. They have chosen the ground—British ground—the only ground on which they can make despots feel the force of their words and actions; and, true to their progressive character, and in glaring contrast with the red man, they go onward, planning improving, accumulating and enlarging.[39] Now, what is to prevent them from living in the future?

As Emigrationists they now live; as business men, they are prospering; as adopted subjects, they cannot fail to grow into favor, as individuals have done before; from the means they bring morally, intellectually, and pecuniarly, the same as are brought by the better class of white emigrants, and the disposition they make of the same.

As a class of men not in service to any man, they must, by common consent, take a position in which they can cheer on the weaker brethren who have just emerged from oppression; and as the bone and sinew of a powerful and increasing class, they will, whether pleasant or otherwise to Americans,

---

[39] Shadd Cary's use of "despots" here might refer to racists in the United States, but because Shadd Cary saw emigration as a strategy that would lead to protection from the British (and not from the American government), I believe the "despots" in question were, in fact, British rulers. If so, it is significant that Shadd Cary acknowledges their capacity to oppress. Critiques of British imperialism and Britain's support for slavery are noticeably absent from Shadd Cary's writings. In this way, her praise for the British appears contradictory. However, this line reveals Shadd Cary's motivations for lauding the British so heavily; she was cognizant that the British were not free from blame, simply the "despots" who may be most amenable to Black people's demands for rights and freedom. Here Shadd Cary also contrasts African Americans' efforts to better their condition with those of Native Americans. Yet she does not acknowledge how settler colonialism and genocide have produced differences in the ways that white supremacy harms indigenous people and African Americans. For more on Shadd Cary's brief and sometimes critical remarks about indigenous people, see Yee, "Finding a Place," 9.

help to shape the destiny of this continent. There is no such thing as driving colored people into the Pacific, nor across to Africa; they must and will make a long proportion of the inhabitants of the New World, and in proportion as they disown the dogged custom of staying in the background, until permission is given to leave, they will gravitate into this freer sphere.

33. "The Emigration Convention," *Provincial Freeman*, July 5, 1856

For many, many years the colored men of the United States, have been assembling in Conventions, at stated periods, in order to devise ways and means by which to improve their condition.[40] Calls are issued—in due time, delegates assemble,—and after making very many speeches (and some of them very excellent ones too,) and passing resolutions of similar tenor, from year to year, they return to their homes with but little hope of any very great amount of good to result from their deliberations; but painfully conscious of a reduction in the pocket. We respect a people who show a disposition to change an uncomfortable position, and we must respect the efforts made by any people, although convinced that the means they use to that end are inadequate to the object, but in so doing, we must not be silent upon the merits of their peculiar theory, much less, must we be expected to endorse their action. The Anti Emigrationists of the States, require not only silence, but the most decided approval, by the people generally, of all they are pleased to advance; now in all kindness we think they require too much. Let them meet Emigrationists on the broad platform of free discussion and inquiry, without bickering, animosity or jealousy, and actuated only by the determination to do NOW for their advancement, what SHOULD NOT be imposed as a burthern [sic] upon coming generations, and our word for it, results will follow different, and of higher character for good, than any that we have yet seen. Now, personal interests and party manoeuvres absorb much of the time in meetings and out of them, and the great questions are made of secondary importance. Let men who clamor for free thought, speech and action, from

[40] Colored conventions emerged during the early 1800s as important sites of Black activism. Delegates to the conventions would make speeches, circulate petitions, debate ideological issues, and pass resolutions concerning Black people. For more, see P. Gabrielle Foreman et al., eds., *The Colored Conventions Movement: Black Organizing in the Nineteenth Century* (Chapel Hill: University of North Carolina Press, 2021); and the Colored Conventions Project, Center for Black Digital Research, https://coloredconventions.org.

their oppressors, tolerate their bretheren [*sic*] in the exercise of these necessary rights, so that when those who do not accept for themselves the old policy of staying at *home* on sufferance, wish to be heard, they may not be made the victims of an opposition for opinion's sake, by a part of their own household, as verily, as the entire people are victims of the slave power.

The Convention to be held in Cleveland in August of the present year, will be held by those who have long since out-grown the policy that has guided the colored people of the States for many years.[41] Emigrationists hold that political elevation, the bone of contention, and which cannot be secured without unnecessay [*sic*] sacrifice of *time*, energy and means in the land of their birth, can be obtained by removal to foreign and more liberal governments. Their positions on this point, should be examined and not be cried down without investigation. They maintain that by emigration they would not only supercede the necessity of colonization to Africa, so strongly insisted upon, and strangely enough, by some white friends, and many colored anti-emigrationists, but that thereby they would be enabled to do Anti-Slavery work more effectually, instead of, as now, remaining where they must, to be popular with some of their leaders, oppose their best interests (to remove) and when in order to get their "bread and cheese," they must actually support their oppressors, and assist in maintaining the government that is in the hands of their enemies a tower of strength. Look calmly and without prejudice at your position anti-Emigration brethren, and you too who are indifferent! Not only are your hands tied against your own redemption from political "thraldom," but you encourage a people to remain, and you remain and accumulate wealth, the very taxes upon which are not only put into the United States Treasury, and used to maintain a government cemented with the blood of your bretheren [*sic*], but a portion of which, actually is appropriated by its legislators to send you to Africa; thus you are forced to go, made to pay the expenses of your own expatriation in part, and made to contribute your quota to return the Burnses, the Simses and other brave fellows, who wish to escape from the tender mercies of its supporters, and, to pay the price demanded by the keepers of the blood hounds human and canine, who seek the fleeing fugitives.[42]·Verily brethren [*sic*] your responsibility is awful!

---

[41] For more on the 1856 National Emigration Convention, see "Abstract of the Minutes of the 1856 Convention," *Provincial Freeman*, November 25, 1856, and "Mode of Publication," *Provincial Freeman*, November 25, 1856.

[42] Shadd Cary refers to Thomas Sims (1834–1902) and Anthony Burns (1834–1862), two Black men who were arrested in Boston under the Fugitive Slave Act and returned to slavery. Sims was

but made more intense by the opposition you show, against those who would reverse this order of things.

Cease to uphold the United States government, if it will, and while it does uphold human slavery. Cease to grapple after the shadow while you disregard the substance. "Come out from" a government that begins its depredations upon the rights of colored men, and ends by destroying the liberties of white men: if they will not regard the members of the household, think you they will listen to you? No verily. Go to the Cleveland Convention, and determine to remove to a country or to countries, where you may have equal political rights, and thus be *elevated* at *once*. Where from the responsibilities of your position as freemen, you will have something else to do, and a higher tone of thought, than to *serve* a class of tyrants for reduced wages, and to speculate upon, and imitate the fashions and follies of a people who despise and decide you. Go up to Cleveland on the 26th of August.

M.A.S.

34. "The Things Most Needed," *Provincial Freeman*, April 25, 1857

By the colored people of Canada, are a good *British* Education, thorough instruction to the young by means of British school books, by teachers British at heart,—and religious instruction in the churches of the Province without distinctions, and by qualified preachers, whether white or black—not as now in some cases little places of our own, and by ignoramuses; these essentials, and a regular indoctrinating in the principles and policy of Canada Conservative politics, make up all to be desired at present.[43] That is, if the people will consent to let American books, teaching, pro-slavery republican

---

arrested in 1851 and abolitionists attempted to rescue him, but their efforts were unsuccessful. He would later escape from slavery again in 1863. Burns was arrested in 1854. Both trials generated considerable public attention. For more, see Stanley W. Campbell, *Slave Catchers: Enforcement of the Fugitive Slave Law, 1850–1860* (Chapel Hill: University of North Carolina Press, 1970), 31–32, 98–100, 117–121, 124–132.

[43] Shadd Cary held complicated views toward Britain, which Yee and Benjamin Fagan have analyzed. Yee highlights the "contradictions and complications" inherent in Shadd Cary's attempts to develop a "black national identity" within British Canada. Yee, "Finding a Place," 2. Among them were Shadd Cary's refusal to acknowledge the existence of racism in Canada and support for integration despite her emigrationism, which is typically understood as a Black nationalist stance.

preaching, negro-hating separate institutions, Yankee old clothes and new clothes, and Yankee habits alone.

—M.A.S.C.

35. "Haytian Emigration," *Weekly Anglo-African,* September 28, 1861[*]

EDITOR OF THE ANGLO-AFRICAN:

Sir—It is extremely gratifying to know that the "Anglo-African" is in circulation once more. When your paper "went out," the hopes of many who had

---

Fagan provocatively suggests that "the *Provincial Freeman* tried to convince its readers that being British was more important than being black." Benjamin Fagan, *The Black Newspaper and the Chosen Nation* (Athens: University of Georgia Press, 2016), 98. He argues, "The newspaper urged readers to . . . consider themselves British before black. Disavowing race and nation would be no easy task, but in the eyes of Mary Ann Shadd and her supporters it was a small price to pay for immediate and enduring freedom and equality." Fagan, *The Black Newspaper*, 118. For additional, detailed discussion of Shadd Cary's stance on British assimilation, see Fagan, 110–118. While Fagan compellingly outlines the reasons why Shadd Cary found Britishness and British Canada so attractive, in Shadd Cary's view, embracing Britishness was a means to an end, not an end in and of itself. Throughout her lifetime, including her tenure with the *Provincial Freeman*, Shadd Cary's priority was to find ways for Black people to live freely and safely. She and the newspaper endorsed Britishness insofar as it held potential for Black liberation; this position did not require them to prioritize Britishness over Blackness, but rather, to pursue both in tandem. Shadd Cary's life and activism after 1863—when she left Canada and returned to the United States—also suggests that there were always limits to her earlier professed interest in Britain and its protections. The Civil War and Reconstruction sufficiently convinced Shadd Cary of the possibility of racial progress in the United States such that she was no longer in pursuit of Britishness. After her return to the United States, Shadd Cary no longer wrote about Britain's potential to guarantee Black freedom, but she continued to advocate specifically for Black people's rights domestically. Shadd Cary saw blackness as an immutable identity, where Britishness was a strategic sociopolitical identity, even during her time as editor of the *Provincial Freeman*.

[*] This piece is one of a series of letters to the editor that Shadd Cary penned for the *Weekly Anglo-African* opposing emigration to Haiti and criticizing its propronents, such as James Redpath (1833–1891). Additional letters appear throughout October, November, and December. In the other letters, Shadd Cary outlines a variety of reasons to oppose Haitian emigration, including, in her view, widespread illness and death in Haiti, untrustworthiness among proponents of Haitian emigration, the incompetence and corruption of the Haitian government, the lack of Christian religion in Haiti, drunkenness, polygamy, and more. Haitian emigration was uniquely objectable to Shadd Cary, and in this series of letters, she also sought "to vindicate Canadian Emigration, Africa civilization, and emigration to Van-Couver's [sic] Island, Jamaica and other British dependencies, from any similarity to this movement." "Haytian Emigration," *Weekly Anglo-African*, October 26, 1861. See also "Haytian Emigration in Canada," *Weekly Anglo-African*, October 19, 1861; "Haytian Emigration," *Weekly Anglo-African*, November 9, 1861; "The Haytian Fever and its Diagnostics in Canada," *Weekly Anglo-African*, December 14, 1861; and "A Correction, A Fact, and a Batch of Wonders," *Weekly Anglo-African*, December 28, 1861.

only heard of it, seemed to die out with it; some feared, they felt by intuition, that mischief was brewing, and very soon the evil was upon them in its full extent.[44]

In the interim, between the transfer of the "Anglo-African" to other parties, and its republication, a doubtful scheme, said to be for the benefit of our much injured people, was securely matured and established, (?) and it has been pushed forward since with a vigor, a tact, and an unscrupulousness worthy of the early days of African Colonization.[45]

For the first time, since colored men dared to canvass questions relating to their own interests, have they been summarily silenced—forbidden to examine both sides; for the first time have they been ruthlessly thrust out of doors by those loud in their protestations of friendship. Not only is this a part of our sad history, but in the prosecution of the Haytian Colonization scheme we have, singularly enough, all of the old, and worn out, and repudiated arguments, about the extinction of our race—extinction from 20 persons in 1620, to 4,000,000 in 1861—the invincibility of American prejudice, common

---

[44] For more on the publication of the *Weekly Anglo-African*, see Fielder et al., "Weekly Anglo-African and The Pine and Palm (1861–1862)," *Just Teach One: Early African American Print* no. 4 (2018), http://jtoaa.common-place.org/welcome-to-just-teach-one-african-american/weekly-anglo-african-and-the-pine-and-palm/#:~:text=The%20Weekly%20Anglo%2DAfrican%E2%80%93%20Pine,world%20deep%20in%20existential%20crisis. The *Weekly Anglo-African* was a newspaper that accompanied a monthly publication, the *Anglo-African Magazine*. The *Weekly Anglo-African* faced various editorial and ownership transitions in 1861. Its original publisher was Thomas Hamilton, an African American writer and activist. Hamilton sold the *Weekly Anglo-African* to James Redpath, a white abolitionist, due to the paper's financial instability. Redpath then took the paper in another direction—one that the paper's readers vehemently opposed. In addition to relaunching the *Weekly Anglo-African* as the *Pine and Palm*, under Redpath's leadership, the paper offered a hearty endorsement of Haitian emigration. This was a controversial position for a variety of reasons. In sum, as Fielder et al. explain, "Hamilton founded the *Weekly Anglo-African* as a black paper, run by black Americans for black Americans. Lawrence and Redpath produced a black paper, owned by a white agent, and financed by the Haitian government. Its articles and iconography centered Haiti, not the United States; its sense of citizenship was based in region, not a nation-state as such." The ideological shift from the *Weekly Anglo-African* to the *Pine and Palm*, as well as fervent opposition to Redpath himself, eventually led to the revival of the *Weekly Anglo-African* under its original configuration.

[45] Here "African Colonization" refers to the movement that advocated for free Black people to relocate to Liberia. Its supporters varied in nature from slaveholders who saw the presence of free African Americans as a threat to the institution of slavery; to abolitionists who were pessimistic about the possibility that African Americans could enjoy equal rights in the United States; to Black people who wanted to establish their own communities while attempting to "civilize" Africa and spread Christianity throughout the continent. Black people held varying positions toward African colonization throughout the nineteenth century. Some were opposed because they thought that African colonization would deprive Black people of their rights in the country that they built. Others were of the view that African colonization was tantamount to abandoning the enslaved, as well as abolition. For more, see Louis R. Mehlinger, "The Attitude of the Free Negro toward African Colonization," *Journal of Negro History* 1, no. 3 (1916): 276–301.

schools, churches, railroads in 1832, and 1861 in States and Canada, the incongeniality of climate—do we not live as long, and are we not as exempt from disease as the pure Anglo-Saxon? We have, with these, the exhumed relics of the past; the fact that instead of unrelenting Democrats and heartless slaveholders, to push forward this new crusade against the best interests of the free colored man of the North, we have Republican abolitionists, and fugitive-slaves, who "once upon a time" fought bravely against the dogma, and when its now cherished arguments were the pet theme of the fierce negro-hater and the great conservators of slave property.

To be consistent, would it not be well for the new colonizationists to dig up their buried foes, and make haste and repair the damage to this generation by singing in praise of their wise foresight, and their genuine friendship for our poor people?

But not only has another doubtful scheme been "set a going," now said to be in the name of the black man, and for black men, but for the first time in thirty years have our Pennington's, our Delaney's[,] our Smith's[,] and Downing[']s, been cuffed into silence.[46] Our so-called enemies, the African Colonizationists, never dared to stigmatize as drunkards, "renegade negroes" and snobs, those of our men known to be among the leaders in defence of our rights.

Once upon a time brave men and women, with bugle-blast of indignation, spoke out against wrong when it was perpetrated against black men, at the risk of the halter. I have a dim recollection of one noble man called William Lloyd Garrison in such peril. Why cannot there be a strong and manly voice now? There has been a slight murmur down about Boston; why does not somebody speak OUT? Are not you recording the dead and buried? Do not you tell of the disappointments? Are not Mother Holly and John Anthony, and numbers, gone? and [sic] have not Mrs. Monroe, Sarah Underwood, Mason, and others spoken?

We are told that only the lazy complain, or tell tales; what must we say of the dead? they [sic] tell no tales.

I have spoken of the sins of commission, in the interim of your silence— now for the sins of omission during the same period: The American Union is one scene of distraction; must we for the same cause be at our wits ends? There never was a time when the colored man could afford to be more calm

---

[46] Shadd Cary is alluding to activists like James W. C. Pennington (1807–1870), Martin Delany, James McCune Smith (1813–1865), and George T. Downing (1819–1903).

and collected than now. There are thousands of "contrabands" peering cautiously from your forests, and skulking behind corners in your cities, not knowing in their extremity what way to go, and finally starved into asking the first "massa," though it may be an enemy, "am this Canada?" Has the North Star, the old beacon light, gone out, that these men cannot be encouraged to follow the ONLY safe and long tried road to freedom? It seems to me that the devil is let loose to hound the poor fugitives for a season. From the faith of our people being in God, and the North Star, a James Redpath and a star never before heard of, a South Star, now dazzle with a sort of "fox fire" light, to the neglect of our duty to God, our true interests, and our obligations to humanity.

Who, may I ask, is this James Redpath, in the hollow of whose hand lies trembling the destiny of our people? This man, who by a species of moral jugglery, beyond my stupid comprehension, has succeeded in throwing glamour over the optics of all our friends, and who has made the bitter pill of colonization sophistry long since discarded by them, a sweet morsel to hundreds of devotees of the god "Palm?" In all sincerity I ask this question. In a letter to the "Planet" of our town, Mr. Redpath complains that the Rev. W. P. Newman, whom he calls a "renegade negro," is trying "to destroy whatever influence my anti-slavery service may have given me with Americans of African descent."

What have been and what are the anti-slavery services of Mr. Redpath, upon which he claims to be entitled to influence with—colored Americans of African descent. In the name of common sense and common fairness what are they? When Wm. Lloyd Garrison, Lewis Tappan, Wendell Phillips, Gerrit Smith, and a host of such speak of services rendered, we know what they mean—they have looked in the opposite direction from Mr. Redpath for thirty years—they toiled in our cause when it cost something, and their noble sacrifices, crop out into a harvest of gratitude from the entire colored people. But what has Mr. Redpath done?[47]

---

[47] For more on Redpath's support for emigration, his acquisition of the *Weekly Anglo-African*, and the eventual collapse of the *Pine and Palm*, see John R. McKivigan, "Commissioner Plenipotentiary for Haiti," in *Forgotten Firebrand: James Redpath and the Making of Nineteenth-Century America* (Ithaca: Cornell University Press, 2018), 61–83. Redpath's biographer portrays him as a benevolent white activist with a genuine commitment to African American freedom. McKivigan summarily dismisses Shadd Cary's legitimate criticisms of Redpath's attempts to frame himself as an abolitionist stalwart and ally to Black people. He writes, "In Canada, Mary Ann Shadd engaged in a campaign of violent abuse against the concept of Haitian emigration and especially against Redpath. Shadd, a Canadian black, had developed her ideological position as an assimilationist through a long battle

Is it this leading men and women by reason of their ignorance and credulity, to untimely graves in the island of Hayti?[48]

A child, say our wise educators should be at least five years old before he should be instructed in the rudiments; it may be that moral precosity entitles Mr. Redpath to some consideration, but keeping in view the fact that John Brown has not been dead three years, and that Redpath for all practical anti-slavery purposes, must have been borne [sic] since then—I cannot forbear again asking what special labor since he came into being entitles him to teach, to dictate a destiny? and [sic] to make of no effect—the work of friendly laborer's [sic] who toiled hard heretofore? Who can tell!

Brother Newman tells you we have some excitement here in Canada, so we have, the most of it, is caused by the advocacy of this Haytian scheme about which I write. It is not that the thousands about which you have heard so much, are going to leave and throw off their British allegiance, but that a few agents, using the name of Brown and talking Redpath have, by working upon an imaginative and hitherto overworked people, set afloat stories of genial skies, plenty to eat, and little to do, and have, at the same time, plied vigorously the old story about their attaining to the "greatest height" among the whites; these rigmaroles, which they have been scattering broadcast for a few months, have caused excitement. Before then, our people in Canada, thanked God for this Asylum; they went on adding to their statement, and were* surely removing the local obstacles to unbounded progress.

A few have gone to Hayti, a few more will go; a few will go to Jamaica; already some have written back from Hayti who are not too well pleased; some more await further advice. Another record of deaths and they will fall back into their former industrious persevering ways; that is what *this new scheme will come to here*, and in the meantime, in answer to the question of a good woman in Wisconsin, who writes to know "what to do with the contrabands,"

---

with Henry Bibb in the mid 1850s." McKivigan, *Forgotten Firebrand*, 73. This description fails to consider that Shadd Cary—and indeed, other Black opponents of Haitian emigration, including Martin Delany and Frederick Douglass—put forth positions that held intellectual weight, regardless of whether Redpath agreed with them. It also reproduces troubling tropes about Black women by describing her ideas and outspokenness as "violent abuse."

[48] Although Shadd Cary is arguing against Haitian colonization, other Black activists did not uniformly share her point of view. As Brandon Byrd has shown, Haiti held several different meanings to African American activists throughout the nineteenth and earlier twentieth centuries. See Brandon Byrd, *The Black Republic: African Americans and the Fate of Haiti* (Philadelphia: University of Pennsylvania Press, 2020).

we say over here, send them to Canada! Send them over here as you have done thousands before, who now sit in the shade of their own noble forests, with none to disturb them. Canada is just as large as ever, and though they may suffer a little for a time, the people will rally to help them; our government will give them one hundred acres of land, in a region where now she gives the same to Norwegians, Irish, English and Scotch, and where colored men can get it if they will, or they can settle down readily, and do well in this western section, with friends and relatives to help them. Do not let the question be asked what shall we do with them? send [*sic*] them along.

M. A. S. CARY

CHATHAM, C.W., Sept. 17, 1861

Part IV
Contextualizing Shadd Cary

36. "Miss Shadd's Pamphlet," *North Star*, June 8, 1849—Excerpt of *Hints to the Colored People of the North*[*]

PHILADELPHIA, April 23, 1849.

FREDERICK DOUGLASS:—DEAR SIR—Miss SHADD has published a small pamphlet, containing twelve pages, called "Hints to the colored People of the North." I had a number of them in my possession to dispose of; but I have not been able, as yet, to sell more than three or four in about two months. As a reader of the North Star, I have been watching very carefully, for the last six months, for some of our able and distinguished writers in this city to take some notice of this little document, but have watched in vain. It has been widely circulated in this city, but I believe very little money has been paid for it. In fact some have said that had they known that the work contained some things which it does, they would not have had it as a gift; but what the objectionable part is, I have yet to learn, unless it be its telling too much truth—particularly in setting the condition of our people in its true light.

I understand that the author of this pamphlet is a daughter of A.D. SHADD, Esq., of Westchester, in this State. She says:—

"Feeling, as I do, that my destiny is that of my people, it is a duty to myself, setting aside the much-ridiculed maxim that 'charity begins at home,' to expose every weakness, to exclaim against every custom that helps prolong our day of depression. I shall, therefore, not by raillery or ridicule, seek to arouse you; but as one who, by assent, if not by actual participation, has aided in this complexion of things, speak plainly and without fear. We thought, in connection with professional men, as the whites had such, we should, as they do, make a grand display of ourselves; we should have processions, expensive entertainments, excursions, public dinners and suppers, with beneficial

---

[*] This letter contains the only extant excerpt of Shadd Cary's first pamphlet, *Hints to the Colored People of the North* (1849).

Mary Ann Shadd Cary. Nneka D. Dennie, Oxford University Press. © Oxford University Press 2024.
DOI: 10.1093/oso/9780197609460.003.0005

institutions, a display of costly apparel, and churches on churches, to minister to our vanity; we forget that 'circumstances alter cases;' we forget that we are, as a people, deficient in the 'needful' to support such things. The praise that would be bestowed upon us, was incense to our susceptible imaginations, instead of gall and wormwood to our souls, as it should have been, and as it really is to our hopes, if we continue to follow this policy. What profits a display of ourselves? Is it to be seen by one another? How does that better our condition as a people? Is it to be seen and admired by the whites? Why, the very people who tell you, 'Your people eclipsed ours on a public occasion;' 'your ladies and gentlemen compare favorably with ours in appearance on the street;' 'your society's regalia looked becoming and neat when Mr. or Mrs. was buried;' say 'the colored people are spending their money for velvet and gold now, and in winter they will be dependent on public charity.' 'The colored caricature the whites, their employers; silly people! they attend all to their exterior!' Negroes and Indians set more value on the outside of their heads than on what the inside needs: 'They (blacks) are glad when one of their number dies, that they may walk in procession, and show their regalia.' There is continual criticism on our actions being indulged in contempt of us, and abuse showered lavishly upon us, by our avowed enemies and pretended friends; while our true friends are sad at heart because of our weakness—this 'grasping at straws.'"

What think you of the language of this young sister, who is now residing in a slave-holding State?[1] Does she tell the truth or not? As one man I am sorry that I have to answer in the affirmative: yes, well may she say that our true friends are sad at heart because of our weakness, which cause she has so handsomely demonstrated in the foregoing extract. I do not know of any of our true friends who give any countenance to these unnecessary and expensive regalia displays; but I do know that whenever one of those regalia institutions turns out in the street to a funeral, or on any other occasion, the pro-slavery newspapers puff them up to a great extent—yes, the very newspapers that, in by-gone days, had aided in the burning of our churches, halls and private dwellings when we had dared to utter a single complaint against the oppressors of our race, and are ready to do it now.

J.B.Y.[2]

---

[1] Shadd Cary lived in Wilmington, Delaware, in early 1849. Slavery was not abolished in Delaware until the 1865 ratification of the Thirteenth Amendment.

[2] It is possible that this letter was written by John B. Vashon (1792–1853), whose initials may have been misprinted as "J. B. Y." Vashon was a veteran, sailor, businessman, abolitionist, and delegate to

37. "Schools in Canada," *Voice of the Fugitive*, July 15, 1852[*]

Dear FUGITIVE,—We have just visited Chatham, Dawn, London, and Buxton, where we have been laboring for the advancement of the cause of temperance and anti-slavery, as a means of elevating our race; but we have only time now to give a brief sketch of our observations on schools among this class.

At Buxton, under the supervision of Rev. Wm. King, they have one of the very best of schools, which is open free to all children without regard to color, and which is attended by all. An interesting church is there erected also, on the same principles, for the worship of the true God. The influence which those institutions are exerting on the community is glorious.

At London, the white and colored children all attend the same schools, and there is no distinction made amongst them; the result is, that a more respectable community of colored people cannot be found in Canada.

From thence we visited the Dawn Institute, which school is in a languishing state. There is evidently something wrong here. Everything seems to be going down hill, so that it is, in fact, unworthy of the name of an Institution. The party that now have it in charge, are doubtless unable to carry it on with propriety. But we are told that its prospects are soon to be revived, under a new board of managers, who have not only the disposition, but the ability also, to make it just what it should be, God speed the day, for a more promising community of colored landholders are seldom seen in any country than is to be found in the vicinity of Dawn.

several colored conventions, including the State Convention of the Colored Citizens of Pennsylvania that was held in December 1848. For more information on Vashon's life and activism, see State Convention of Colored Citizens of Pennsylvania (Harrisburg, PA, 1848), "Minutes of the State Convention of Colored Citizens of Pennsylvania, Convened at Harrisburg, December 13–14, 1848," *Colored Conventions Project Digital Records*, accessed October 30, 2022, https://omeka.coloredconventions.org/items/show/241; Paul N. D. Thornell, "The Absent Ones and the Providers: A Biography of the Vashons," *Journal of Negro History* 83, no. 4 (1998): 284–301; and Samantha de Vera, "John B. Vashon," *Mural Exhibit: The Colored Conventions Movement and beyond in Philadelphia*, https://coloredconventions.org/mural-arts/biographies/john-b-vashon/.

[*] Although this article was unsigned, it was likely written by *Voice of the Fugitive* editor Henry Bibb and his wife Mary Bibb (1820–1877), who repeatedly engaged in conflicts with Shadd Cary. Shadd Cary and the Bibbs shared a cordial, working relationship in 1851, but by the following year, their dynamic had soured. See Rhodes, *Mary Ann Shadd Cary*, 34–43. Shadd Cary's pamphlet *A Plea for Emigration* was published in June 1852, and "Schools in Canada" appeared in the *Voice of the Fugitive* approximately one month later. In this context, the article is best understood not simply as a discussion of educational opportunities for Black students in Canada, but also as a subtle objection to Shadd Cary's decision to publish *A Plea for Emigration*, as well as some of the claims contained within. This article reveals the nature of the challenges Shadd Cary faced to her leadership as both an educator and an outspoken Black woman writer.

At Chatham they have a large school consisting of from 60 to 80 scholars. But unfortunately it is just like it is at Windsor, a *colored school*[3]—a mark of prejudice uncalled for by the Government under which we live and which has a tendency to perpetuate that prejudice against color, that has always kept our children under the feet of the whites. The only difference between these schools is, that the one at Chatham is supported by the Free Mission Baptist Society, while the one at Windsor is supported by the American Missionary Association. We are happy to be able to say that the Chatham school is well conducted by these devoted teachers, who should be better compensated than they are, for we learn that they do not both together receive more than $160 from the above society. We must indulge in a single remark just here respecting an article which appeared in one column a short time since with regard to the colored school at Windsor, and the support of its teacher.

At this we understand, that there was an offence taken by Miss Shadd, (the teacher), where there was none intended by us. We heard her say that she was receiving "three york shillings, from each of her pupils per month," which sum was not enough to support her from about 20 children, and after we learned that the above society had granted her the sum of $125, we thought that they did well, and we ventured to give publicity to the fact, for the encouragement of our people in Windsor as they were entirely ignorant of it up to that time, so this was good news to them, and as our business is to give the news, and not knowing that she wished this information kept from the parents of the children, we gave publicity to it and for which Miss Shadd has said and written many things which we think will add nothing to her credit as a lady, for there should be no insult taken where there is none intended.[4]

---

[3] Here the article is referring to Shadd Cary's school. Although she repeatedly decried race separatism and published articles in the *Provincial Freeman* that advertised the school as being open to all, her school had a predominantly, if not entirely, Black population. Black Canadians in the early 1850s we embroiled in fierce debates about whether schools should be integrated or segregated, which inspired Bibb's pointed critique. For more on Shadd Cary's attempts to open and fund a school in Windsor, see Rhodes, *Mary Ann Shadd Cary*, 36–41.

[4] Contemporaneous critiques of Shadd Cary simultaneously pertained to her actions, her perspectives, and her tendency to depart from socially acceptable performances of nineteenth-century Black womanhood. Elizabeth Cali notes that "contentions played out between Shadd Cary and the Bibbs, by way of disparaging Shadd Cary's womanhood and virtue. . . . The discourse employed in the Bibbs's critique offers an early glimpse of what would become a gendered pattern of admonishment of Shadd Cary's public voice and presence vis-à-vis respectability politics." Cali, "'Why does not SOMEBODY speak out?,'" 34. Likewise, Rhodes explains that "Bibb and his supporters were equally disturbed by Mary Ann's independence and her refusal to be submissive to Canada's more established, black male leadership." Rhodes, *Mary Ann Shadd Cary*, 43.

38. "For Frederick Douglass' Paper," *Frederick Douglass' Paper*, January 4, 1855

FREDERICK DOUGLASS: DEAR SIR:—I hope that in my taking this liberty of asking a place in your paper, I do not trespass on your views of those of the readers of your paper. What I am about to say, I do with the very best of motives, especially those who may think with me on the great matters that pertain to our general welfare. The only regret and fear with me is, that we are too inactive on our part, while those that think differently are on the watch tower at their post, proclaiming the scheme of emigration in every town and village in our State. The people of this city have had four lectures on the plan, prospects and success of emigration. Three by Miss Shadd, and one by Wm. E. Walker.[5] Permit me to say that these individuals differ widely on the place to go, to the lady for Canada and the gentleman for Liberia, both assuming high grounds to sustain the possession they pretend to assume. Miss Shadd took the ground that the people of color reach every station in the government that is now held by any class of the people which she said could not be had in the United States any where, some of which was mentioned, such as justices of the peace, stations in the army, and such like; and the reason that more were not filled by men of color, was incapability.

I must say it is a great pity that woman is not admitted in the Assembly of the law making power. There would be at least two out of the forty thousand people of color who might be admitted into that department of the government. The idea of a colored nationality is out of the question. If this be true, then all the great ado at Cleveland will prove abortive; and the money spent by the Pittsburghers will be nothing more than to enrich the railroad companies. The position that Miss Shadd took in relation to the Canadas being annexed to the United States, was folly, and never could be done, specially if the people of color would go to that place, which would put a stop to any plan of annexation. If one could have dropped down in the midst of the assembly at any time during the evenings that were occupied by Miss Shadd, and not being acquainted with the aims of the people of the city, would come

---

[5] William E. Walker (n.d.) was a Black minister who supported emigration, but nevertheless believed in African Americans' right to remain in the United States. He also introduced a petition for Florida to become a territory that would be reserved for Black people. For more, see Sebastian N. Page, *Black Resettlement and the American Civil War* (New York: Cambridge University Press, 2021), 267–268, and "Letter from William E. Walker," *Pine and Palm*, December 28, 1861.

to the conclusion that the people was in favor of going to Canada. The next day, on the second evening, she gave the product, climate and soil of the country, and promised to exhibit some of the products of the sale. This was not done. The time taken up on the last evening, was a reply to Mr. Walker. At the close of the meeting, the Rev. A.R. Green offered a resolution complimentary to the lady, and endorsing the ability of the editors of the *Provincial Freeman*, recommending the same to the people of the city. This was done, when no one expected. Mr. J.I. Gaines made an effort to present the passage of the resolutions, but failed. He, however, made one true statement, and that was, that the emigrationists always skulk behind everything, to effect[ively] carry out their ends. I have already said more than I intended, and must content myself by saying nothing at present, touching Mr. Walker's position, as his plan is out of the question. Then, in conclusion, I must say I have not heard anything that has had a tendency to change my mind on remaining in the United States, under the tree that we have planted.

D. JENKINS

CINCINNATI, O. DEC 25 '54

39. "From Our Philadelphia Correspondent," *Provincial Freeman*, December 1, 1855[*]

No. XII.

———

PHILADELPHIA, Nov. 17, 1855.
Miss M.A. Shadd's Visit in Philadelphia—Immensely large Meeting for her benefit—The audience disappointed in not seeing Passmore Williamson, Esq.— The Black Swan, &c. &c.

At an Anti-Slavery Meeting, addressed by Miss Shadd, at the Shiloh Church, it was suggested that she had lectured on several occasions in this city, but had never had a *single Dollar* tendered her towards defraying her heavy travelling and other expenses; consequently, in view of her faithful services in the cause of Reform, it was unanimously voted by the house, to call a meeting expressly for her benefit, hence, the first steps being then

[*] The Philadelphia correspondent may have been William Still, but due to the effusive nature of this particular article, as well as Shadd Cary's penchant for writing anonymously or publicly crediting others for organizing meetings that she orchestrated herself, I find it prudent to acknowledge the possibility that Shadd Cary authored parts of this statement herself.

taken, in the course of a few days a Committee of Twenty respectable ladies and gentlemen, were selected to carry into effect the proposed object, and Friday evening, 9th inst., was announced for the occasion.

It was proposed to have *Anti-Slavery Speeches, Music, and Refreshments.* In the meantime, while the arrangements were thus being carried into effect, Mr. Williamson was unexpectedly *released.*[6] Consequently, on being visited by one of the committee, on the day following, he was told of the contemplated meeting, its object, &c., and at the same time was invited to be present. He replied that he desired not to be "lionized, or take part in any meeting got up for that purpose." He was assured that among the colored people, on his behalf, the most intense interest was felt, and that it would be gratifying to them in the extreme simply to *see* him, though he should not speak or participate in the exercises. On further consultation, therefore, Mr. W. said; "you may announce that Passmore Williamson will be present." Accordingly, he was simply *so* announced: but on the assembling of the audience, unhappily they were disappointed in not seeing him. For some cause or other, his mind changed and he did not come.

In making this statement, however, far be it from the Committee to reflect upon Mr. W. His labors and services on behalf of the oppressed, to say nothing of the cruel outrage which has just been inflicted upon him by Judge Kane, are too well known not to be appreciated by them. He had justifiable reasons, in his own opinion, they charitably inferred for being absent. Still they were not unconscious of the fact that many would feel that his name had been used without authority, and the public duped, designedly; hence, the discomfiture of the moment can better be imagined than expressed. Two eminent speakers had engaged to speak, and the celebrated Miss Greenfield, the *"Black Swan,"* had kindly volunteered her services, besides the ladies had Ice Cream, and other refreshments, in great abundance.[7] Thus, at half past seven, the *Sanson Street Hall* was literally packed to overflowing, with a

[6] Passmore Williamson (1822–1895) was a white abolitionist and secretary of the Pennsylvania Abolition Society. He was arrested under the Fugitive Slave Act for helping to liberate an enslaved woman, Jane Johnson (d. 1872), and her two sons. For more see *Narrative of Facts in the Case of Passmore Williamson,* (Philadelphia: Pennsylvania Anti-Slavery Society, 1855), https://lccn.loc.gov/10034487.

[7] The "Black Swan" refers to Elizabeth Taylor Greenfield (1824–1876), a Black concert singer. For more, see Kristin Moriah, "'A Greater Compass of Voice': Elizabeth Taylor Greenfield and Mary Ann Shadd Cary Navigate Black Performance," *Theatre Research in Canada* 41, no. 1 (2020): 20–38, and Julia Chybowski, "Becoming the 'Black Swan' in Mid-Nineteenth-Century America: Elizabeth Taylor Greenfield's Early Life and Debut Concert Tour," *Journal of the American Musicological Society* 67, no. 1 (2014): 125–165.

mixed audience of white and colored, all waiting impatiently for the exercises to commence.

Thus in the hour of disappointment, but for Miss Gree[n]field's liberality and charming melodies, one can scarcely imagine to what extent confusion must have been witnessed by the audience. On no previous occasion since her extraordinary acquirements and triumphs, as a Vocalist, have the citizens of Philadelphia ever had the opportunity of hearing her sing for less than 50 cts., consequently it was quite apparent that the audience felt that they could easily get the worth of their 25 cts., notwithstanding the disappointment. So the house remained packed, observed good order, and by their frequent and hearty applause seemed highly delighted throughout the evening.

In justice to Miss Greenfield, to whom the audience, and especially the Committee and Miss. S., were so largely indepted [*sic*] for her admirable music, Anti-Slavery Songs, too much praise cannot be expressed. To her credit be it said, instead of singing only "too ballads," for which a handsome sum was offered, when first invited, she very magnanimously *sung more than she is accustomed to do at her ordinary Concerts*, evidently desiring to do her full share, not only in making the occasion interesting, but likewise, in making it as beneficial to Miss S. as possible, refusing to receive any thing for her services. Besides she engaged the services of two competent young ladies to perform on the Piano, and an excellent gentleman amateur also, all of whom cheerfully performed their parts.

In addition to the good music, brief speeches were made by Mr. McKim, Miss Shadd, Mr. Douglass, Mr. Bowers, and others. Mr. McKim, in his remarks, referred to the object of the meeting; the disappointment felt on account of Mr. Williamson's absence, the labors of Miss Shadd, in Canada, &c., strongly recommending her to the public. Miss S., though not intending before going to the meeting, to have any thing to say, on the occasion, made quite an interesting speech, in which she complimented Miss Greenfield as the "Jenny Lind of America," &c.; also spoke considerably on the favourable condition and privileges of the colored people of Canada—contrasting their situation with that of the same class in the States. Mr. Bowers' remarks were strongly opposed to Emigration to Canada, or elsewhere, believing it to be the duty of the colored people to "remain here," at all hazards.

Mr. Douglass aimed to show that abolitionists fail to patronize colored men in business, &c., and reflected upon them severely.

With regard to Miss Shadd, whose good fortune it was to be the recipient of so unexpected a compliment, perhaps it may be well for the information of those unacquainted with her labors in the cause of Reform, to briefly refer to her services during the last two years, saying nothing of her usefulness as a school teacher, her exemplary character and superior intelligence before leaving this State for Canada, which in so doing, the motives of the Council, in volunteering in her behalf, will also be the better understood.

As she stands connected with the press, she is justly entitled, doubtless, to the credit of being the *first* colored woman on the American Continent, to Establish and Edit a weekly newspaper.

In 1853, seeing the great need of a paper among the colored people, to represent their true condition, increase their love for education, to inspire them to diligence and self-reliance in business; as well as to counteract grievances brought upon them by those who, for sinister motives, had grossly misrepresented them. Through no ordinary zeal and exertion, in March, 1854, she was ready to commence publishing the *Provincial Freeman*, placing this significant motto at its head: '*Self-reliance is the true road to Independence.*' She promised that the "*Freeman* should live one year," at all events; firmly resolving not to beg, or countenance begging on the part of others, for fugitives in Canada, &c., she took upon herself the arduous re-sponsibility of Editress, Publishing Agent, Financier, &c., which experi-ment, however naturally enough, brought multiplied trials, hardships and sacrifices, such as but few even in the unpopular cause of Anti-Slavery, have been made to feel.

In order to promote the good of the cause, and sustain the *Freeman*, she has not only had to forego the ordinary recreation and rest so essential to health, but not unfrequently has been obliged to take long journeys on Rail Roads and Steam Boats (some times on the burthen trains or upper deck, to save expenses,) in the most inclement weather, even when in delicate health. Sometimes without a dollar, though having regularly to meet the weekly expenses of the office. When in the office, the drudgery as well as the Editing, &c., she has been obliged to perform. Last winter, while on a Lecturing and Canvasing tour, in Indiana and Ohio, she was quite severely frosted about her face, to say nothing of the insults and injuries which she was frequently subjected to, on Railroads, &c., by insolent Conductors and others, on the score of prejudice. However, as indignant as she has felt, on account of these personal grievances, she has invariably declined publishing them, reserving the room in her paper for what she regarded as of more importance to the cause[.]

While on Lecturing tours, to defray her expenses, and procure aid for her enterprise, she has mainly been obliged to depend on the sale of her small book, and subscriptions to the paper, eschewing to ask favors or indicate her straitened circumstances; consequently, except in one or two instances, Public Meetings at which she has lectured, have done nothing in the way of collections, so she declares.

Notwithstanding, the *Freeman* lived its year out, making its usual visits from week to week, with as much regularity as ordinary papers regularly established; and indeed it still continues to live, though for the last few months has been considerably embarrassed.

It is but just to state that a sister of Miss S., for a time, while she was canvasing in the west, very creditably filled her post, in the office as Editress, &c.

On the subject of Canada; the condition of the Fugitives; progress and prosperity of the Free Colored man, in Canada or the States, she is perfectly familiar; having studied these questions with absorbing interest from childhood.

Therefore, the Committee in tendering to Miss S. the proceeds of the meeting, felt assured that she was justly entitled, not only to their pecuniary aid, but also to their fullest confidence and esteem.

COMMITT[E]E'S NAMES

Mrs. Stephen Smith,	Mrs. Webb,
" Nazrey,	" Dorsey,
" Dunson,	" Nichols,
" Bivans,	" Gordon,
" Dutierte,	Miss Hinton,
" Still,	" Mapps,
" Wilkins,	" Beckett,
" Burr,	Mr. J. C. White,
" Laws,	" H. Shadd,
" Hawkins	" M. Hall,

Mr. Wm. Still.

WM. STILL.

40. "For the Provincial Freeman," *Provincial Freeman*, December 22, 1855

PHILADELPHIA, NOV. 1855

Interesting Discussion on Emigration to Canada, between Miss M.A. Shadd, of Canada, on the Affirmative, and Mr. J.C. Wears, of Philadelphia, on the Negative

On Monday and Tuesday evenings, 5th and 6th instant, in this City, the following question was discussed in a very spirited manner, before large and intelligent audiences, by the parties above named: *"Shall the Free Colored People of the United States, Emigrate to Canada?"*

For a number of years, Mr. Wears had been regarded by many, as one of *"our leaders,"* as well as one of our *most able debators*, and withal an un-flinching opponent of emigration to Canada, or elsewhere; on the other hand, the ability of Miss Shadd, as a speaker and writer, and especially as an advocate of Canadian Emigration, the public were also familiar with.[8] Hence no small amount of interest were manifested to hear the question fairly discussed. On the first evening, therefore, at the suggestion of Mr. W., three competent and respectable gentlemen were appointed as Judges on the occasion.

Miss S. being on the affirmative, of course opened the discussion. In rising, with her notes in her hand, she commenced her remarks by complimenting the high character, as a debator, of her opponent, obviously leaving room for the audience to infer that she was fully sensible of the responsibility she oc-cupied; however, she proceeded to state, that she had *"Twelve Reasons* to offer on the present occasion, in favor of Emigration to Canada," adding, at the same time, that if another opportunity should occur, she would obligate to produce *"twelve additional reasons."*

Accordingly, she read her reasons, consecutively, emphasizing each one strongly; after which, she occupied her half hour in their support—saying many good things in favor of Canada—the impartiality of the laws of the country—the fine agricultural advantages—cheapness of the soil—health of the climate—character of the inhabitants, and condition of the colored man, especially; frequently contrasting his chances, as a British subject, with

---

[8] The newspaper article misprinted the initials of the man who debated Shadd Cary. It refers to Isaiah C. Wears (c. 1820–1900), a Black activist from Philadelphia. For more see Anna Lacy et al., "From the Stage: Isaiah C. Wears," in *The Fight for Black Mobility: Traveling to Mid-Nineteenth-Century Conventions*, Colored Conventions Project, https://coloredconventions.org/black-mobility/delegate-lecture-circuits/isaiah-c-wears/.

his condition and chances in the United States, under oppression, proscription, &c.

Miss S.'s half hour having expired, Mr. W. took the floor, doubtless entertaining the opinion, as did not a few of his friends, that he would very triumphantly demolish all her *en masse emigration notions*—would place emigration to Canada in the same category with African colonization, and thereby bring both schemes equally into bad odor. Consequently, after paying a polite tribute to Miss Shadd's ability and sincerity, he took occasion to give notice that he should *treat her in the discussion precisely as he would a gentleman, occupying her position*; assuring the audience that his opponent, though a lady, was too high spirited to crave any *special favor* or *courtesy*, as in fact she was not entitled to any; hence, he wished all to understand, that there were to be no compromises in the matter.

Having thus got fairly under way, without troubling himself however with replying to the "*Twelve Reasons*," he eloquently set forth what he conceived would be the disastrous consequences of *en masse emigration*, viz: the slave in his chains would be forsaken, the fugitive would be left unprotected, the ends of colonization would be satisfied, and, in short, the humiliating concession would then appear, as our enemies have said, that the colored man could not be elevated in this country. The speaker also mentioned, that prejudice existed to a great extent in Canada, to the colored man's disadvantage. As evidences of encouragements, he declared that great progress were to be witnessed amongst the colored people, and that by remaining, their elevation would ultimately be effected, &c., &c. Though this was Mr. W.'s first speech, obviously, it was his most effective one; all his "thunder" in it was exhausted.

Miss S., in entering upon her second half hour, in a felicitous mood, charged her opponent with having *shunned the issue*; in which she was reminded of the "Irishman's flea." "When he went to put his finger on it, it was not there."

The pertinency of the illustration seemed obvious, and much amused the audience. In further reviewing his remarks, she showed, that although *en masse emigration* were feasible, and the doctrine sound, nevertheless it could not reasonably be inferred that a spontaneous uprising would universally be resorted to by the people, prepared or unprepared.

As to the slave and the fugitive being left in his chain and forsaken, she argued that it would be quite the reverse; taking the position that the colored man's increase of character, wealth, influence, education, &c., in Canada, where his manhood would be recognized, would afford opportunities to aid to a far greater extent than could be done under present circumstances; while poor, and unprotected, being obliged to fill menial occupations, with but poor pay, taxed heavily to support schools, public institutions, State and General Government; while Common School privileges are withheld, the right of franchise denied! without being allowed the slightest liberty or say, in making the laws by which he is ruled; besides being hourly exposed to the infamous fugitive slave law, and countless other outrages. With regard to colonization, her position was, that emigration would be just the antidote for that vile scheme. Though the colonizationists wanted to get rid of the black man, they had no wish or idea of his going to Canada, where he would occupy precisely the same position enjoyed by the whites, socially, politically, and religiously. Under those circumstances, their doctrines and aims would all be brought to naught.

Also, by emigrating, she held up the idea, that in the event of the colored man's gaining power, being on the confines of the slave territory, he might, in a *time* of *need, be on hand to settle accounts with his oppressors.*

"Instead of having to wait five hundred years for his rights," as Dr. Smith, and others amongst the leaders have said, "he could enjoy them immediately." Instead of the young colored man having to put up with being a *barber*, and other pursuits, by which he is unable to make a respectable livelihood, he could be a respectable and successful farmer, mechanic, or professional man in Canada. Many instances of very rapid progress in the various callings in life, by those who went pennyless, were enumerated by the speaker. Likewise, on the score of prejudice, she replied to Mr. W., acknowledging that it did exist, and in some places had been very malignant; but having *no law to back it up, the colored man had nothing to fear*; there, it was manageable, not like it is in the States. Even the *waiters* in St. Catherines, only two years ago, had put an effectual stop to the omnibus proscription; so now, where Bishop Payne, two years ago was refused a ride, by the same omnibuses, colored men are daily being accommodated, without distinction. In other places also, she referred to the existence of prejudice a few years back, but by colored people settling in the neighborhood, and making improvements, it had been easily dispelled. In the large towns and districts, amongst the most respectable inhabitants, schools, churches, colleges, offices, &c., &c., &c., were all acceptable to the colored man, if he would only avail himself of the privileges. Quite a number of instances were cited, showing that capable men were already filling responsible and lucrative positions in office, having been duly elected thereto.

In conclusion, she scouted the idea entertained by many, that *because here is our birth-place, here, we must abide, fare well or fare ill; for spite, if for no other reason.*

Mr. W.'s second half hour, evidently by this time he realized; that in attempting to answer Miss S.'s *reasons*, and at the same time, attend to some little incidental points, he would have quite an *uphill* job of it; a performance which he had not contracted for. In Pennsylvania, the slave hunting ground, especially in Philadelphia, the residence of the notorious *kidnapper, Alberti*; the dead *Engraham*, the infamous *Judge Kane*, &c., &c., even the astute and gifted Mr. W. could not readily find plausible arguments in favor of a country tolerating such *monsters*, and the diabolical laws they administer.

Mr. W. however, remained on the "*old platform*," throughout, warmly contending that it was not the business of the colored man to emigrate under any circumstances, in view of his present condition.

The hour of adjournment having again arrived, and all parties being willing for the discussion to close, it only remained for the judges to give their decision in the matter; which, in a very *able, fair*, and *impartial* manner, they proceeded to do—*all agreeing that Miss Shadd had fully sustained her positions*.

While the judge was delivering the opinion part of which had been written, Mr. W., seeing that there was no chance for himself, and wishing to defeat the "ends of justice," he very abruptly called him to account; also a friend or two of Mr. W. suggested that the house should decide; but neither the house nor the judges heeded the suggestion of Mr. W. or his friends; consequently they were obliged to bear their defeat as well as they could under the circumstances.

Yours, &c.,

C. W.

41. "Anti-Slavery Lectures," *Provincial Freeman*, March 29, 1856[*]

On Tuesday evening last, the citizens of this place were visited and addressed by Miss M. A. Shadd, a conductor of the *Freeman*, published at Chatham, Canada West, and Mr. H.F. Douglass who is engaged in furthering the cause of the paper.

---

[*] The first half of this article is reprinted from the *Elkhorn Independent*, a newspaper based in Wisconsin. As I have written elsewhere, the practice of reprinting articles that were first published in another city, especially cities in the United States, was a common editorial feature of the *Provincial Freeman* and helped to situate the paper and Shadd Cary herself as transnational entities. See Dennie, "Leave That Slavery-Cursed Republic," 484–486.

A large audience was in attendance, which was highly pleased with the efforts of the speakers.

They are light mulatoes, comely in their appearance, and intelligent.

Mr. Douglass' delivery is extremely musical and eloquent, and his efforts gave universal satisfaction.

Miss Shadd's effort was nervous, hurried, and not so eloquent as Mr. Douglass, but it was replete with original ideas and soundest logic, and unmistakeably showed that she is a woman of superior intellect, of high literary cultivation, and of the most persevering energy of character. Her manner is modest, and in strict keeping with the popular nations of the "sphere of women." She is truly a superi[o]r woman.

They will speak hereafter at Burlington, Rochester, Mukwonago, Fast Troy, Spring Prairie, Troy, Sugar Creek, Walworth, Sharon, and Allen's Grove, and the people are assured of being well paid for their attendance.

Remember that they belong to a class denied all social and political rights, and after they have been listened to, will the people say they are inferior to *any* of the lecturers among their white fellow citizens?

O! why will the people not be just!—*Elkhorn Independent*

It will be seen by the above notice, cut from a Western paper, that our co-workers in this office, H. F. Douglass and M. A. Shadd, are not idle. But that while working for the *Freeman*, they are doing good work for our oppressed brethren in the States[.] We have had the best of evidence lately of their efficiency in the list of names and subscriptions they have forwarded to us. The prompt response and the ready testimony in favor of their labors in a field almost or quite uninhabited by colored people, should not be without significance to those among us who wish the paper well, and who "intend" to work for the overthrow of oppression; but who never do more than *talk*.[9]

42. "Meeting of Colored Canadians," *Pine and Palm*, April 3, 1862[*]

The following article is republished from the Chatham (Canada West) *Planet*.

MEETING OF COLORED CANADIANS.—At a public meeting held in the town of Chatham on Monday, December 16, 1861, Mr. J. C. Brown was

[9] The final line of this unsigned editorial is reminiscent of Shadd Cary's earlier assertion that Black activists should "do more, and talk less." Letter to Frederick Douglass, *North Star*, March 23, 1849, included in Part 1. It is possible that she penned the second half of this piece herself.

[*] This article appeared in multiple newspapers as early as January 30, 1862. It spurred Shadd Cary to write a response, "An Unmitigated Falsehood," published in the *Weekly Anglo-African* on February

called to the chair, and J. W. Menard, secretary. The objects of the meeting were to give an expression against the system of begging for refugees and public institutions in Canada. After the objects of the meeting ere stated, the following named gentlemen were appointed as a committee to prepare business for the meeting—Isaac Holden, Edmund Doston, Thomas Hickerson, Henry Green, J. W. Menard.

During the absence of the committee, the audience was addressed by the chairman, who reviewed in detail the past and present history of self-constituted beggars in Canada, several of whom were named; and concluded by summing up the vast amount of injury emanating from such persons. The committee, after a long absence, reported the following resolutions, which were unanimously received and adopted:

Whereas, we, the colored people of Chatham, have been repeatedly imposed upon by being misrepresented abroad by certain persons in Chatham, who go about begging in behalf of the fugitives, and necessary public institutions for the elevation of the same; and whereas we are of opinion that such institutions are not necessary, owing to the advantages of the public school system; and whereas we have been informed that the means so collected have been misused by these persons in purchasing sites for the erection of these said institutions, and deeding the same to persons as *private property*; and whereas we are informed that some of the beggars have obtained important official signatures under false pretenses, for the purpose of going across the waters to gull the philanthropists of Great Britain; and whereas this system of fraud calls loudly upon us for redress in behalf of a change, therefore, be it

Resolved, That we will use every means in our power to exhibit to the world the true condition of all such beggars or pretended agents, and repudiate the base slanders they fabricate for the purpose of obtaining a livelihood.

Resolved, That we emphatically denounce the action of one Mary Ann Shadd Cary, in collecting means for the purpose of purchasing a site for the erection of a mission school, which site has already been purchased and deeded in fee simple to one I. D. Shadd, a brother of the said Mrs. Shadd Cary.

15, 1862 (included in Part 1). Shadd Cary regularly turned to newspaper columns to defend her character and her work when faced with opposition from her contemporaries.

Resolved, That all such impositions have a tendency to injure the character of the colored people of Chatham, and also to rob the benevolent public.

Resolved, That copies of these resolutions be forwarded to the United States and England for publication.

J. C. BROWN, Chairman.

J. W. MENARD, Secretary.

43. Letter from Martin Delany, February 24, 1864[*]

To All Concerned

This is to certify, that Mrs. M. A. S. Cary is Authorized and Empowered as my Agent, to obtain men for Connecticut Volunteers, now forming near New Haven, Conn. to report to me, subject to all orders and inst. instructions given by me, unless located.

New Albany, Ind.

Feb. 24th 1864

M. R. Delany

Sup. Rctg. [Nestr.] Dept.

for B. S. Pardee, Esqr.

Lt. Col. Of Vol. Regt. of

U.S. Col. Sold. [4.G.G.][10]

[*] Martin Delany was a Black activist, author, physician, soldier, and recruiting agent for the Union army during the Civil War. His relationship with Shadd Cary predates this letter. For instance, Delany wrote favorably about Shadd Cary in the *Provincial Freeman* as early as 1856, and he "delighted in introducing her at lectures and in writing about her, for she personified all that he had expressed concerning the intellectual potential of his people, both female and male." Ullman, *Martin R. Delany*, 188. Shadd Cary and Delany also exchanged correspondence during the Civil War as Shadd Cary recruited Black troops for the Union army at Delany's request. Ripley et al., *Black Abolitionist Papers*, 520. Shadd Cary's willingness to contribute to the war effort in this fashion evidences her support for Black armed resistance, albeit in a formal, militarized capacity. For more on Delany's life, military service, and work with Shadd Cary, see Ullman, *Martin R. Delany*, and Martin R. Delany, "Martin R. Delany to Mary Ann Shadd Cary," in *Black Abolitionist Papers*, ed. Peter C. Ripley et al. (Chapel Hill: University of North Carolina Press, 1985), 520–522. M. R. Delany to All Concerned, February 24, 1864, Mary Ann Shadd Cary Collection 13, Box 1, MSRC Division, Moorland-Spingarn Research Center, Washington, DC.

[10] Delany's signature identifies him as a recruiting officer for Benjamin S. Pardee (c. 1830—c. 1900), the lieutenant colonel of the Volunteer Regiment of U.S. Colored Soldiers. Shadd Cary also communicated directly with Pardee, who requested her continued service in an unspecified "new field" that would pay her "handsomely" if she were successful. See "Correspondence- Pardee, Benjamin S.," Mary Ann Shadd Cary Papers, Moorland-Spingarn Research Center, https://dh.howard.edu/mscary_corres/7/.

44. Letter from Frederick Douglass, July 4, 1871*

Rochester, N.Y. July 4th 1871

My Dear Madam:

Your kind letter reached me here. It came too late for the preparation of an article announcing your purpose of making a southern tour in the New National Era article will be published tomorrow. I will however, in next weeks [*sic*] paper, give you a suitable introduction to my southern readers and bespeak for you the cordial and respectful welcome which you so well deserve, not only because of your talents but because of your many and efficient labors for the freedom, education and elevation of our still oppressed people. Go to the South, my freind [*sic*], go with words of cheer. [G]o with words of wisdom to our newly emancipated people and help them in their travels through the wilderness and to all who know me or know of me, I commend you in all earnestness and truth.

Your Friend and fellow worker
Frederick Douglass

Mrs. M. A. Shadd Cary.

45. "Mrs. Mary A. S. Cary," *New National Era*, July 13, 1871

The school term of this successful teacher and student (for she is both) being ended, she avails herself of the interval for a short tour of active service through the South and West.[11] We give our readers in those regions the benefit of this announcement with unaffected satisfaction. They are to be visited by no ordinary person. The fact that Mrs. CARY undertakes the tour southward at this fiery season is an indication of her sterling and

---

* This document is pictured in Figure 4.1. Frederick Douglass to Mary Ann Shadd Cary, July 4, 1871, Mary Ann Shadd Cary Collection 13, Box 1, MSRC Division, Moorland-Spingarn Research Center, Washington, DC.

[11] The article references Shadd Cary's status as a law student at Howard University. Although she was the first Black woman to enroll in law school in the United States, she was not, in fact, the first to complete a law degree. It ultimately took Shadd Cary fourteen years to complete the two-year program. The precise reasons for the delay continue to elude scholars. As Jane Rhodes has explained, it is possible that Shadd Cary was not permitted to graduate due to her gender, which Shadd Cary once suggested. Yet it is also possible that demands on Shadd Cary's time, labor, finances, and/or health prevented her from completing her degree within two years. For more on Shadd Cary's time at Howard University, see Rhodes, *Mary Ann Shadd Cary*, 185–191.

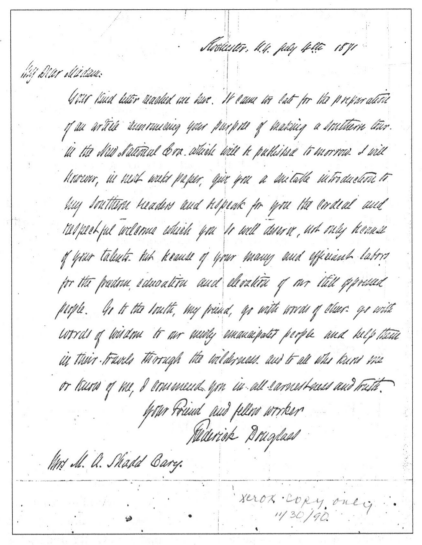

Figure 4.1 Frederick Douglass to Mary Ann Shadd Cary. July 4, 1871. Mary Ann Shadd Cary Collection 13, Box 1, MSRC Division, Moorland-Spingarn Research Center, Washington, DC.

stirring character. When other teachers, students, and literary persons are seeking rest, repose, and recreation, she proposes to go straight to work, devoting herself to traveling and lecturing among our newly-emancipated people. In the work of their education, improvement, progress, and elevation, her zeal is unflagging and her industry untiring. Her head is fully equal to her heart and hands. With voice and pen she is equally able and eloquent, while she is just such a woman, in all moral qualities, as may be safely commended to the hearths and homes of good people everywhere. In all the relations of life Mrs. CARY has acquitted herself in a manner to receive the respect and esteem of upright men and honorable women. We have not met any colored woman in the United States who combines so much knowledge with so much ready talent for affairs. In the conduct of the Provincial Freeman, a paper long published and edited by Mrs. CARY, in Canada, she displayed industry, financial capacity, and literary ability of a high order. We, perhaps, regard this lady with all the more admiration because she was the first woman of our race in this country who had the nerve to enter upon the duties and labors of journalism. Until Mrs. CARY, we could not point to one colored lady among us who in this way vindicated the mental dignity and capacity of colored women. White women had this field all to themselves, and colored women were unknown to literary fame. Thanks to Mrs. CARY this darkness is broken, if only by a single ray. She is a pioneer among colored women, and every colored lady in the country has a right to feel proud of her. Such a woman demonstrates the possibilities of her sex and her class. It is idle to hope for much refinement and civilization among our colored young men until there shall be more of solid character, education, and refinement among colored women. When our mothers, sisters, wives, and sweethearts are cultivated and intelligent, with their thoughts and conversations lifted above the trifles and follies of dress and amusements, and above the physical intoxications of the camp-meeting, their sons, brothers, and husbands will be encouraged to make greater and better efforts in the same direction. We have no doubt that those who meet with and listen to Mrs. CARY will be in all respects the better for such seeing and hearing. Her eloquence is not of the spread-eagle kind, but chaste, argumentative, thoughtful, earnest, and yet animated. We could not allow our friend to depart on her mission southward, where she may meet with some things to discourage her, without sending after her our earnest words of commendation and our heartiest assurance of respect and sympathy. We call upon our friends everywhere to do what may be in their power to make Mrs. CARY's visit a complete success.

46. "Teachers Assignment. 'One by One the Roses Fall.'" *Washington Bee*, September 20, 1884

The annual assignment of teachers in the public schools for the seventh and eight divisions took place respectively at the Sumner and Jno. F. Cook school buildings.

The ladies at the Sumner were apparently uneasy and exhibited but little warmth towards trustee Brooks, whom most of them entertain the utmost contempt for. Supt. Cook made his usual statistical speech and amazed his listeners with the astonishing announcement that there existed a difference of 6.3% between the two divisions in Corporal punishment.

The question which seemed most to puzzle the teachers was who was the pupil and what part of his body received the 3 thus administered. Mr. Brooks read the assignments and volunteered an entirely unnecessary statement, to wit that "he was responsible for the changes made." We say unnecessary for it is a well-known fact that if a mean or contemptible act is to be perpetrated upon a teacher, Mr. Brooks yields to no one the opportunity of showing himself at his best. His attempts at sophistry, like his swaggering man-of-war manners, were both futile of effect as was his lascivious leer disgusting. If he were at all gentlemanly he would profit by the example in deportment, modesty, and good breeding shown by Messrs. Cardoza and Terrell. The idea of a school officer introducing officially a gentleman to a corps of teachers as one likely "to set their hearts fluttering." No one but an ill-bred person would indulge in such expressions in presence of educated and refined ladies. The most notable change in this division was transferring and reducing in grade Mrs. A. P. Spencer from *Stevens* to *Chamberlain* building. Mrs. Spencer has taught continuously and successfully since 1869, and have served acceptably as principal of the Jno. F. Cook and Sumner buildings, two of the largest buildings in the District. Her degrading is another case of spite work on part of Mr. Brooks. Miss Lucy Barbour, was sent from Stevens to Minor in order to find a soft place for one of Mr. Brooks' relations. This *model* trustee also served notice that all the places for males in the schools had been filled and it was useless for any more to apply. Eight Division—The ladies teaching in this Division assembled at 4 p.m. at Jno. F. Cook building in anxious expectancy as to where they would be assigned for their year's work. Not many changes were made in this division, the most notable and commendable was relieving Mrs. M. A. S. Cary, of the principalship of the Banneker building. Mrs. Cary has taught in these schools since 1869, and has caused the trustees considerable annoyance.[12] Her retention was mainly due to services rendered two

---

[12] Shadd Cary's conflicts with the school board were documented in the *Washington Bee* as early as the summer of 1883. For instance, after one board member's departure, a columnist wrote, "You know that I am glad. He never would let the poor school marms have any rest. There was an old grudge he had against our dear old friend M. A. S. C. It is hoped that the new board will see that she is cared for. You have no idea what fun the girls had over his defeat." "Louise to Clara," *Washington Bee*, July 21, 1883. It appears, however, that by the following year, there remained tension between Shadd Cary and other administrators.

generations ago to the cause of liberty as represented then by the anti-slavery societies. Her youthful bloom and charming manners were only equaled then by her trenchant pen and eloquent sayings. Of late years she has grown dyspeptic, with voodoo tendencies and imagined persons were endeavoring to *root* her, and went provided with counter irritants in a green bag.[13] *Tibi seris, tibi metis.* The assignment of Miss Anna L. Foote to succeed her as principal gives general satisfaction in the division.

Miss Foote is not only a good teacher but a pleasant affable lady, and no doubt will bring the building up to a higher standard. The promotion of Miss Nalle to the vacancy in the Jno. F. Cook, made by Miss Foote's promotion, is a deserved one in every respect and is well received by parents. Miss Nalle is one of the best equipped and most brainy teacher in the corps and is deserving of a higher position than yet assigned her. Several other changes, among them Misses Sara Lewis, Mamie Nichols, Lina Jean, Ella Barrier, and Fannie Barrier, were made without any special significance. The meeting between trustee Smith and the teachers was quite cordial and in marked contrast to that accorded his colleague in the seventh division. The Supervising principals were present at their respective divisions looking on and taking mental notes.

47. Attorney General Endorsement, *Washington Bee*, September 27, 1884[*]

Should Mrs. Belva Lockwood be elected President, we know that the colored people would receive great recognition.[14] In that event the BEE will support Miss M. A. S. Cary for Attorney General of the United States.

[13] This announcement indicates how public attitudes toward Shadd Cary had begun to shift once she was an aging activist. She had long been a polarizing figure who received effusive praise from some and fierce critiques from others (which she typically rebuffed with equal ferocity). By September 1884, however, some Washingtonians simultaneously recognized Shadd Cary's former prominence and dismissed her as a paranoid, irritable, elderly woman. Shadd Cary first began to field personal attacks approximately thirty years earlier as she encountered backlash for having the audacity to speak out about the most pressing issues of the day. It is perhaps no surprise, then, that after decades of defending her ideas, and after decades of airing her grievances about perceived slights through writing publicly, she appeared to be concerned about potential sabotage. These vestiges of days long past likely continued to influence Shadd Cary's point of view throughout her lifetime.

[*] This endorsement was published in the *Washington Bee* one week after it printed the previous piece, "Teachers Assignment. 'One by One the Roses Fall.'" Public perceptions of Shadd Cary continued to vary throughout her lifetime. The *Washington Bee* gave voice to both favorable and critical evaluations of Shadd Cary.

[14] Belva Lockwood (1830–1917) was a white suffragist and lawyer who ran for president in 1884 and 1888. She was also the first woman to argue a case before the Supreme Court. Lockwood, among

48. "Mrs. Carey in Mississippi," *New York Age*, April 11, 1885

Reduction of School Term.

TO THE EDITOR OF THE FREEMAN:—It is so seldom that any event happens to ruffle the dead-sea level of life in this corner of the world that when it was announced last week that [M]rs. M. A. Shadd Cary, a colored lady lawyer, and lecturer on Temperance and other reforms, of Washington, D. C., would lecture at the court house on a subject of vital importance to everybody, the populace turned out en masse. The subject of the lecture was "Race Pride and Co-operation."[15] How well the subject was treated was evidenced by the frequent rounds of hearty applause that greeted the speaker. During the course of her deeply interesting discourse, she also touched on temperance and other reforms. After the conclusion of the lecture the Rev. M. H. Moore of the M. E. Church, South, heartily endorsed the words of the lecturer.

Mrs. Cary is one of the three ladies who have passed the post-graduate course in law and is the only colored lady who has passed that course. She was the guest of our Town Clerk and Treasurer, Mr. D. T. Williamson (her nephew) while in town.

The schools of this county (Issaquena) are in good condition but the school term, though longer than in some parts of this State, is still too short to do much practical good. Pupils have seven months to forget—only five to learn. The six months session of last year has this year been reduced to five, and for no apparent cause. If there is a cause for the reduction it is one of those things which no man knows.

AFRICANUS.

Mayersville, Miss., March 14

---

others, coauthored the "Report on Woman's Labor" that she and Shadd Cary prepared for the 1869 Colored National Labor Convention. For more, see Jill Norgren, *Belva Lockwood: The Woman Who Would Be President* (New York: New York University Press, 2008).

[15] Though there are few surviving documents written by Shadd Cary during the latter decades of her life, this article grants insight into her work during the 1880s. By this point in time she was delivering lectures around the country on topics including temperance and racial pride, indicating her continued efforts to ensure the well-being of Black communities.

49. "Locals," *Washington Bee*, June 10, 1893

WANTED: At this office two ladies to learn the printing business. Permanent work. Apply at once.

_____

Mrs. Mary Shadd Carey an old and respected citizen died Monday Morning at 4:50.

Mrs. Carey was one of the few lady lawyers in which profession she had an active practice and was an honor to the profession.

The funeral took place from Isreal [*sic*] C. M. E. Church Wednesday at three oclock [*sic*].

_____

DEATH OF MRS. CAREY

:—

Mrs. M. S. Carey one of the best known women in this country died at her residence on last Monday morning at 4:50 a.m.

Mrs. Carey was a woman of excellent traits of character and loved by all who knew her. While she may have been excentric [*sic*] at times, she was a women [*sic*] of kind disposition.[16]

Mrs. Evans her only surviving daughter has the sympathy of the BEE.

_____

[16] Shadd Cary's historical stature stands in stark contrast to the brief and somewhat wry obituary that calls more attention to her perceived eccentricity than her decades of activism on behalf of Black people. The obituary's framing of Shadd Cary's death underscores the ways that her work was underappreciated in both life and death.

Conclusion

"Why Not Go Farther?"

In March 1857, the Supreme Court issued its infamous Dred Scott decision. The decision essentially contained three parts. First, the Supreme Court ruled that enslaved African Americans who entered free states and territories were not granted their freedom upon entry. Second, it ruled that African Americans were not citizens of the United States. Third, it ruled that the Missouri Compromise, which restricted the expansion of slavery beyond a particular latitude line, was unconstitutional. Approximately one month later in a newspaper article titled "Meetings at Philadelphia," Mary Ann Shadd Cary offered a succinct reflection on how Black and white activists should address racial inequality. In response to a meeting that was held "to express condemnation of the Dred Scott decision," she writes, "The resolutions are strong and pointed, but why not go farther?"[1] This question—why not go farther?—encapsulates Shadd Cary's lifelong approach to advocating for Black people in general, and Black women in particular. She determined that activism on behalf of Black people was worth the struggle, regardless of what sacrifices they might make or what the consequences may be.

Shadd Cary knew that Black activists' labors would occasionally come at great personal cost. She repeatedly wrote in defense of herself, both publicly and privately, amid attacks on her character and reputation. For example, Shadd Cary was embroiled in an ongoing feud with Reverend C. C. Foote, Henry Bibb, and Mary Bibb due to her criticisms of the Refugees' Home Society (RHS) and their dissatisfaction with her bold entry into Black Canadian activism. On December 28, 1852, Shadd Cary wrote a nine-page letter to George Whipple to assure him that she was not spreading lies, as Foote claimed. Shadd Cary declared,

---

[1] Shadd Cary, "Meetings at Philadelphia," *Provincial Freeman*, April 18, 1857.

Mary Ann Shadd Cary. Nneka D. Dennie, Oxford University Press. © Oxford University Press 2024.
DOI: 10.1093/oso/9780197609460.003.0006

I will proceed to take up Mr. F's charges in their order and in the outset deny
ever having written "slanderous["] letters to abolitionists concerning their
society and agents. I have written truthful[,] private letters to friends, to
which his attention has been called, and which contained what Rev. C. C.
Foote knew to be true. I have not given my opinion merely, but have given
facts; when it was a matter of opinion, only, I said nothing.

She then explained that many RHS agents had kept a substantial portion of
the donations that were intended for fugitives. Shadd Cary claimed that "few
of the officers are anti-slavery men," and that the RHS—which she conceded
was originally established for the good of the community—now operated primarily for the individual financial benefit of its agents.[2] This prolonged battle
continued into March 1853, when she published an article, "'The Colored
People in Canada—Do They Need Help?,'" that responded to Foote's article
of the same name and offered a detailed account of alleged wrongdoing by
the RHS.[3]

In April, Shadd Cary wrote to Whipple again—but this time, her tone
was far more dejected than defensive. Shadd Cary's letter was a response to
prior communication from Whipple, which indicated that the American
Missionary Association—a key funder of her school—had called her religious beliefs into question. Shadd Cary's disappointment is clear: "I do not
see the justice in raising a question now that was settled to your minds last
year. . . . Allow me to ask why it was thought necessary to raise the question?
If my views of the RHS did not cause it[,] what did?" By this point in time,
Shadd Cary had grown weary from constantly fending off opposing forces.
Sadly, she explained:

A regular and well[-]executed series of attacks might be resisted by a man
of strong physical constitution but I am not equal to it I confess; the mental
and physical suffer, and I would that it were at an end. I must say though,
I hope ever to have unrestricted liberty of opinion on all matters of general
interest—never to allow interest to become master of principle; and always
to act as God requires.

<hr/>

[2] Mary Ann Shadd Cary, Letter to George Whipple, December 28, 1852.
[3] "'The Colored People in Canada—Do They Need Help?'" is included in Part 1 of this volume.

In Shadd Cary's view, she took a principled stand against the RHS, and as a result, her relationship with the AMA had suffered. This not only posed a threat to her financial livelihood, but also, as she indicates, her mental and physical health. By 1853, Shadd Cary was well acquainted with the challenges that could accompany activism. However, that did not stop her from asking "why not go farther?" four years later.

Throughout her lifetime, Shadd Cary confronted personal crises alongside the systemic crises that she sought to combat in her work. While in Canada, for example, she experienced difficulties like contracting cholera, receiving insufficient income, and navigating the death of her husband.[4] Despite a pandemic, financial anxieties, and grief, Shadd Cary continued to publish the *Provincial Freeman*, write, and teach; I see her perseverance under these circumstances as simultaneously tragic and inspirational. Shadd Cary's advocacy for Black people was not without suffering. She, like other activists and intellectuals, had to confront the simultaneity of personal and political challenges. She, like other ancestors, deserved rest. Nevertheless, she persisted. Shadd Cary's dedication and accomplishments are worthy of admiration; the struggles she endured are worthy of sympathy. Despite the personal toll that Shadd Cary's writing and activism took on her at a relatively early stage of her career, in the decades to come, she continued to live by a core principle: "Why not go farther?"

The nature of Shadd Cary's archive complicates the matter of understanding her interior life, as well as her intellectual thought. Shadd Cary's work is housed in several archives rather than a single repository. For example, her personal papers are housed at the Moorland-Spingarn Research Center (MSRC) in Washington, DC,; the Shadd family records are located at the Archives of Ontario; copies of the *Provincial Freeman* are available at the Kislak Center for Special Collections at the University of Pennsylvania; and the Amistad Research Center at Tulane University is home to Shadd Cary's correspondence with the American Missionary Association. Additional articles by Shadd Cary and discussions of her work are available in newspapers like the *Weekly Anglo-African*, the *Washington Bee*, and other local African American newspapers around the country. Shadd Cary's records are geographically diverse, and her papers do not exist alongside one another in a single, central collection.

---

[4] Mary Ann Shadd Cary, Letter to George Whipple, August 18, 1852; Mary Ann Shadd Cary, Letter to George Whipple, March 28, 1853; Rhodes, *Mary Ann Shadd Cary*, 135–136, 215.

Shadd Cary's archives are best described as "disorderly distributed archives," a term that Ashley Farmer coined in order to name the phenomenon where Black women's "records are spread across formal and informal collection sites and therefore rendered illegible when viewed through traditional archival processing and research practices."[5] Farmer aptly suggests that the seemingly disorganized dispersal of Black women's archives sometimes makes it difficult to understand them as radicals and as intellectuals. She explains,

> This supposed archival scarcity and historical incoherence stems from what I call a *disorderly distribution* of archival material, or when the documentation of their ideas and lives are literally located everywhere and strewn across multiple archival spaces. . . . The absence of a traditional archival collection has had important implications for the histories that scholars produce. Such Black women theorists are often left out of the historical record all together due to claims about the "lack" of the "right kind" of sources to write them into histories. Or, if they are included, scholars frame them as incongruous, incomplete, or enigmatic figures because their lives and thoughts are not neatly collected and processed in manuscript collections. If their archive is discordant, then their activism and theorizing must be too. . . . Such an archival fragmentation is common for other radical Black women organizers.[6]

In Shadd Cary's case, her disorderly distributed archive has led to an overwhelming emphasis on the early period of her work as editor of the *Provincial Freeman* during the 1850s, with some attention to her pamphlet *A Plea for Emigration* and a lesser focus on the broad range of her writings throughout her lifetime. Despite the longevity of her career and breadth of her activism, she has yet to be widely regarded as an intellectual equal to some of her contemporaries, such as Frederick Douglass, Martin Delany, and Frances Harper. By uniting disparate moments across Shadd Cary's career, this book hopes to mend some of the fissures in her historical and philosophical framing. Shadd Cary may not appear radical when certain aspects of her life are viewed in isolation, but closer examination of her larger body of work over the course of four decades reveals that she was a Black radical thinker.

[5] Ashley D. Farmer, "Disorderly Distribution: The Dispersal of Queen Mother Audley Moore's Archives and the Illegibility of Black Women Intellectuals," *Black Scholar* 52, no. 4 (2022): 6.

[6] Farmer, "Disorderly Distribution," 6.

This shift in how we understand Shadd Cary is only possibly by engaging with her archive in a way that seeks to grapple with its fullness rather than its fragments.

Shadd Cary's disorderly distributed archive is not inherently problematic; rather, it is a feature of her historical preservation that scholars must be cognizant of in order to fully reckon with its effects. As Farmer notes, "There is also promise in this disorderly distribution."[7] In some ways, the structure of Shadd Cary's archive reinforces her 1849 claim: "Though native of a different State, still in anything relating to our people, I am insensible of boundaries."[8] It also reflects her movements throughout the United States and Canada, as well as the transnational scope of her work. Shadd Cary's archive encourages us to consider how she continually navigated space and place, and how her search for Black freedom across borders impacted the documentation of her work.

Recent strides in digitizing Shadd Cary's archive offer exciting opportunities to pursue further research into her life and intellectual thought. Various digital databases, like Accessible Archives; Slavery and Anti-Slavery: A Transnational Archive; and Women and Social Movements, 1600–2000 host a wealth of material by and about Shadd Cary. Other repositories, like the MSRC and the Kislak Center, have made their holdings freely available online. In addition, the Center for Black Digital Research at Pennsylvania State University, organized Douglass Day 2023 around Shadd Cary, which allowed thousands of volunteers nationwide to transcribe her records in celebration of Frederick Douglass's chosen birthday, February 14. Digital collections have great potential for encouraging new approaches to Shadd Cary's archive and facilitating future research about Shadd Cary. There are also, at the time of this writing, multiple upcoming essay collections on Shadd Cary being edited by scholars, including Kristin Moriah and Meena Krishnamurthy. Both volumes are necessary interventions in order to situate Shadd Cary within literary and philosophical studies more broadly, and foster deeper engagement with her intellectual thought.

Increased possibilities for archival research, digital humanities projects, and essays will hopefully precipitate more monographs that have a singular focus on Shadd Cary, as Jane Rhodes's biography of Shadd Cary continues to

---

[7] Farmer, "Disorderly Distribution," 10

[8] Shadd Cary, "Letter to Frederick Douglass," *North Star*, March 25, 1849. This letter is included in Part 1 of this volume.

stand alone nearly three decades after its publication. In the spirit of scholars like Sharon Harley and Alison M. Parker, who describe Mary Church Terrell as a "genteel militant" and "unceasing militant," future research into Shadd Cary should also situate her among other Black women in the long nineteenth century who were the unsung radicals of their generation.[9] Such work can grant greater insight into nineteenth-century Black women's theorizing and activism. By learning more about Shadd Cary and her intellectual labor, we can develop more capacious views of nineteenth-century Black women *and* arrive at a fuller understanding of Black women's radicalism.

Shadd Cary embraced a Black radical ethic of care through her analyses of racial uplift, women's rights, and emigration. As she advocated for racial uplift, she put forth a comprehensive view of what Black people most needed in order to live freely and protect their civil rights: education, self-reliance, racial integration, and economic self-determination. Throughout her career, Shadd Cary also prioritized Black women's specific needs, such as protection from slavery, the right to participate in activism alongside Black men, broader labor opportunities, and the right to vote. When Shadd Cary endorsed emigration, she was chiefly concerned with how it would advance the cause of abolition, ensure that African Americans could exercise their rights in another country, and prevent US expansion of slavery into the Caribbean. Shadd Cary wrote about racial uplift, women's rights, and emigration while she adopted other strategies like teaching, editing the *Provincial Freeman*, delivering lectures, and joining organizations. She adopted multifaceted approaches to merging Black radical theory and praxis throughout her career.

Shadd Cary's work has significant implications for how scholars interpret nineteenth-century Black women's radicalism. First, a closer analysis of Shadd Cary's writing, editorship, and organizational work throughout her lifetime disrupts the dichotomous framing of Black women activists as either respectable *or* radical. Nineteenth-century Black women's radicalism is often illegible because they expressed it in ways that differ from more commonly recognized forms of radicalism that arose during the twentieth century. Their invocations of religion, morality, femininity, and temperance, for instance, can overshadow their powerful calls for liberty and justice. However,

[9] Sharon Harley, "Mary Church Terrell: Genteel Militant," in *Black Leaders of the Nineteenth Century*, ed. Leon Litwack and August Meier (Urbana: University of Illinois Press, 1991), 307–321; Alison M. Parker, *Unceasing Militant: The Life of Mary Church Terrell* (Chapel Hill: University of North Carolina Press, 2020).

as we see from Shadd Cary's works, Black women embraced Black radical positions throughout the nineteenth century.

Second, Shadd Cary's discussions of labor show that economic self-determination was central to her conceptualization of Black and women's rights. Her writings suggest that African Americans could secure their economic independence by emigrating or by empowering Black people to pursue a broader range of labor opportunities. For Shadd Cary, Black people's rights in general and Black women's rights in particular were intertwined with their class status. Her work illustrates how Black radical analyses of labor have existed outside of the Black communist frameworks that would later grow synonymous with Black radicalism during the twentieth century.

Third, greater attention to Shadd Cary's work can reveal the ways in which nineteenth-century Black women constructed transnational networks and participated in transnational activism. While scholars and activists today often grapple with how to pursue Black feminism across geopolitical boundaries, Shadd Cary—through advocating for emigration, expatriating to Canada, publishing internationally, and later returning to the United States—offers a model for how we may transnationalize Black, feminist, and Black feminist movements. Furthermore, her work highlights how early Black women pursued transnationalism as a strategy for pursuing Black freedom.

Mary Ann Shadd Cary shows us that Black women have been saying the same thing for hundreds of years. We have a right to mobilize on behalf of Black people. We experience oppression in ways that simultaneously overlap with and remain distinct from other Black people and women of all races. We need self-determination. We want our ideas to be taken seriously. And, most importantly, we matter.

Recommended Reading

This recommended reading list identifies works that offer deep analyses of Shadd Cary's work and further locate Shadd Cary within the dominant debates and ideological currents that she engaged throughout her lifetime. Some texts specifically examine Shadd Cary's life and work by interrogating her activism, publishing practices, and perspectives on emigration and women's rights. Others situate Shadd Cary alongside her contemporaries through their discussions of abolition, Black print culture, and nineteenth-century Black women's roles in public culture. Additional texts that are included do not directly address Shadd Cary's writing and activism, but nevertheless lend insight into early Black intellectual thought in ways that help to clarify Shadd Cary's significance as a Black radical thinker. Finally, some readings are anthologies that include work by Shadd Cary. The texts here comprise journal articles, book chapters, books, blog posts, news articles, and digital exhibits from various disciplinary perspectives. Collectively, these works offer a fuller sense of the political landscape that Shadd Cary navigated and the ways that she positioned herself as an activist and intellectual.

Journal Articles

Cali, Elizabeth. "'Why Does Not SOMEBODY Speak Out?': Mary Ann Shadd Cary's Heteroglossic Black Protofeminist Nationalism." *Vitae Scholasticae* 32, no. 2 (2015): 32–48.

Calloway-Thomas, Carolyn. "Mary Ann Shadd Cary: Crafting Black Culture through Empirical and Moral Arguments." *Howard Journal of Communications* 24, no. 3 (2013): 239–256.

Conaway, Carol B. "Racially Integrated Education: The Antebellum Thought of Mary Ann Shadd Cary and Frederick Douglass." *Vitae Scholasticae* 27, no. 2 (2010): 86–104.

Conaway, Carol B. "Rhetorically Constructed Africana Mothering in the Antebellum: The Racial Uplift Tradition of Mary Ann Shadd Cary." *Journal of Pan African Studies*, no. 1 (2007): 4–18.

Dennie, Nneka D. "'Leave That Slavery-Cursed Republic': Mary Ann Shadd Cary and Black Feminist Nationalism, 1852–1874." *Atlantic Studies: Global Currents* 18, no. 4 (2021): 478–493.

Fraser, Rebecca J., and Martyn Griffin. "'Why Sit Ye Here and Die'? Counterhegemonic Histories of the Black Female Intellectual in Nineteenth-Century America." *Journal of American Studies* 54, no. 5 (2020): 1005–1031.

Mehlinger, Louis R. "The Attitude of the Free Negro toward African Colonization." *Journal of Negro History* 1, no. 3 (1916): 276–301.

Mann, Regis. "Theorizing 'What Could Have Been': Black Feminism, Historical Memory, and the Politics of Reclamation." *Women's Studies* 40, no. 5 (2011): 575–599.

Moriah, Kristin. "'A Greater Compass of Voice': Elizabeth Taylor Greenfield and Mary Ann Shadd Cary Navigate Black Performance." *Theatre Research in Canada / Recherches Théâtrales au Canada* 41, no. 1 (2020): 20–38.

Olbey, Christian. "Unfolded Hands: Class Suicide and the Insurgent Intellectual Praxis of Mary Ann Shadd." *Canadian Review of American Studies* 30, no. 2 (2000): 151–174.

Paul, Heike. "Out of Chatham: Abolitionism on the Canadian Frontier." *Atlantic Studies* 8, no. 2 (2011): 165–188.

Pease, William H., and Jane H. Pease. "Organized Negro Communities: A North American Experiment." *Journal of Negro History* 47, no. 1 (1962): 19–34.

Scott, David. "On the Very Idea of a Black Radical Tradition." *Small Axe* 17, no. 1 (2013): 1–6.

Walcott, Rinaldo. "'Who Is She and What Is She to You?' Mary Ann Shadd Cary and the (Im)Possibility of Black/Canadian Studies." *Atlantis: Critical Studies in Gender, Culture & Social Justice* 24, no. 2 (2000): 137–146.

Yee, Shirley J. "Finding a Place: Mary Ann Shadd Cary and the Dilemmas of Black Emigration to Canada, 1850–1870." *Frontiers: A Journal of Women Studies* 18, no. 3 (1997): 1–16.

Book Chapters

Casey, Jim. "Parsing the Special Characters of African American Print Culture: Mary Ann Shadd and the * Limits of Search." In *Against a Sharp White Background: Infrastructures of African American Print*, edited by Brigitte Fielder and Jonathan Senchyne, 109–126. Madison: University of Wisconsin Press, 2019.

Conaway, Carol B. "Mary Ann Shadd Cary: A Visionary of the Black Press." In *Black Women's Intellectual Traditions: Speaking Their Minds*, edited by Kristin Waters and Carol B. Conaway, 216–245. Lebanon: University Press of New England, 2007.

Dennie, Nneka D. "Black Women and Africana Abolitionism." In *The Routledge Companion to Black Women's Cultural Histories*, edited by Janelle Hobson, 184–193. New York: Routledge, 2021.

Rhodes, Jane. "At the Boundaries of Abolitionism, Feminism, and Black Nationalism: The Life and Activism of Mary Ann Shadd Cary." In *Women's Rights and Transatlantic Antislavery in the Age of Emancipation*, edited by Kathryn Kish Sklar and James Brewer Stewart, 346–366. New Haven: Yale University Press, 2007.

Silverman, Jason H. "Mary Ann Shadd and the Search for Equality." In *Black Leaders of the Nineteenth Century*, edited by August Meier and Leon Litwack, 87–100. Urbana: University of Illinois Press, 1988.

Simpkins, Ann Marie Mann. "Rhetorical Tradition(s) and the Reform Writing of Mary Ann Shadd Cary." In *Calling Cards: Theory and Practice in the Study of Race, Gender, and Culture*, edited by Jacqueline Jones Royster and Ann Marie Mann Simpkins, 229–241. Albany: State University of New York Press, 2005.

Solomon, Nassisse. "Calling to Her Brethren: Immigration, Race, and Female Representation in the Life and Writings of Mary Ann Shadd Cary." In *Women in the Promised Land: Essays in African Canadian History*, edited by Nina Reid-Maroney, Boulou Ebanda de B'béri, and Wanda Thomas Bernard, 13–42. Toronto: Women's Press, 2018.

Steadman, Jennifer Bernhardt. "Traveling Uplift: Mary Ann Shadd Cary Creates and Connects Black Communities." In Steadman, *Traveling Economies: American Women's Travel Writing*, 85–111. Columbus: Ohio State University Press, 2007.

Stone, Andrea. "Ancient Ideals and the Healthy Self: Mary Ann Shadd's Plea for Emigration and Martin Robison Delany's Condition, Elevation, Emigration, and Destiny." In Stone, *Black Well-Being: Health and Selfhood in Antebellum Black Literature*, 51–83. Gainesville: University Press of Florida, 2016.

Wilson, Ivy G. "The Brief Wondrous Life of the Anglo-African Magazine: Or, Antebellum African American Editorial Practice and Its Afterlives." In *Publishing Blackness: Textual Constructions of Race since 1850*, edited by George Hutchinson and John K. Young, 18–38. Ann Arbor: University of Michigan Press, 2013.

Books

Asaka, Ikuko. *Tropical Freedom: Climate, Settler Colonialism, and Black Exclusion in the Age of Emancipation*. Durham: Duke University Press, 2017.

Bay, Mia, Farah J. Griffin, Martha S. Jones, and Barbara D. Savage eds. *Toward an Intellectual History of Black Women*. Chapel Hill: University of North Carolina Press, 2015.

Bearden, Jim, and Jean Butler, Linda. *Shadd: The Life and Times of Mary Shadd Cary*. Toronto: NC Press, 1977.

Broyld, dann j. *Borderland Blacks: Two Cities in the Niagara Region during the Final Decades of Slavery*. Baton Rouge: Louisiana State University Press, 2022.

Dabel, Jane E. *A Respectable Woman: The Public Roles of African American Women in 19th-Century New York*. New York: Basic Books, 2010.

Fagan, Benjamin. *The Black Newspaper and the Chosen Nation*. Athens: University of Georgia Press, 2016.

Foreman, P. Gabrielle. *Activist Sentiments: Reading Black Women in the Nineteenth Century*. Urbana: University of Illinois Press, 2009.

Foreman, P. Gabrielle, Jim Casey, and Sarah Lynn Patterson, eds. *The Colored Conventions Movement: Black Organizing in the Nineteenth Century*. Chapel Hill: University of North Carolina Press, 2021.

Glass, Kathy L. *Courting Communities: Black Female Nationalism and "Syncre-Nationalism" in the Nineteenth-Century North*. New York: Routledge, 2006.

Guy-Sheftall, Beverly, ed. *Words of Fire: An Anthology of African-American Feminist Thought*. New York: New Press, 1995.

Jackson, Kellie Carter. *Force and Freedom: Black Abolitionists and the Politics of Violence*. Philadelphia: University of Pennsylvania Press, 2019.

Jones, Martha S. *All Bound Up Together: The Woman Question in African American Public Culture, 1830–1900*. Chapel Hill: University of North Carolina Press, 2007.

Litwack, Leon F., and August Meier. *Black Leaders of the Nineteenth Century*. Urbana: University of Illinois Press, 1988.

Moody, Joycelyn. *Sentimental Confessions: Spiritual Narratives of Nineteenth-Century African American Women*. Athens: University of Georgia Press, 2003.

Parker, Alison M. *Articulating Rights: Nineteenth-Century American Women on Race, Reform, and the State*. DeKalb: Northern Illinois University Press, 2010.

Peterson, Carla L. *Doers of the Word: African-American Women Speakers and Writers in the North*. New Brunswick: Rutgers University Press, 1998.

Power-Greene, Ousmane. *Against Wind and Tide: The African-American Struggle against the Colonization Movement*. New York: New York University Press, 2014.

Ripley, C. Peter, Jeffery S. Rossback, Roy E. Finkenbine, Fiona E. Spiers, and Debra Susie, eds. *The Black Abolitionist Papers*. Vol. 1: *The British Isles, 1830–1865*. Chapel Hill: University of North Carolina Press, 1985.

Shadd, Mary A. *A Plea for Emigration, Or, Notes of Canada West*. Edited by Richard Almonte. Toronto: Mercury Press, 1998.

Shadd, Mary Ann. *A Plea for Emigration; Or Notes of Canada West*. Edited by Phanuel Antwi. Peterborough: Broadview Press, 2016.

Sinha, Manisha. *The Slave's Cause: A History of Abolition*. New Haven: Yale University Press, 2017.

Spires, Derrick R. *The Practice of Citizenship: Black Politics and Print Culture in the Early United States*. Philadelphia: University of Pennsylvania Press, 2019.

Sterling, Dorothy. *We Are Your Sisters: Black Women in the Nineteenth Century*. New York: Norton, 1984.

Streitmatter, Rodger. *Raising Her Voice: African-American Women Journalists Who Changed History*. Lexington: University Press of Kentucky, 2014.

Tate, Gayle T. *Unknown Tongues: Black Women's Political Activism in the Antebellum Era, 1830–1860*. East Lansing: Michigan State University Press, 2003.

Terborg-Penn, Rosalyn. *African American Women in the Struggle for the Vote, 1850–1920*. Bloomington: Indiana University Press, 1998.

Tomek, Beverly C. *Colonization and Its Discontents: Emancipation, Emigration, and Antislavery in Antebellum Pennsylvania*. New York: New York University Press, 2011.

Waters, Kristin. *Maria W. Stewart and the Roots of Black Political Thought*. Jackson: University Press of Mississippi, 2021.

Waters, Kristin, and Carol B. Conway, eds. *Black Women's Intellectual Traditions: Speaking Their Minds*. Burlington: University of Vermont Press, 2007.

Yee, Shirley J. *Black Women Abolitionists: A Study in Activism, 1828–1860*. Knoxville: University of Tennessee Press, 1992.

Yellin, Jean Fagan, and Cynthia D. Bond. *The Pen Is Ours: A Listing of Writings by and about African-American Women before 1910 with Secondary Bibliography to the Present*. New York: Oxford University Press, 1991.

Zackodnik, Teresa, ed. *African American Feminisms, 1828–1923*. New York: Routledge, 2007.

Zackodnik, Teresa. *Press, Platform, Pulpit: Black Feminist Publics in the Era of Reform*. Knoxville: University of Tennessee Press, 2011.

Zackodnik, Teresa. *"We Must Be Up and Doing": A Reader in Early African American Feminisms*. Peterborough: Broadview Press, 2010.

Blog Posts and News Articles

Davis, Jennifer. "Mary Ann Shadd Cary: Lawyer, Educator, Suffragist." February 28, 2019. https://blogs.loc.gov/law/2019/02/mary-ann-shadd-cary-lawyer-educator-suffragist/.

Hassan, Huda. "How Mary Ann Shadd Cary Set the Blueprint for Abolitionist Feminist Writing." *CBC*, October 27, 2022. https://www.cbc.ca/arts/how-mary-ann-shadd-cary-set-the-blueprint-for-abolitionist-feminist-writing-1.6631709.

Specia, Megan. "Overlooked No More: How Mary Ann Shadd Cary Shook up the Abolitionist Movement." *New York Times*, June 6, 2018. https://www.nytimes.com/2018/06/06/obituaries/mary-ann-shadd-cary-abolitionist-overlooked.html.

Digital Exhibits

Black Women's Organizing Archive. Center for Black Digital Research. https://bwoaproject.org/.

Colored Conventions Project. Center for Black Digital Research. https://coloredconventions.org/.

Locke, Brandi, Samantha Q. de Vera, P. Gabrielle Foreman, Nneka D. Dennie, and Rachel Fernandes. "Mary Ann Shadd Cary's Herstory in the Colored Conventions." Colored Conventions Project. Center for Black Digital Research. https://coloredconventions.org/mary-ann-shadd-cary/.

Bibliography

"A Protest from the Colored People." *Voice of the Fugitive*, May 20, 1852.

"About Belva Lockwood." George Washington University Law School. Accessed June 13, 2020. https://www.law.gwu.edu/about-belva-lockwood.

"Abstract of the Minutes of the 1856 Convention." *Provincial Freeman*, November 25, 1856.

"Adieu." *Provincial Freeman*, June 30, 1855.

"Aid to Fugitives in Canada." *Liberator*, December 10, 1852.

Ames, Mary Clemmer. "A Woman's Letter from Washington." *New York Independent*, January 25, 1872.

Basch, Norma. *In the Eyes of the Law: Women, Marriage and Property in Nineteenth-Century New York*. Ithaca: Cornell University Press, 1982.

Bay, Mia, Farah J. Griffin, Martha S. Jones, and Barbara D. Savage, eds. *Toward an Intellectual History of Black Women*. Chapel Hill: University of North Carolina Press, 2015.

Beasley, Nancy M. *The Underground Railroad in DeKalb County, Illinois*. Jefferson, NC: McFarland, 2013.

Beckles, Hilary. *How Britain Underdeveloped the Caribbean: A Reparation Response to Europe's Legacy of Plunder and Poverty*. Mona: University of the West Indies Press, 2021.

Berlin, Ira. *Slaves without Masters: The Free Negro in the Antebellum South*. New York: Pantheon Books, 1976.

Blackett, R. J. M. *Samuel Ringgold Ward: A Life of Struggle*. New Haven: Yale University Press, 2023.

Bonilla-Silva, Eduardo. *Racism without Racists: Color-Blind Racism and the Persistence of Racial Inequality in America*. 5th ed. New York: Rowman & Littlefield, 2017.

Bridgen, Lorene. "On Their Own Terms: Temperance in Southern Ontario's Black Community (1830–1860)." *Ontario History* 101, no. 1 (2019): 64–82.

Bumsted, J. M. "Thomas Douglas, 5th Earl of Selkirk." *The Canadian Encyclopedia*. Historica Canada. January 22, 2008; last modified March 4, 2015. https://www.thecanadianencyclopedia.ca/en/article/thomas-douglas-5th-earl-of-selkirk.

Burke, Meghan. "Racing Left and Right: Color-Blind Racism's Dominance across the U.S. Political Spectrum." *Sociological Quarterly* 58, no. 2 (2017): 277–294.

Byrd, Brandon. *The Black Republic: African Americans and the Fate of Haiti*. Philadelphia: University of Pennsylvania Press, 2020.

Cali, Elizabeth. "'Why Does Not SOMEBODY Speak Out?': Mary Ann Shadd Cary's Heteroglossic Black Protofeminist Nationalism." *Vitae Scholasticae* 32, no. 2 (2015): 32–48.

Camp, Stephanie M. H. *Closer to Freedom: Enslaved Women and Everyday Resistance in the Plantation South*. Chapel Hill: University of North Carolina Press, 2004.

Campbell, Stanley W. *Slave Catchers: Enforcement of the Fugitive Slave Law, 1850–1860*. Chapel Hill: University of North Carolina Press, 1970.

Careless, James Maurice Stockford. "Province of Canada (1841–67)." *The Canadian Encyclopedia*. Historica Canada. February 7, 2006; last modified March 21, 2022. https://www.thecanadianencyclopedia.ca/en/article/province-of-canada-1841-67.

Carter, Marie. "Reimagining the Dawn Settlement." In *The Promised Land: Historiography of the Black Experience in Chatham-Kent's Settlements and Beyond*, edited by Boulou Ebanda de B'béri, Nina Reid-Maroney, and Handel Kashope Wright, 176–192. Toronto: University of Toronto Press, 2014.

Casey, Jim. "Parsing the Special Characters of African American Print Culture: Mary Ann Shadd and the * Limits of Search." In *Against a Sharp White Background: Infrastructures of African American Print*, edited by Brigitte Fielder and Jonathan Senchyne, 109–126. Madison: University of Wisconsin Press, 2019.

Christian, Barbara. "The Race for Theory." *Feminist Studies* 14, no. 1 (1987): 67–79.

Chybowski, Julia. "Becoming the 'Black Swan' in Mid-Nineteenth-Century America: Elizabeth Taylor Greenfield's Early Life and Debut Concert Tour." *Journal of the American Musicological Society* 67, no. 1 (2014): 125–165.

Colored Conventions Project. Center for Black Digital Research. 2012. https://colored conventions.org/.

Collins, Patricia Hill. *Black Feminist Thought: Knowledge, Consciousness, and the Politics of Empowerment*. New York: Routledge, 2000.

Conaway, Carol B. "Mary Ann Shadd Cary: Visionary of the Black Press." In *Black Women's Intellectual Traditions: Speaking Their Minds*, edited by Kristin Waters and Carol B. Conaway, 216–248. Lebanon: University Press of New England, 2007.

Cooper, Afua. *The Hanging of Angélique: The Untold Story of Canadian Slavery and the Burning of Old Montréal*. Athens: University of Georgia Press, 2007.

Cooper, Brittney. *Beyond Respectability: The Intellectual Thought of Race Women*. Urbana: University of Illinois Press, 2017.

Cooper, Valerie C. *Word, Like Fire: Maria Stewart, the Bible, and the Rights of African Americans*. Charlottesville: University of Virginia Press, 2011.

"Correspondence- Pardee, Benjamin S." Mary Ann Shadd Cary Papers. Moorland-Spingarn Research Center, https://dh.howard.edu/mscary_corres/7/.

Dabel, Jane E. *A Respectable Woman: The Public Roles of African American Women in 19th-Century New York*. New York: Basic Books, 2010.

de Vera, Samantha. "John B. Vashon." In *Mural Exhibit: The Colored Conventions Movement and beyond in Philadelphia*. Colored Conventions Project. 2022. https://col oredconventions.org/mural-arts/biographies/john-b-vashon/.

DeBow, J. D. B. *Statistical View of the United States, Embracing its Territory, Population—White, Free Colored, and Slave—Moral and Social Condition, Industry, Property, and Revenue; The Detailed Statistics of Cities, Towns, and Counties; Being a Compendium of the Seventh Census; To Which Are Added The Results of Every Previous Census, Beginning with 1790, in Comparative Tables, with Explanatory and Illustrative Notes, Based upon the Schedules and Other Official Sources of Information*. Washington, DC: Beverley Tucker, Senate Printer, 1854.

Delany, Martin R. M. R. Delany to All Concerned. February 24, 1864. Mary Ann Shadd Cary Collection 13, Box 1, Manuscript Division, Moorland-Spingarn Research Center, Washington, DC.

Delany, Martin R. "Martin R. Delany to Mary Ann Shadd Cary." In *Black Abolitionist Papers*, edited by Jeffery S. Rossback, Roy E. Finkenbine, Fiona E. Spiers, and Debra Susie, 520–522. Chapel Hill: University of North Carolina Press, 1985.

Dennie, Nneka D. "'Leave That Slavery-Cursed Republic': Mary Ann Shadd Cary and Black Feminist Nationalism, 1852–1874." *Atlantic Studies: Global Currents* 18, no. 4 (2021): 478–493.

Donovan, Ken. "Slavery and Freedom in Atlantic Canada's African Diaspora: Introduction." *Acadiensis* 43, no. 1 (2014): 109–115.

Douglass, Frederick. Frederick Douglass to Mary Ann Shadd Cary. July 4, 1871. Mary Ann Shadd Cary Collection 13, Box 1, Manuscript Division, Moorland-Spingarn Research Center, Washington, DC.

"The Extension of the Provincial Freeman." *Provincial Freeman*, March 1, 1856.

Ewing, K. T. "Tricksters, Biographies, and Two-Faced Archives." *Black Perspectives.* African American Intellectual History Society. June 2, 2022. https://www.aaihs.org/tricksters-biographies-and-two-faced-archives/.

Fagan, Benjamin. *The Black Newspaper and the Chosen Nation.* Athens: University of Georgia Press, 2016.

Farmer, Ashley D. "Disorderly Distribution: The Dispersal of Queen Mother Audley Moore's Archives and the Illegibility of Black Women Intellectuals." *Black Scholar* 52, no. 4 (2022): 5–15.

Faulkner, Carol, and Laurie Olin, *Women's Radical Reconstruction: The Freedmen's Aid Movement.* Philadelphia: University of Pennsylvania Press, 2007.

Feimster, Crystal N. *Southern Horrors: Women and the Politics of Rape and Lynching.* Cambridge: Harvard University Press, 2011.

Fielder, Brigitte, and Jonathan Senchyne, eds. *Against a Sharp White Background: Infrastructures of African American Print.* Madison: University of Wisconsin Press, 2019.

Fielder, Brigitte, Cassander Smith, and Derrick Spires, eds. "Weekly Anglo-African and the Pine and Palm (1861–1862)." *Just Teach One: Early African American Print,* no. 4 (2018), http://jtoaa.common-place.org/welcome-to-just-teach-one-african-american/weekly-anglo-african-and-the-pine-and-palm/#:~:text=The%20Weekly%20Anglo%2DAfrican%E2%80%93%20Pine,world%20deep%20in%20existential%20crisis.

Foote, C. C. "The Colored People in Canada—Do They Need Help?" *Liberator,* December 24, 1852.

Foreman, P. Gabrielle. *Activist Sentiments: Reading Black Women in the Nineteenth Century.* Urbana: University of Illinois Press, 2009.

Foreman, P. Gabrielle, Jim Casey, and Sarah Lynn Patterson, eds. *The Colored Conventions Movement: Black Organizing in the Nineteenth Century.* Chapel Hill: University of North Carolina Press, 2021.

Garnet, Henry Highland. "Self-Help.—The Wants of Western New York." *North Star,* January 19, 1849.

Glass, Kathy L. *Courting Communities: Black Female Nationalism and "Syncre-Nationalism" in the Nineteenth-Century North.* New York: Routledge, 2006.

Hall, Rebecca. "Not Killing Me Softly: African American Women, Slave Revolts, and Historical Constructions of Racialized Gender." *Freedom Center Journal* 1, no. 2 (2009): 1–44.

Harley, Sharon. "Mary Church Terrell: Genteel Militant." In *Black Leaders of the Nineteenth Century,* edited by Leon F. Litwack and August Meier, 307–321. Champaign: University of Illinois Press, 1991.

Harris, Robert L., Jr. "H. Ford Douglas: Afro-American Antislavery Emigrationist." *Journal of African American History* 62, no. 3 (July 1977): 217–234.

Hartman, Saidiya V. *Scenes of Subjection: Terror, Slavery, and Self-Making in Nineteenth Century America.* New York: Oxford University Press, 1997.

Haynes, April R. "Flesh and Bones." In Haynes, *Riotous Flesh: Women, Physiology, and the Solitary Vice in Nineteenth-Century America,* 132–162. Chicago: University of Chicago Press, 2015.

Henson, Josiah. *The Life of Josiah Henson, Formerly a Slave, Now an Inhabitant of Canada, as Narrated by Himself.* Boston: A. D. Phelps, 1849.

Hepburn, Sharon A. Roger. "Following the North Star: Canada as a Haven for Nineteenth-Century American Blacks." *Michigan Historical Review* 25, no. 2 (1999): 91–126.

Higginbotham, Evelyn Brooks. *Righteous Discontent: The Women's Movement in the Black Baptist Church, 1880–1920.* Cambridge: Harvard University Press, 1993.

Hooker, Juliet. "How Can the Democratic Party Confront Racist Backlash? White Grievance in Hemispheric Perspective." *Polity* 52, no. 3 (2020): 355–369.

hooks, bell. *Feminist Theory from Margin to Center.* Boston: South End Press, 1984.

Horton, James Oliver, and Lois E. Horton. *In Hope of Liberty: Culture, Community, and Protest among Northern Free Blacks, 1700–1860.* New York: Oxford University Press, 1997.

Ice-T. (@FINALLEVEL). "For the record. I am not a Democrat and I am not a Republican so you can miss me with all your Left-Right talk..[*sic*] Both Wings are on the same Bird." Twitter, June 1, 2020, 4:26 PM, https://twitter.com/FINALLEVEL/status/1267 553159364268032.

Ingraham, Christopher. "Black Men Sentenced to More Time for Committing the Exact Same Crime as a White Person, Study Finds." *Washington Post,* November 16, 2017. https://www.washingtonpost.com/news/wonk/wp/2017/11/16/black-men-senten ced-to-more-time-for-committing-the-exact-same-crime-as-a-white-person-study-finds/.

Jabali, Malaika. "Pete Buttigieg Has a Race Problem. So Does the Democratic Party." *The Guardian,* November 22, 2019. https://www.theguardian.com/commentisfree/2019/nov/22/pete-buttigieg-race-us-elections-2020-democrats.

Jackson, Kellie Carter. "'Dare You Meet a Woman': Black Women, Abolitionism, and Protective Violence, 1850–1859." *Slavery and Abolition* 42, no. 2 (2021): 269–292.

Jones, Martha. *All Bound Up Together: The Woman Question in African American Public Culture, 1830–1900.* Chapel Hill: University of North Carolina Press, 2007.

Jones, Martha. *Birthright Citizens: A History of Race and Rights in Antebellum America.* New York: Cambridge University Press, 2018.

Lacy, Anna, Jessica D. Conrad, Jake Alspaugh, and Samantha de Vera. "From the Stage: Isaiah C. Wears." In *The Fight for Black Mobility: Traveling to Mid-Nineteenth-Century Conventions.* Colored Conventions Project. https://coloredconventions.org/black-mobility/delegate-lecture-circuits/isaiah-c-wears/.

Landon, Fred. "The Negro Migration to Canada after the Passing of the Fugitive Slave Act." *Journal of Negro History* 5, no. 1 (1920): 22–36.

Lee, Cynthia. "Making Race Salient: Trayvon Martin and Implicit Bias in a Not Yet Post-racial Society." *North Carolina Law Review* 91, no. 5 (2013): 1555–1612.

"Letter from William E. Walker." *Pine and Palm,* December 28, 1861.

Lichen, Faith. "That Woman's Letter from Washington." *New National Era,* February 22, 1872.

Lindsey, Donal F. *Indians at Hampton Institute, 1877–1923.* Urbana: University of Illinois Press, 1995.

Lindsey, Treva. *Colored No More: Reinventing Black Womanhood in Washington.* Urbana: University of Illinois Press, 2017.

Locke, Brandi, Samantha Q. de Vera, P. Gabrielle Foreman, Nneka D. Dennie, and Rachel Fernandes. "Mary Ann Shadd Cary's Herstory in the Colored Conventions: Abraham Shadd." In Colored Conventions Project. Center for Black Digital Research. 2023. https://coloredconventions.org/mary-ann-shadd-cary/making-a-delegate/abraham-shadd/.

Locke, Brandi, Samantha Q. de Vera, P. Gabrielle Foreman, Nneka D. Dennie, and Rachel Fernandes. "Mary Ann Shadd Cary's Herstory in the Colored Conventions: Family Tree." In Colored Conventions Project. Center for Black Digital Research. 2023. https://coloredconventions.org/mary-ann-shadd-cary/making-a-delegate/family-tree/.

"Louise to Clara." *Washington Bee*, July 21, 1883.

Marx, Karl. *The Communist Manifesto.* Edited by Frederic L. Bender. New York: Norton, 1988.

Masur, G. Straussmann. "Simón Bolívar." *Encyclopedia Britannica.* July 20, 1998; last modified December 13, 2022. https://www.britannica.com/biography/Simon-Bolivar.

Masur, Kate. *An Example for All the Land: Emancipation and the Struggle over Equality in Washington.* Chapel Hill: University of North Carolina Press, 2010.

Maynard, Robyn. *Policing Black Lives: State Violence in Canada from Slavery to the Present.* Black Point: Fernwood Publishing, 2017.

McGuire, Danielle. *At the Dark End of the Street: Black Women, Rape, and Resistance: A New History of the Civil Rights Movement from Rosa Parks to the Rise of Black Power.* New York: Vintage, 2011.

McKivigan, John R. "Commissioner Plenipotentiary for Haiti." In McKivigan, *Forgotten Firebrand: James Redpath and the Making of Nineteenth-Century America*, 61–83. Ithaca: Cornell University Press, 2018.

McLaren, Kristin. "'We Had No Desire to Be Set Apart': Forced Segregation of Black Students in Canada West Public Schools and Myths of British Egalitarianism." In *The History of Immigration and Racism in Canada*, edited by Barrington Walker, 69–81. Toronto: Canadian Scholars' Press, 2008.

Mehlinger, Louis R. "The Attitude of the Free Negro toward African Colonization." *Journal of Negro History* 1, no. 3 (1916): 276–301.

Melton, Tracy Matthew. *Hanging Henry Gambrill: The Violent Career of Baltimore's Plug Uglies, 1854–1860.* Baltimore: Maryland Historical Society, 2005.

Milteer, Warren Eugene, Jr. *Beyond Slavery's Shadow: Free People of Color in the South.* Chapel Hill: University of North Carolina Press, 2021.

"Mode of Publication." *Provincial Freeman*, November 25, 1856.

Moldow, Gloria. *Women Doctors in Gilded-Age Washington: Race, Gender, and Professionalization.* Urbana: University of Illinois Press, 1987.

Moody, Joycelyn. *Sentimental Confessions: Spiritual Narratives of Nineteenth-Century African American Women.* Athens: University of Georgia Press, 2003.

Moore, Darnell L. "Black Radical Love: A Practice." *Public Integrity* 20, no. 4 (2018): 325–328.

Moriah, Kristin. "'A Greater Compass of Voice': Elizabeth Taylor Greenfield and Mary Ann Shadd Cary Navigate Black Performance." *Theatre Research in Canada / Recherches Théâtrales au Canada* 41, no. 1 (2020): 20–38.

Morris, J. Brent. *Oberlin, Hotbed of Abolitionism: College, Community, and the Fight for Freedom and Equality in Antebellum America.* Chapel Hill: University of North Carolina Press, 2014.

Narrative of Facts in the Case of Passmore Williamson. Philadelphia: Pennsylvania Anti-Slavery Society, 1855. https://lccn.loc.gov/10034487.

"Naturalization Certificate of Mary Ann Shadd Cary." September 9, 1862. R4182-1-1-E, Mary Ann Shadd Cary Collection. Library and Archives of Canada. https://recherche-collection-search.bac-lac.gc.ca/eng/home/record?app=fonandcol&IdNumber=5793102.

Norgren, Jill. *Belva Lockwood: The Woman Who Would Be President*. New York: New York University Press, 2008.

Page, Sebastian N. *Black Resettlement and the American Civil War*. New York: Cambridge University Press, 2021.

Parker, Alison M. *Unceasing Militant: The Life of Mary Church Terrell*. Chapel Hill: University of North Carolina Press, 2020.

Patterson, Orlando. *Rituals of Blood: The Consequences of American Slavery in Two Centuries*. New York: Basic Books, 1999.

"Pay us what you Owe." *Provincial Freeman*, February 28, 1857.

Pelletier, Kevin. *Apocalyptic Sentimentalism: Love and Fear in U.S. Antebellum Literature*. Athens: University of Georgia Press, 2015.

Peterson, Carla. *"Doers of the Word": African-American Women Speakers and Writers in the North (1830–1880)*. New Brunswick: Rutgers University Press, 1998.

Petrino, Elizabeth A. "'We Are Rising as a People': Frances Harper's Radical Views on Class and Racial Equality in *Sketches of Southern Life*." *ATQ: 19th Century American Literature and Culture* 19, no. 2 (2005): 133–154.

Power-Greene, Ousmane. *Against Wind and Tide: The African-American Struggle against the Colonization Movement*. New York: New York University Press, 2014.

Rhodes, Jane. *Mary Ann Shadd Cary: The Black Press and Protest in the Nineteenth Century*. Bloomington: University of Indiana Press, 1998.

Rhodes, Jane. "At the Boundaries of Abolitionism, Feminism, and Black Nationalism: The Activism of Mary Ann Shadd Cary." In *Women's Rights and Transatlantic Antislavery in the Era of Emancipation*, edited by Kathryn Kish Sklar and James Brewer Stewart, 346–366. New Haven: Yale University Press, 2007.

Richardson, Marilyn, ed. *Maria W. Stewart, America's First Black Woman Political Writer: Essays and Speeches*. Bloomington: Indiana University Press, 1987.

Ripley, C. Peter, Jeffery S. Rossback, Roy E. Finkenbine, Fiona E. Spiers, and Debra Susie, eds. *The Black Abolitionist Papers*. Chapel Hill: University of North Carolina Press, 1985.

Ritchie, Andrea. *Invisible No More: Police Violence against Black Women and Women of Color*. Boston: Beacon Press, 2017.

Robinson, Cedric. *Black Marxism: The Making of the Black Radical Tradition*. Chapel Hill: University of North Carolina Press, 2005.

"Schools in Canada." *Voice of the Fugitive*. July 15, 1852.

Shadd, Mary Ann. "'The Colored People in Canada—Do They Need Help?'" *Liberator*, March 4, 1853.

Shadd, Mary Ann. "Editorial Cor. for the Provincial Freeman." *Provincial Freeman*, April 26, 1856.

Shadd, Mary Ann. "The Emigration Convention." *Provincial Freeman*, July 5, 1856.

Shadd, Mary Ann. Letter to Frederick Douglass. *North Star*, March 23, 1849.

Shadd, Mary Ann. "Our Free Colored Emigrants." *Provincial Freeman*, May 20, 1854.

Shadd, Mary Ann. *A Plea for Emigration, Or, Notes of Canada West*. Edited by Richard Almonte. Toronto: Mercury Press, 1998.

Shadd, Mary Ann. *A Plea for Emigration; or, Notes of Canada West, in its Moral, Social, and Political Aspect: with Suggestions Respecting Mexico, West Indies, and Vancouver's Island, for the Information of Colored Emigrants*. Detroit: George W. Pattison, 1852.

Shadd, Mary Ann. *A Plea for Emigration; Or Notes of Canada West*. Edited by Phanuel Antwi. Peterborough: Broadview Press, 2016.

Shadd Cary, Mary Ann. "Advancement of Women." *New York Age*, November 11, 1887.

Shadd Cary, Mary Ann. Colored Women's Progressive Franchise Association Minutes. February 9, 1880. Mary Ann Shadd Cary Collection 13, Box 1, Manuscript Division, Moorland-Spingarn Research Center, Washington, DC.

Shadd Cary, Mary Ann. Colored Women's Progressive Franchise Association Statement of Purpose. c. 1880. Mary Ann Shadd Cary Collection 13, Box 1, Manuscript Division, Moorland-Spingarn Research Center, Washington, DC.

Shadd Cary, Mary Ann. "A Correction, A Fact, and a Batch of Wonders." *Weekly Anglo-African*, December 28, 1861.

Shadd Cary, Mary Ann. Diversified Industries a ~~National~~ Necessity." n.d. Mary Ann Shadd Cary Collection 13, Box 1, Manuscript Division, Moorland-Spingarn Research Center, Washington, DC.

Shadd Cary, Mary Ann. "Editorial- by M. A. S. Cary (Editor)." *Provincial Freeman*, Spring Edition 1866.

Shadd Cary, Mary Ann. "A First Vote, Almost." 1871. Mary Ann Shadd Cary Collection 13, Box 1, Manuscript Division, Moorland-Spingarn Research Center, Washington, DC.

Shadd Cary, Mary Ann. "A Good Boarding House Greatly Needed by the Colored Citizens of Canada." *Provincial Freeman*, December 6, 1856.

Shadd Cary, Mary Ann. "Haytian Emigration." *Weekly Anglo-African*, September 28, 1861.

Shadd Cary, Mary Ann. "Haytian Emigration." *Weekly Anglo-African*, October 26, 1861.

Shadd Cary, Mary Ann. "Haytian Emigration." *Weekly Anglo-African*, November 9, 1861.

Shadd Cary, Mary Ann. "Haytian Emigration in Canada." *Weekly Anglo-African*, October 19, 1861.

Shadd Cary, Mary Ann. "The Haytian Fever and its Diagnostics in Canada." *Weekly Anglo-African*, December 14, 1861.

Shadd Cary, Mary Ann. "The Last Day of the 43 Congress." c. 1875. Mary Ann Shadd Cary Collection 13, Box 1, Manuscript Division, Moorland-Spingarn Research Center, Washington, DC.

Shadd Cary, Mary Ann. "Letter from Baltimore." *New National Era*, August 10, 1871.

Shadd Cary, Mary Ann. "Letter from Wilmington, DE." *New National Era*, August 24, 1871.

Shadd Cary, Mary Ann. "Letters to the People—No. 1 Trade for Our Boys!" *New National Era*, March 21, 1872.

Shadd Cary, Mary Ann. "Letters to the People—No. 2 Trade for Our Boys!" *New National Era*, April 11, 1872.

Shadd Cary, Mary Ann. "Meetings at Philadelphia." *Provincial Freeman*, April 18, 1857.

Shadd Cary, Mary Ann. "Petition of Mary Shadd Cary, a citizen of Washington, District of Columbia, praying for the removal of her political disabilities." c. 1878. Accessed May 2, 2020. https://search.alexanderstreet.com/view/work/bibliographic_entity%7Cbibliographic_details%7C4689860.

Shadd Cary, Mary Ann. "School for ALL!!" *Provincial Freeman*, June 13, 1857.

Shadd Cary, Mary Ann. Sermon [Break Every Yoke], April 6, 1858, Mary Ann Shadd Cary fonds, F 1409-4-0-153, Archives of Ontario.

Shadd Cary, Mary Ann. "Should We Economise?" n.d. Mary Ann Shadd Cary Collection 13, Box 1, Manuscript Division, Moorland-Spingarn Research Center, Washington, DC.

Shadd Cary, Mary Ann. "Speech to the Judiciary Committee Re: The Right of Women to Vote." Mary Ann Shadd Cary Collection 13, Box 1, Manuscript Division, Moorland-Spingarn Research Center, Washington, DC.

Shadd Cary, Mary Ann. "The Things Most Needed." *Provincial Freeman*, April 25, 1857.

Shadd Cary, Mary Ann. "An Unmitigated Falsehood." *Weekly Anglo-African*, February 15, 1862.

Shadd Cary, Mary Ann. "Would Woman Suffrage Have a Tendency to Elevate the Moral Tone of Politics." n.d. Mary Ann Shadd Cary Collection 13, Box 1, Manuscript Division, Moorland-Spingarn Research Center, Washington, DC.

Shadd Cary, Mary Ann, Caroline E. G. Colby, Joseph P. Evans, Belva A. Lockwood, and J. S. Griffing. "Report on Woman's Labor." In *Proceedings of the Colored National Labor Convention*, 21–22. Washington, DC: New Era, 1870.

Shakur, Assata. *Assata: An Autobiography.* Chicago: L. Hill, 2001.

Silver, Nate, and Alison McCann. "Are White Republicans More Racist Than White Democrats?" *Five Thirty-Eight*, April 30, 2014. https://fivethirtyeight.com/features/are-white-republicans-more-racist-than-white-democrats/.

Simien, Evelyn. *Gender and Lynching: The Politics of Memory.* New York: Palgrave, 2011.

Sklar, Kathryn Kish, and James Brewer Stewart, eds. *Women's Rights and Transatlantic Antislavery in the Era of Emancipation.* New Haven: Yale University Press, 2007.

Spires, Derrick. *The Practice of Citizenship: Black Politics and Print Culture in the Early United States.* Philadelphia: University of Pennsylvania Press, 2019.

"Spirited Meeting of the Colored Citizens of Philadelphia." *Liberator*, April 10, 1857.

State Convention of Colored Citizens of Pennsylvania (1848: Harrisburg, PA). "Minutes of the State Convention of Colored Citizens of Pennsylvania, Convened at Harrisburg, December 13–14, 1848." *Colored Conventions Project Digital Records.* Accessed October 30, 2022, https://omeka.coloredconventions.org/items/show/241.

Sterling, Dorothy. *We Are Your Sisters: Black Women in the Nineteenth Century.* New York: Norton, 1997.

Streitmatter, Rodger. *Raising Her Voice: African-American Women Journalists Who Changed History.* Lexington: University Press of Kentucky, 1994.

Stewart, Maria W. "Lecture Delivered at the Franklin Hall." In *Maria W. Stewart, America's First Black Woman Political Writer: Essays and Speeches*, edited by Marilyn Richardson, 45–49. Bloomington: Indiana University Press, 1987.

Tate, Gayle. *Unknown Tongues: Black Women's Political Activism in the Antebellum Era, 1830–1860.* East Lansing: Michigan State University Press, 2003.

Thornell, Paul N. D. "The Absent Ones and the Providers: A Biography of the Vashons." *Journal of Negro History* 83, no. 4 (1998): 284–301.

"To our Friends in the Western States." *Provincial Freeman*, February 17, 1855.

"To Our Readers West." *Provincial Freeman*, June 9, 1855.

"To Travelling Agents and Subscribers." *Provincial Freeman*, May 13, 1854.

Tomek, Beverly C. *Colonization and Its Discontents: Emancipation, Emigration, and Antislavery in Antebellum Pennsylvania.* New York: New York University Press, 2011.

Toronto History Museums. "Luminary: Mary Ann Shadd." Accessed October 22, 2021. https://www.toronto.ca/explore-enjoy/history-art-culture/museums/luminary-mary-ann-shadd/.

Toronto History Museums. "Awakenings Reflections with Adeyemi Adegbesan." August 10, 2021. 6:07. https://www.youtube.com/watch?v=5tqvYAGlTIQ.

Ullman, Victor. *Martin R. Delany: The Beginnings of Black Nationalism.* Boston: Beacon Press, 1971.

"Underground Railroad." Wheaton History A to Z. Accessed June 9, 2020. http://a2z.my.wheaton.edu/underground-railroad.

W. S. "Letter to the Editor." *Provincial Freeman,* September 2, 1854.

W. S. "Letter to the Editor." *Provincial Freeman,* March 7, 1857.

Walcott, Rinaldo. "'Who Is She and What Is She to You?': Mary Ann Shadd Cary and the (Im)possibility of Black/Canadian Studies." *Atlantis: Critical Studies in Gender, Culture, and Social Justice* 24, no. 2 (2002): 137–146.

Walker, Barrington. *Race on Trial: Black Defendants in Ontario's Criminal Courts, 1858–1961.* Toronto: University of Toronto Press, 2010.

Ward, Samuel Ringgold. *Autobiography of a Fugitive Negro: His Anti-slavery Labours in the United States, Canada, & England.* London: John Snow, 1855.

Waters, Kristin, and Carol B. Conaway, eds. *Black Women's Intellectual Traditions: Speaking Their Minds.* Burlington: University of Vermont Press, 2007.

Watkins, Frances Ellen. "The Free Labor Movement." *Frederick Douglass' Paper,* June 29, 1855.

Watkins, Frances Ellen. "The Burial of Moses." *Provincial Freeman,* May 24, 1856.

Watkins, Frances Ellen. "Died of Starvation." *Provincial Freeman,* March 7, 1857.

White, Deborah Gray. *Too Heavy a Load: Black Women in Defense of Themselves, 1894–1994.* New York: Norton, 1999.

Whitley, William Bland, and the *Dictionary of Virginia Biography.* "Joseph P. Evans (1835–1889)." *Encyclopedia Virginia.* Virginia Humanities. Last modified December 22, 2021. https://encyclopediavirginia.org/entries/evans-joseph-p-1835-1889/.

"Woman's Rights." *Provincial Freeman,* May 6, 1854.

"Women's Suffrage in New York State." New York Assembly. Accessed May 31, 2020. https:// nyassembly.gov/member_files/058/20090226/.

Yee, Shirley. *Black Women Abolitionists: A Study in Activism, 1828–1860.* Knoxville: University of Tennessee Press, 1992.

Yee, Shirley. "Finding a Place: Mary Ann Shadd Cary and the Dilemmas of Black Emigration to Canada, 1850-1870." *Frontiers: A Journal of Women Studies* 18, no. 3 (1997): 1–16.

Zackodnik, Teresa. *African American Feminisms, 1828–1923.* New York: Routledge, 2007.

Zackodnik, Teresa. *Press, Platform, Pulpit: Black Feminist Publics in the Era of Reform.* Knoxville: University of Tennessee Press, 2011.

Ziparo, Jessica. *This Grand Experiment: When Women Entered the Federal Workforce in Civil War-Era Washington, D.C.* Chapel Hill: University of North Carolina Press, 2017.

Index

For the benefit of digital users, indexed terms that span two pages (e.g., 52–53) may, on occasion, appear on only one of those pages.